Christian W. Thomsen **Visionary Architecture**

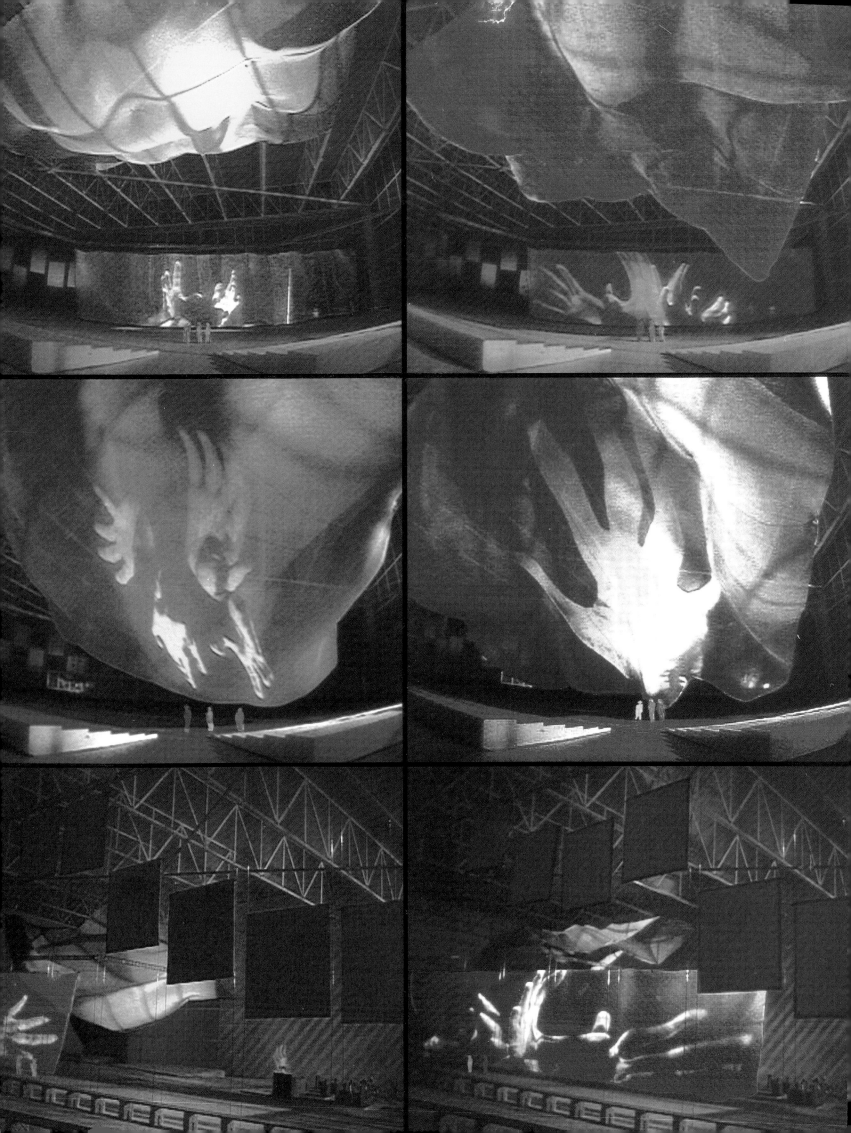

Christian W. Thomsen

Visionary Architecture

**FROM BABYLON
TO VIRTUAL REALITY**

Prestel
Munich · New York

© Prestel-Verlag, Munich and New York, 1994
© of works illustrated by the artists, their heirs and assigns, except in the following cases:
Peter Behrens, Robert Delaunay, George Grosz, El Lissitzky, and Adolf Loos
by VG Bild-Kunst, Bonn, 1994

Photograph credits on p. 190

Translated from the German by John William Gabriel
Copyedited by Simon Haviland

Front cover: *Pyramid City TRY 2004* (see p. 165)
Back cover: Pieter Bruegel the Elder, *The Building of the Tower of Babel* (see p. 12)
        Master of the Barberini Panels, *Presentation of the Virgin in the Temple*
        (see p. 53)
        Frank R. Paul, *City of the Future* (see p. 159)
        Angus McKie, *Hyperspace-Troop Carrier, 5.16.2526* (detail; see p. 155)
        Rem Koolhaas, model for the Center for Art and Media Technology (ZKM),
        Karlsruhe (detail; see p. 176)
Frontispiece: ag4 Cologne, The Stuff that Dreams Are Made of, 1994

Prestel-Verlag · Mandlstrasse 26 · D-80802 Munich, Germany
Tel. (89) 381709-0 · Fax (89) 381709-35
and 16 West 22nd Street, New York, NY 10010, USA
Tel. (212) 6278199; Fax (212) 6279866

All books published by Prestel-Verlag are distributed worldwide.
For information on distribution in your country, please contact
Prestel at either of the above addresses.

Cover design by F. Lüdtke, A. Volohonsky, Munich
Lithography by PHG Lithos, Munich
Typeset by Uhl+Massopust, Aalen
Printed by Aumüller Druck KG, Regensburg
Bound by Buchbinderei Salzburg, Almesberger GmbH, Salzburg

Printed in Germany

ISBN 3-7913-1425-4 (English edition)
ISBN 3-7913-1397-5 (German edition)

CONTENTS

People need shelter, whether it be a cave or a tent, a mobile home or a spaceship. Not having a roof over one's head is a terrible thing, as the sight of streams of homeless refugees crossing our television screens every night brings home to us. This explains why architecture is one of the oldest and most important arts devised by humanity. And even its mythical originator, Daedalus, was a visionary architect, not only building the Cretan labyrinth but envisioning flying machines to escape the embroilments of this earthly life. His act became a program for his successors. When architects cannot build, or are prevented from doing so for whatever reason, they concoct architectural fantasies or write manifestos. A demiurgic ambition to reshape the world in accordance with their ideas has characterized architects since time began. Their activity combines a free play of imagination with a desire for order and meaning, spontaneity with a love of experiment and a scientific testing of new materials, forms, and functions.

Architecture is generally distinguished from its visionary, utopian, or fantastic cousin, the ideal city, science-fiction projection, or urban utopia, by drawing a sharp line between reality and fiction. According to this definition, what is actually built cannot be visionary. The distinction, I believe, is obsolete. By now almost everyone will have realized that human imagination contributes materially to the construct or image of reality that we hold in our minds, and hence that it is no longer possible to draw a clear distinction between imagination and reality. Living in a period in which borderlines are being transgressed in every field, we should be prepared to question accepted aesthetic categories as well, to rethink them in terms of process, and to define them flexibly. In situations of political, economic, or cultural crisis, visionary thinking is especially important, because it enables us to challenge hidebound conventions and to open a path for innovative approaches and solutions.

If I had held to established definitions and categories in writing this book, I would have had to dispense with bizarre architecture and architectural eccentricities, with houseboats and tree houses, cave dwellings, hermits' eyries and ivory towers, with movie architecture and the seemingly science-fiction space station designs that are actually in the planning stages at this moment. The examples extend from Duke Orsini's enigmatic sculptures and the apparently occult and crazy structures in the park at Bomarzo (ca.

Heinz Birg, *Ancestral Tower.* Drawing, 1986

Hannsjörg Voth, *Stairway to Heaven*. Drawing on tracing paper, 1985

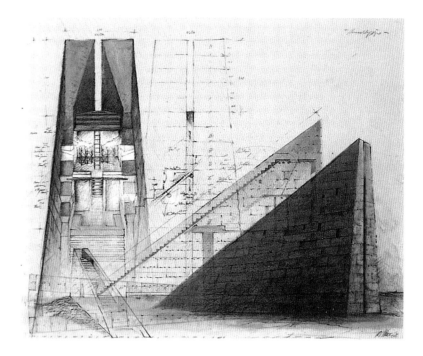

ag4, Office for "Mediatecture," Cologne. Streetcar stop with media shelter, Hauptplatz, Linz. Design by Kronhagel, Lepel, and Singer for Ars Electronica, 1993

Lebbeus Woods, *A City, Sector 1576 N*. Drawing, 1988

1525) all the way down to H. R. Giger's spaceship models for the *Alien* films. Visions of even the most daring kind have at times been given real shape. If in the past these were usually castles or palaces, in the modern era they often take the form of museums or theaters, research institutes or skyscrapers. Or they have been the private aesthetic dreams of compulsive outsiders like Ferdinand Cheval, or of experimental creators of a *Gesamtkunstwerk* like the Austrian architect Günther Domenig. Frequently, political, economic, or personal difficulties prevent the execution of some carefully planned project, which is then relegated to the realm of fantasy. In this case we speak of an "architectural vision" rather than of "visionary architecture."

The history of architecture has been accompanied from the beginning by poets, writers, and philosophers, the master builders of language, who must also be considered in our discussion. Language, literature, and building have a great deal in common, from their basic structure or framework down to the tiniest building block, from a combination of parts to form larger wholes to the finished design, including its ornamentation. In addition, writers have long shown a penchant for projecting visionary architecture in their works, and painters and filmmakers are increasingly doing the same. As the borderline between yesterday and tomorrow incessantly advances, erasing the present moment and relegating it to the past, architectural trends, fashions, and styles seem to be changing more rapidly than ever before. Yet architectural fantasies are among those creations of the human mind that attempt to link today with tomorrow, suffuse the present with a taste of the future. Thanks to the accelerating transformation of our societies into a media and information culture, thanks to a transition from analogue to digital and a change of paradigm from a material to an immaterial aesthetic, our entire cultural system may be largely determined by media developments in future. In fact, the very concept of "reality" has already become one of the fuzziest terms in current usage.

Self-styled "reality television" is only one example of the way in which imagination, fact, and fiction can be blended into the mixed reality constructs of new types of television production. In architecture, too, we now justifiably talk about "virtual architectures," something that only a short time ago sounded like castles in the air, a contradiction in terms. Cyberspace, for instance, is architecture, possesses an architecture, contains architecture. Immaterial, virtual, telematic spaces are increasingly suffusing, overlaying actual built spaces. Media interfaces, "intelligent" or "thinking" architectures are changing the vocabulary, grammar, and rhetoric of traditional architecture, and compelling its practitioners to reconsider their activity and partially redefine it. In the final chapters of the book I shall attempt to explore the frontiers between present and future and ask whether certain architectural visions located here can expect to be realized or not. In any case, such visions do contribute to development, suggest alternatives, and, through their stylistic inconsistencies and expansions, encourage innovation and, ultimately, even the creation of new jobs. The wishes and dreams they contain express the *Zeitgeist* of the current avant-garde. The architectural visions of cranks and cross-discipline thinkers, dreamers, and eccentrics, men and women who live with their heads in the clouds, who

Nils Ole Lund, *The Tower of Babel.* Collage, after 1970

9

Hans Scharoun, *Concert Hall.* Watercolor, ca. 1920

Gerd Winner, *Times Square.* Silkscreen print, 1987–88

are ensconced in ivory towers, or who rave over high tech, ecology, or the blessings of the modern media — visionaries of whatever stamp all fulfil a crucial function for society. They form the critical, sometimes ironic, crafty, playful catalyst for a saturated establishment, putting it to the test by asking embarrassing questions and making astonishing suggestions. They point out new ways of doing things, experiment in their heads, on canvas, on the drawing board, and increasingly on the computer. Architecture urgently requires new conceptions to bring high tech, the media, and ecology into some sort of working relationship with one another, in order to be able to develop new approaches and applications, new forms of living and working, and perhaps in the end a new architectural aesthetic.

In the meantime some governments, like the German state of North Rhine-Westphalia, have established institutes to research the future, with the mission of investigating the links, interfaces, and interpenetrations between art and science in the hope of being able to recognize new trends and innovations at an early point and turn them to commercial ends. International competition makes such efforts imperative today. By the same token, the architectural visions and visionary architecture described in the following pages, in a survey by no means complete but certainly comprehensive, increasingly are taking on a key and quite concrete significance for the intellectual, artistic, and economic welfare of modern societies.

From the "Whore of Babylon" to the "New Jerusalem" to the Ideal Cities of the Renaissance

The names of the cities of Babylon and Jerusalem are among those concepts of Judeo-Christian, Oriental, and Occidental culture which have long been divorced from their original, historic sources.[1] Babylon has become a metaphor for the big city per se, and its tower a symbol of the hubris of human science and the pioneer spirit in architecture. Jerusalem, in contrast, came to serve as a model for religiously inspired conceptions of the ideal city and a long series of social utopias. Both names are associated with emotions and ideas which for over two millennia now have continued to fuel the artistic and architectural imagination.

In the Bible, the two cities are chained to one another by a bond of hate and political rivalry. The conquest of Jerusalem and destruction of Solomon's temple by Nebuchadnezzar II, who in 597 and 587 B.C. ravaged Palestine and enslaved much of the Jewish populace in the Babylonian Captivity,[2] explains why Old Testament references to Babylon have the aggressive tone of political polemics. The city cannot have been nearly so depraved as its religious and political opponents claimed. Similarly, a reaction to the political situation at that time may be imputed to the Book of Revelation, where St. John speaks of Babylon as an embodiment of a godless world power and means Rome. Still, for all the disgust John feels for the Whore of Babylon, seat of religious and moral perversion and profligate unchecked capitalism, between the lines one can sense much of the glory of the city, which must have been an architectural jewel of antiquity. Babylon's role was later taken over by Rome, and it was the love-hate relationship of the religious zealot that drove the prophet to castigate it. A man who fears the temptations of such a place simply declares it a hotbed of sin and predicts its downfall:

And the merchants of the earth shall weep and mourn over her; for no man buyeth their merchandise any more: the merchandise of gold, and silver, and precious stones, and of pearls, and fine linen, and purple, and silk, and scarlet, and all thyine wood, and all manner vessels of ivory, and all manner vessels of most precious wood, and of brass, and iron, and marble, and cinnamon, and odours, and ointments, and frankincense, and wine, and oil, and fine flour, and wheat, and beasts, and sheep, and horses, and chariots, and slaves, and souls of men (Revelation 18.11–13).

Reconstruction of the Ishtar Gate of Babylon. Pergamon Museum, Berlin

Pieter Bruegel the Elder, *The Building of the Tower of Babel.* Oil on wood, 1563

What city is like unto this great city! And they cast dust on their heads, and cried, weeping and wailing, saying, Alas, alas that great city, wherein were made rich all that had ships in the sea by reason of her costliness! for in one hour is she made desolate (Revelation 18.18–19).

In discussing the architectural visions of Classical Antiquity and the Middle Ages, we generally have little more than literary sources to rely on. There were of course builders and architects, but their written plans and conceptions were either lost, were recorded less frequently than is now the case, or were simply ignored by a historiography concerned principally with the hierarchical matters of ruling dynasties and victories in war.

Our present-day picture of Babylon as a negative symbol of the metropolis has been influenced equally by the biblical denunciation of the city and by modern urban developments since the nineteenth century, especially the unplanned growth of gigantic urban agglomerations, initially in Europe and the United States, and then on every continent. The proliferating megalopolises of the past few decades have led their critics, with Alexander Mitscherlich, to speak of the "unlivability of cities," with reference to the entire range of problems symbolically associated with Babylon: the multilingual babble, the housing shortages, slums, crime, unemployment, traffic jams, waste-disposal crisis, sinking water table, smog, noise, and other typical big-city troubles. Yet despite all this, great cities have apparently lost very little of their cultural and commercial attractiveness.

Domenico di Michelino, *Dante and His "Divina Commedia."* Fresco, Florence Cathedral, 1465

The historical Babylon and other cities of antiquity indeed faced many of the same, or similar, problems. The first relatively reliable report on Babylon was provided by Herodotus, who visited it in 458 B.C., when the city had already passed the apex of its economic power and its heyday was over. This did not prevent him from exclaiming, "Babylon is not only a larger city, but also a more glorious one than any other city known to me." Nebuchadnezzar, who had transformed Babylon into the dominant power of the Near East, had been dead for over a hundred years by the time Herodotus arrived. Babylon then had a population of about 300,000; the Euphrates, which bisected the town, insured good profits from waterborne trade. The straight streets flanked by three- and four-story houses abutted the riverbank at right angles. There was a single drawbridge on stone piers, pulled up at night, that linked the two great halves of the city. The core of the city had an area of about one-and-a-half square miles and was surrounded by a massive wall. Four further concentric walls protected the entire city territory, at whose nucleus were the temple district, Nebuchadnezzar's palace, and the Hanging Gardens of Semiramis, traditionally one of the Seven Wonders of the World. The innermost core was occupied by the Tower of Babylon, a stepped pyramid or ziggurat, three hundred feet in height. Access to it was provided by a broad avenue, the renowned Processional Road, which in terms of size and glory outshone everything that had gone before.

Classical descriptions of great cities were free of the religious and moral connotations found in biblical descriptions of Babylon. Even Homer in *The Odyssey* already showed a keen eye for architectural details such as gates and towers and battlemented walls, and he profusely described the marvellous palaces he visited on his journeys. The imposingness of fortifications like those of Carthage played a key part in Virgil's *Aeneid* as well. On the other hand, Seneca and the Roman historians put more emphasis on a realistic depiction of big-city life, describing the bustling traffic of Rome, the land, building and rent speculation that beset it, its inadequate streets and sanitation, its apartment buildings rising up to a hundred feet in height, its Spartan private dwellings and ostentatious public edifices — metropolitan features and problems, in short, that strike one as astonishingly modern.

To return to Babylon, the secular literary descriptions of the city given in the Middle Ages surprisingly emphasized its positive aspects almost to the exclusion of its seamier side. While the eleventh-century *Annolied* made do with a brief, objective description that praised the city's precise mathematical layout, the *Weltchronik* of

View of Babylon. From Hartmann Schedel's *World Chronicle*, 1493

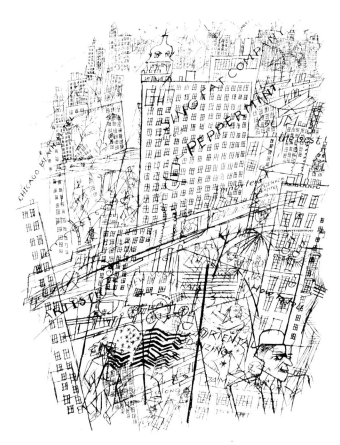

George Grosz, *Memory of New York*. Drawing, 1916–17

Rudolf von Ems, written in the thirteenth century, waxed enthusiastic about Babylon's glory. Admittedly, Rudolf's vision altered the city of the scriptures to conform with medieval notions and ideals, giving it invincible circular fortifications and a hundred bronze gates and massive towers. More objectively but also in line with the ideal city of the Middle Ages, Babylon's prosperity was explained by the economic utility of the river and the city's sway over numerous vassal peoples.

In his *Alexander*, Rudolf cut entirely free of biblical tradition and solicited his contemporaries' sympathy for Babylon by describing the splendor of its court and an enjoyment of life's pleasures that recalls *Carmina Burana*. Architecture of a visionary nature was subsequently projected by Heinrich von Neustadt, in *Apollonius*, where despite having been laid waste by the curse of God, Babylon nevertheless shines with a fairy tale splendor of medieval-style marble walls, embellished pinnacles, and streets paved in marble and precious stones.

The modern, negative image of Babylon really did not begin to gel until the nineteenth century, with the emergence of great industrial

George Grosz, *White Slaver*. Watercolor, 1918

cities. Charles Dickens was among the first authors to lend Babylonian connotations to, and predict a Babylonian fate for, their amorphously proliferating tenements, unhealthy climate, and the effects of urban working conditions on the populace. In *Great Expectations* he described Smithfield Market, the London stockyards, as a bloody symbol of a mercantile world in which human relationships were brutalized and adapted to the conditions of the slaughterhouse. *Our Mutual Friend*, a work of Dickens' old age, showed the big city suffused with a miasma of fog, darkness, dirt, and death. When the offices and shops closed for the night, he wrote, they exuded "an air of death"; the working-class inhabitants of the East End were like prisoners; and the huge Newgate Prison, in which many novelistic episodes had been set since the eighteenth century, appeared as the central bastion of the ruling class.

If Dickens spoke of the big city in anthropomorphic terms, Emile Zola applied the naturalist's scalpel to its ills. As the nineteenth century wore on, the capitals of Europe and their life came increasingly to be pictured in literature as organisms with a complex web of functions, where the entire range of human activities and mores was compressed in a constricted space, and where the architectural range extended from teeming slums to railway stations and crystal palaces, the symbols of a new industrial prosperity.

In the twentieth century, German Expressionist poets took the metropolis à la Babylon as one of their key motifs. Even before the First World War, they seismographically sensed the imminent apocalypse and associated it with the Moloch of the great city. Kurt Pinthus' famous anthology, *Menschheitsdämmerung* (Twilight of Humanity), uniting authors like Georg Heym, Theodor Däubler, Johannes R. Becher, Ernst Stadler, René Schickele, Jakob van Hoddis, and Gottfried Benn, abounded with disparaging Babylonian allusions and images of soot-blackened buildings, smoke-belching chimneys and faceless masses of human beings who sweat, gripe, groan and cry out in despair — the city as a swamp, its denizens as creatures who wallow helplessly in the mire, condemned to suffer, fornicate, and die. They all painted the city in two colors, black and red: black standing for hopelessness, depression, and death, and red standing for blood and the apocalyptic fires. By comparison to medieval literature, the modern poems employed far more emotional and psychological metaphor, and in describing the city they limited themselves to very few architectural features like towers, smokestacks, and canals. The city as a whole was seen more strongly from the point of view of a sensitive, suffering consciousness, which generally lent its architecture mythical and demoniac traits and suppressed its actual appearance. The result in both cases, medieval and modern, was a visionary architecture, with the difference that the modern "literarchitecture" of the city conveys — at least for architects — only a vague sense of repugnance. In the modern poems, mythical and religious aspects are overshadowed by societal ones.

Taddeo di Bartolo, *San Gimignano with the Model of the City Named after Him*, ca. 1400

The City of Rottweil, ca. 1435

Such gloomy visions stand in contrast to the urban utopias of the philosophers, Thomas More's *Utopia* (1516), Tommaso Campanella's *La Città del Sole* (1602), and Francis Bacon's *New Atlantis* (1624). In the nineteenth century this line of thinking was continued in the garden-city idea and William Morris's longings for a lost paradise state. The first decades of our own century brought the generally euphorically tinged urban designs of the great planners and architects, Walter Gropius and Le Corbusier in particular. Writers and artists, on the other hand, were often quick to sense the dangers in the well-meant, philanthropic projects of such men, realizing that in practice, unpredictable conflicting interests could easily turn their intentions inside out.

Lyrical jeremiads against the modern urban Babel were by no means as common in English, French, or American poetry as they were in German. At least, poets in those countries seemed to be aware of the positive myths that surrounded the metropolis, be it Berlin, Paris, London, or New York.

Babylon also provided the key metaphor for one of the greatest epic novels in German literature of the first half of the twentieth century, Alfred Döblin's *Berlin Alexanderplatz*. Projecting a complex urban panorama, the demiurgic narrator behind Franz Biberkopf, his working-class, ex-con hero, who in the middle of the book quotes the Whore of Babylon passage from the Bible, re-creates urban life and architecture from a plethora of subjective facets. Döblin's American counterpart, John Dos Passos, was more intent on tempering subjectivity with an objective view. In *Manhattan Transfer*, a precursor of his great, stylistically revolutionary trilogy, *U.S.A.*, Dos Passos attempted to adapt the techniques of the new media to literary ends — movies, newsreels, newspaper reports, and his aesthetic of the fleeting moment captured, his "camera eye."

At about the same time, in 1924, Fritz Lang visited America, where he conceived the idea for *Metropolis*, one of the most successful silent films of all time. It, too, relied on the Babylon metaphor, interpreted in sequences whose visual power and use of innovative camera tricks were matched only by the major works of Sergey Eisenstein. *Metropolis* has remained perhaps the most influential film based on architectural motifs in the history of the medium. It engendered an entire genre of disaster movies with Babylonian overtones, released at ever-shorter intervals ever since. The same ambience — the staccato tempo of the Jazz Age, political crises, stock-market crashes, the Babylonian lust for life of the 1920s and 1930s — was also captured by artists of the day. Let the names Max Beckmann, Christian Schad, and George Grosz stand for many others.

But to return to Dos Passos and his evocation of the ambiguous fascination of the big city, with all of its temptations and opportunities, its exploitation, depravity, nerve-jangling pace, its dog-eat-dog attitudes, smell of smoke and decay, and its glory, glitter, and rags-to-riches hopes. More intensively than in comparable specimens of

German literature, an awareness is created of the positive aspects and attractiveness of the modern Babylon, a tendency which has remained characteristic of New York fiction to this day. With epic breadth and in a mosaic of countless news fragments Dos Passos invokes the history of the great city and its architecture:

> There was Babylon and Nineveh, they were built of brick, Athens was gold-marble columns. Rome was held up on broadarches of rubble. In Constantinople the minarets flame like great candles round the Golden Horn....
>
> O there's one more river to cross. Steel, glass, tile, concrete will be the materials of skyscrapers. Crammed on the narrow island the millionwindowed buildings will jut, glittering pyramid on pyramid, white cloudsheads piled above a thunderstorm....
>
> And it rained forty days and forty nights
> And it didn't stop till Christmas
> And the only man who survived the flood
> Was longlegged Jack of the Isthmus....
>
> Kerist I wish I was a skyscraper.[3]

George Grosz, *Before Sunrise.* Watercolor, 1922

And with the skyscraper we come to the second part of the Babylon theme, the Tower of Babel, which has been carefully skirted until now and will be treated in the next chapter. While the Whore of Babylon motif tends to belong to "literarchitecture," the Tower involves a theme that has always fueled the imagination of artists and architects more than that of writers.

THE HEAVENLY JERUSALEM AND MEDIEVAL CONCEPTIONS OF THE IDEAL CITY

In the prophet's description of the Apocalypse, the vision of the Holy City, the New Jerusalem, shines like a diamond in the gloom. So glorious, exquisite, and sensuously present was this city brought down to earth by God that its vision has never ceased to preoccupy the thoughts of preachers, poets, and architects concerned either with a metaphorical evocation of religious community or with actual designs for ideal cities. Even if the latter have not always been aware of it, the New Jerusalem is a visual matrix embedded deep in our cultural consciousness, whether it be specifically Christian-oriented or not.

In the ecclesiastical and secular writings of the Middle Ages, the motif complex of *Jerusalem caelestis* (Heavenly Jerusalem) was the most frequently employed stock theme of all relating to sacred architecture. Illustrators and authors were aided by the fact that in its mixture of concrete reference and more general, allusive terms the biblical description left much room for the imagination:

View of Nuremberg. Woodcut, 1493

Wolfgang Katzheimer the Elder, *The Leave-Taking of the Apostles.* Oil on wood, 1483

And he carried me away in the spirit to a great and high mountain, and showed me that great city, the holy Jerusalem, descending out of heaven from God, having the glory of God: and her light was like unto a stone most precious, even like a jasper stone, clear as crystal; and had a wall great and high, and had twelve gates, and at the gates twelve angels,... And he that talked with me had a golden reed to measure the city, and the gates thereof, and the wall thereof. And the city lieth four-square, and the length is as large as the breadth.... (Revelation 21.10–12, 15–16).

Even this brief passage contains much that was to become familiar from medieval views of art and architecture: the high wall protected by towers, the square layout alluding to that of the actual Jerusalem, the glory and marvels of a royal residence. Throughout the Middle Ages, key images evoking the Heavenly Jerusalem suffused sermons and hymns, and the numerous commentaries on the Apocalypse. These included such formulas as *"taz himelriche," "Diu himelisge gotes burg," "daz gotes ebenerbe,"* and *"diu haimuot...der himeliscen Jerusalem,"* which point, among other things, to the identity of castle and city that still obtained in the Late Middle Ages.

While church literature provided detailed descriptions of the religious architecture of the ideal city, secular writings contained both occa-

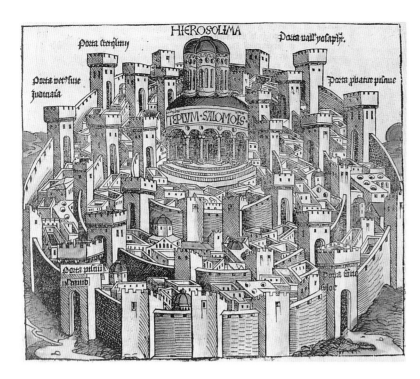

sional passages on the Heavenly Jerusalem and remarkable transpositions of the topic to profane, indeed quite real cities. The multifarious nuances of description involved might be illustrated by a few examples. In visual depictions, any comparatively large town might become Jerusalem, and the equation "Bamberg is Jerusalem" is reasonable enough when one considers that familiar locales were used to help the faithful understand the Passion of Christ.[4] Still, artists of the day had difficulties in translating complicated three-dimensional configurations into two-dimensional terms. Initially architectural features remained mere set pieces in ecclesiastical art, and interiors were unknown. In the medieval period the city was considered primarily as a form of life which differed fundamentally from that of the country, and which in book illumination or on seals could be abbreviated to walls and towers symbolizing the protected nature of the former.

The City of God in the Augustinian sense, with express emphasis on *Jerusalem caelestis,* first became a motif in German religious literature in the eleventh and twelfth centuries. It already emerged full-blown in Hildegard von Bingen's allegorical visions of the world, and then, in the latter half of the eleventh century, the City of God was introduced, prolifically detailed, into the medieval context in *Himmel und Hölle* (Heaven and Hell), a work probably written by a Bamberg clergyman. Religious and visionary factors still predominated in the architecture described: "The heavenly palace of God needs neither the senses nor human light to be resplendent...." Its foundations, gates and walls were made of precious stones. The saints and the greatest defenders of the faith served as vassal princes of the monarch of the city, whose streets were paved with shimmering reddish gold: indeed the entire city was suffused by a lovely

Hildegard von Bingen, *Cosmic Visions.* Seventh Vision, ca. 1230

19

golden glow, as if from transparent glass. This description is architecturally noteworthy especially on account of its lavish reference to glass, then still exorbitantly costly, which was meant to symbolize the pure and profound virtuousness of the Heavenly City's inhabitants.

In medieval religious literature, art and theology blended. Heaven was the unutterable, incapable of being imagined in real terms; so authors turned to figurative language. Participating in the Heavenly Jerusalem meant being permitted to come face to face with God — a mystical vision, in other words, to represent which medieval authors often adopted architectural motifs.

As researchers have known for quite some time, many of the basic elements of the City of God motif can be traced back through Christianity and Judaism to Babylonian and ancient Oriental mythology. What became characteristic for the Middle Ages, then, was an interchangeability of almost all of the architectural motifs mentioned in the Bible, as these were seen to convey identical meanings: city, temple, king's house, king's court, kingdom, homeland, paradise. In ecclesiastical writings, architectural imagery invariably referred to the House of God and the blessed, not to actual, built structures.

This, of course, did not prevent medieval architects from emulating the architectural visions of the Bible and religious literature and attempting to transform them into reality. Great numbers of Romanesque churches, which were frequently built and rebuilt over the course of centuries to conform to changing period tastes, were intended to make manifest, in the House of God, the ideal of the City of God and the New Jerusalem. Some of the most beautiful examples are found among the Romanesque churches of Cologne. There the Church of the Holy Apostles, St. Gereon, and Great St. Martin still bear witness to the intensity with which medieval master builders

Censer of Gozbertus, Trier. Cast gilt bronze, early twelfth century

Limbourg Brothers,
Les Très Riches Heures,
1416. Month of October,
showing peasants plowing
and sowing on the bank
of the Seine, with
the Louvre in the background

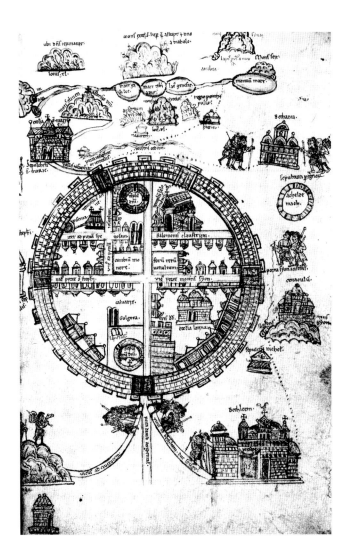

Miscellany, latter half of the twelfth century. This map, named for Fulco, the chronicler of the first crusade, reduces Jerusalem to the familiar, symbolically charged scheme of the quartered circle.

and church fathers strove to ⋯ ⋯s into reality.

In the *Annolied* and the poem *Hochzeit* (Nuptials) of the thirteenth century, the Heavenly Jerusalem found another broad, symbolic and spiritual interpretation. The closely guarded gates described in *Hochzeit*, made of shimmering precious stones and leading from four sides to the Kingdom of God, set striking architectural accents that played a key role in visual depictions of the motif. The decisive step towards a largely realistic description of the divine, ideal city was taken in the thirteenth-century poem, *Vom Himmelreich* (The Realm of Heaven). Its heavenly city, built of living stone and growing by the day, teemed with bustling medieval life. It had twelve gateways giving access from four sides, twelve towers with jewelled battlements echoing with songs of praise, and battlemented walls on which scores of angels stood watch, singing the praises of the Lord. Here the author supplemented the Revelation vision of the City of God with a compelling picture of an ideal medieval city of the chivalric age.

Yet as visual depictions of the period indicate, there was not one but several types of ideal city layout — rectangular, polygonal, round — with streets of various types. This is clearly corroborated by historical research.[5] After all, architectural manifestations of the Heavenly Jerusalem idea were not intended to be sheer fantasies but represented attempts to render visible, by poetic means, a realm beyond the human imagination that nevertheless materially affected human life.

It was typical of the Middle Ages that the concreteness of such depictions increased whenever the city was described as a fortified castle. At this point, religious and secular literature converged, as may be seen in Wolfram von Eschenbach's *Parzival* and Heinrich von Veldeke's *Eineide*. The building metaphor, on the one hand, was a key part of the storehouse of imagery and ideas with which the church reflected upon itself and represented its mystical essence. On the other, the motifs associated with the City of God filtered down into the secular realm of city, castle, and palace. This was a politically logical reference, to the Christian ruler by divine right, and to an interaction of political and religious domains in which it was a matter of course for Christian prince and Christian king to employ architectural metaphors that spirited them from the sphere of mere mortals into a divine realm.

While the Heavenly Jerusalem motif did not come to an end with its translation into medieval ideals, its significance diminished in the further course of history, except perhaps for the field of mystical literature, where it was frequently reactivated. Also, it later sometimes merged with other ideal notions, such as that of Eternal Rome. Nor has the New Jerusalem vanished from men's imagination even today, especially where visions of social utopias are concerned. In English literature, for instance, a train of thought can be discerned that leads from Plato's *Republic* through St. Augustine's *Civitas Dei*, the sacred and profane literature of the Middle Ages, to John Bunyan's *The Pilgrim's Progress*, William Blake's *Jerusalem*, William Makepeace Thackeray's *Vanity Fair*, and finally, in our own day, to Arnold Wesker's *Their Very Own and Golden Cities* and David Edgar's *Maydays*. With an ironic twist it even appears in Tom Wolfe's satirical novel *The Bonfire of the Vanities* (1987), a lasting monument to New York's yuppie culture of the 1980s.

Yet these contemporary authors were preceded by another who transformed the motif of the City of God on earth into a brilliant satirical vision of Ireland, Europe's most medieval country, where long into the twentieth century every fifth male was still a clergyman or a monk. This was James Joyce, in *Ulysses*:

> BLOOM: My beloved subjects, a new era is about to dawn. I, Bloom, tell you verily that it is even now at hand. Yea, on the word of a Bloom, ye shall ere long enter into the golden city which is to be, the new Bloomusalem in the Nova Hibernia of the future.

> (Thirtytwo workmen wearing rosettes, from all the counties of Ireland, under the guidance of Derwan the builder, construct the New Bloomusalem. It is a colossal edifice, with crystal roof, built in the shape of a huge pork kidney, containing forty thousand rooms. In the course of its extension several buildings and monuments are demolished. Government offices are temporarily transferred to railway sheds. Numerous houses are razed to the ground. The inhabitants are lodged in barrels and boxes, all marked in red with the letters: L.B. Several paupers fall from a ladder. A part of the walls of Dublin, crowded with loyal sightseers, collapses.)⁶

In secularized form the idea of the New Jerusalem also flowered in several interesting ways in twentieth-century architecture, particularly in cases where democratic ideas were to be given shape in new capital cities located outside developed centers. Canberra, Australia, and Brasília, Brazil, are only two examples, which also go to show the difficulties involved in bringing utopian vision into congruence with national and municipal realities.

St. Gereon, Cologne. Copperplate engraving, 1646

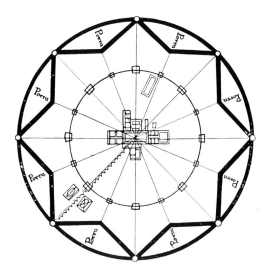

Filarete, Plan for the Ideal City of Sforzinda, ca. 1465

Palmanova (map) and Antonio Lupicini (ground plan), both sixteenth century

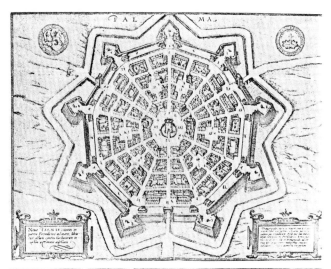

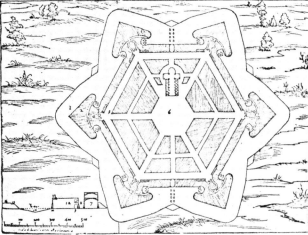

RENAISSANCE CONCEPTIONS OF THE IDEAL CITY

The cultural differences between the Middle Ages and the Renaissance are enormous, and nowhere do they become more obvious than in architecture, especially in architectural designs. In the Renaissance, a Christian, allegorical image of the ideal city was supplanted by that of a city planned according to rational, aesthetic, and military criteria. Compared to the walled-in chaos of medieval towns, even Babylon's layout may look planned; but compared to the theoretically grounded feasibility propagated by Leon Battista Alberti (1404–72), the leading Renaissance theorist, Babylon seems amorphous. Admittedly, *Roma quadrata* had gone before, but what is striking about the ideal city designs of the Renaissance is the relative absence of the principles of Roman city planning. Even Dürer's ideal city of 1527, despite its stringent geometric plan and square overall area, owed more to the military camps of Rome than to its cities. Yet the most obvious difference between Renaissance plans and those of the Middle Ages consisted in the replacement, at city center, of the House of God by the princely palace, the church being relegated to the periphery. A more striking illustration of the shift in values and ideals would be hard to imagine.

Alberti based his *Ten Books on Architecture (De re aedificatoria libri X)*, written between 1443 and 1452, on Vitruvius, the father of architectural theory, and on Platonic ideas, while taking account of his own and contemporaries' experiences and needs.[7] At the center of his urban design there now stood man, not God.

The buildings have been erected for men's sake, whether out of necessity or requirement or to enhance their lives, or whether it be to serve their passing pleasure. Human society is variously divisioned, wherefrom variety springs and whence also we must begin (IV.1).

Utility and a practical approach to life are supplemented here by precise ideas about the organizational form of the city, whose hierarchical structure is reflected even in the arrangement of the buildings. Still, Alberti's fundamental considerations on the meaning and use of cities deserve to be framed and hung on the wall of every urban planner's office today:

The ideal of a city and its tasks, according to the philosophers, may be seen in the fact that here the inhabitants lead a peaceful life, as free as possible of worries and care (IV.2).

And so I maintain, further, that a city should be conceived such that of all the disadvantages…none at all should be in evidence. And of all the things desirable for the necessities of life, none should lack (IV.2).

In his ideal city plans Alberti took account of geographical location, and the advantages and disadvantages of mountains, plains, and coasts. Even climate played an important role in his considerations.

Alberti's sixth book discussed the dignity of buildings, their charm and elegance, proportions and ornamentation. Their meaning, he said, lay in the creation of beauty, which he defined as the "regular conformity of all parts." This, too, was a dictum which held valid for Renaissance art in its entirety.

The Italian sculptor and architect Antonio di Pietro Averlino, alias Filarete (1400–69), served as court architect to Francesco Sforza in Milan. In his *Treatise on Architecture* (*Trattato d'architettura*; 1460–64), he designed an ideal city, Sforzinda, naming it for his patron. It had a star-shaped plan formed of two rotated, superimposed squares. "Rather," Filarete explained, "one corner must lay precisely midway between two others" (Book II). He also determined the exact position of streets, plazas, markets, cathedral, and princely palace. In his dialogue novel, however, many a clear conception was blurred by his imaginings of stately edifices for the nobleman. The city center was to be occupied not by a palace or church but by a tower of virtue, a public building with a moral purpose. Its two lower stories were reserved for the physical pleasures, containing a bordello, restaurants, baths, prostitutes' quarters, and police station. The seven upper stories were to house a library, a theater, and facilities for the study of the seven sciences. While a steep stairway made access to the halls of virtue rather arduous, once one was there, one could take an inclined ramp down to the rooms reserved for the sensual joys.

Leonardo da Vinci (1452–1519) sketched a modern-looking city built on two traffic levels in which the buildings were arranged with reference to streets, squares, and canals. Good water drainage and hygienic conditions also played an important role. Leonardo devoted much space to fortification structures, which were to gain increasing influence on Italian city planning; waging war, after all, was one of the favorite pastimes of the numerous monarchies and republics of Italy. In the sixteenth century, the design of entire cities was predicated on their fortifications.

Ground plan of the fortification of Casale, near Mantua. Built 1589–95

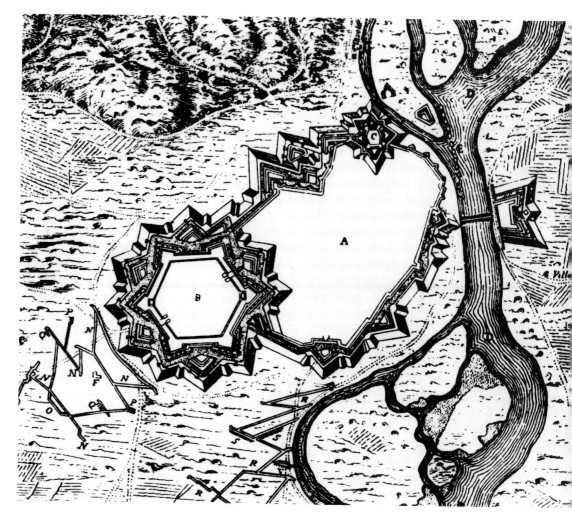

With Vincenzo Scamozzi (1552–1616), another gifted master builder attempted to solve the problem of the ideal city. His work *L'idea dell'architettura universale* (1615), published in many editions and languages, had a great influence on seventeenth-century architects both in Europe and beyond. In the second book, Scamozzi projected an ideal city on a twelve-sided plan whose stringent layout was based on the needs of defense. As this example shows, Alberti's successful mixture of social, aesthetic, and military components was increasingly supplanted in the late Renaissance by the dictates of geometry. Other examples are found in the numerous ideal city plans in the Italian tradition published by Jacques Perret, a Frenchman, in his manual *Des fortifications et artifices* of 1601. Ranging in shape from rectangular to twenty-four pointed star, his plans foresaw radial streets from center to periphery, blocks of buildings, and right-angled intersections that anticipated Baroque and American urban planning (if seeming exuberantly inventive by comparison to the latter's grids). Perret also designed palaces and houses, including one centrally located royal palace in a high-rise form that represented an astonishing harbinger of the future.

In the Late Renaissance and Early Baroque periods, conceptions of the ideal city were increasingly transferred to the field of the perspective stage, as well as entering theories of the state and philosophical novels about ideal states. Alberti's versatility and balance were never again reached, not even by the scenarios of Sebastiano Serlio (1475–1554). Even though none of the city designs mentioned above was ever actually built, the visionary architecture of the Renaissance did not remain without practical consequences, and it exerted considerable influence on Central European architecture in the period from the sixteenth to the eighteenth century. Absolutistic Baroque plans — like those of Karlsruhe, Mannheim and many other royal residence towns of the eighteenth century that emulated Versailles with any means at their disposal — translated quite faithfully into reality what two centuries before had been audacious imaginings.

Jacques Perret, A Royal Palace in the Form of a High-Rise, 1601

In the truest sense of the word, towers are among the most outstanding, imposing architectural structures, and they consequently have preoccupied and inspired architects, writers, artists, philosophers, engineers, and even prophets, preachers, and priests for centuries. Whatever towers may have antedated it, the Tower of Babel took on a myth-forming function, its name entering the language as a metaphor for the advancement, expansion, and transgression of human limitations.

No other building in history has ever assumed such fantastic dimensions as this tower, which in reality was an enormous block with a ground area of a thousand square feet, was more than six stories high, had a 200-foot-long and 30-foot-wide central stairway, and measured 295 feet (some estimates say 300) to its peak. As it was visible from a great distance over the flat plains, it may well have seemed that the tower indeed wished to wed itself with the heavens. In short, the Tower of Babel was a stepped pyramid, a ziggurat, a temple about whose cultic significance many interesting theories exist, but no surviving text that would prove or disprove them. Biblical tradition, in an odd chronology, places its construction immediately following the Flood and the story of Noah in the Book of Genesis; the real tower apparently went up at the beginning of the second millennium B.C. Still, the biblical tower's lack of basis in historical fact has only served to enhance its magnetism as a myth.

Two stories intertwine in the report on the building of the Tower of Babel: its actual construction and the confounding of tongues brought down upon its builders by the Lord. Here language met architecture, and in their common tendency to hubris, a presumptuous belief born of inventiveness and religious zeal in men's ability to surpass themselves and become godlike, the edifice of language crumbled with the tower. The Old Testament God watched jealously over his privileges, and dealt harsh punishment to those who sinned against them:

Reconstruction of the Tower of Babel, east elevation. After Busink, 1938; colored by Erwin Heinle, 1986

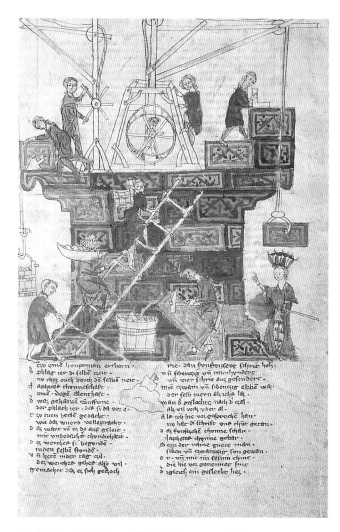

The Building of the Tower of Babel, Bohemia, ca. 1340

Ambrogio Lorenzetti, View of a Fortified City (Città sul Mare). Oil on wood, ca. 1346

And they said one to another, Go to, let us make brick, and burn them thoroughly. And they had brick for stone, and slime had they for morter. And they said, Go to, let us build us a city and a tower, whose top may reach unto heaven; and let us make us a name, lest we be scattered abroad upon the face of the whole earth (Genesis 11.3–4).

Yet what to some seemed collective delusion, an attempt to leave behind the temporal and spatial limitations imposed on mankind and aspire to a godlike measure in order to plumb the immeasurable, was for others the focus of a religious cult. From the beginning, in other words, the Tower of Babel bore religious, sacred, and literary connotations of a positive nature. There are salient reasons to assume that the mountain-shaped temple of Babylon, consecrated to the city god Marduk, was intended to symbolize the world mountain that according to Babylonian religion stood at the beginning of Creation. Thus the tower presumably signified the opposite of hubris to the Babylonians, namely harmony with the universe and a reminder of human limits. It was also certainly a masterpiece of engineering and architectural art, and there is good reason to believe that in its late period, before the Persians destroyed it, the Tower of Babylon served scientific purposes as well. Indeed the Babylonians' influence on the sciences — especially in the fundamentals of weights and measures, and in the fields of mathematics, astronomy, medicine, linguistics, and law — has remained important to this day.

In medieval literature the Tower of Babel is described in the Genesis poems of the eleventh and twelfth centuries, in the *Annolied,* in Lamprecht's *Tobias,* in the chronicles of Rudolf von Ems and Jansen Enikel, and in *Reinfried von Braunschweig.* In the course of time the height of the tower grew in authors' imaginations to 4,000 fathoms in the *Annolied,* and to 5,047 fathoms for Jansen Enikel; most credited Nimrod, founder of the Babylonian empire, with its construction. In Enikel's case, fantasy got the upper hand in every respect. The incredibly rich king of Babylon, he relates, built the tower so that he could conveniently climb to heaven; seventy-two master masons trained a further one hundred masters each, and then worked until the king's treasury had been transformed into stone.

In sum, the highly symbolic story in Genesis was divested of its imaginative significance for human history and, seen through the eyes of medieval building activity, the

Tower of Babel took on the character of an architectural vision. This vision, in turn, was superimposed on contemporary tower structures, sublimating them to fairy tale proportions, as countless illustrations of the period confirm.

The hubris motif also played a role in the actual tower architecture of the period. In the twelfth and thirteenth centuries, the appearance of important Italian towns was dominated by the battle towers of the local nobility. As Stanislaus von Moos writes, the streets of most of these towns must have been plunged in shadow, cast by the massive shafts and jutting projections of such towers.[8]

Famed far and wide were those of Pavia — the City of a Hundred Towers — Vicenza, and Ascoli Piceno. Visiting Pisa in 1159, Benjamin von Tudela maintained that he had counted 10,000 towers there, though his imagination must have got the better of him. In Bologna, on the other hand, it is said that there were at least 180 family towers and that the streets often resounded with the rumbling of siege machines on the way to some private war. Towers and dwellings were crowded together, and when attackers managed to demolish a tower, the consequences for the inhabitants were horrifying. The highest of them, the Torre Asinelli in Bologna, is said to have been 318 feet tall, higher than the Tower of Babel, in other words. Those of Florence were only slightly shorter, and from a report of the year 1248 we know that noble families fought each other day and night from their battlements.

While such towers had military advantages, they were also a means of demonstrating family prestige and power. When ambition and pride impelled them to too great a height, their usefulness as fortifications dwindled. As families sometimes ensconced themselves for years in such towers in wartime or when one of their members was threatened by a vendetta, they may be viewed as predecessors of the modern apartment building in many respects, although the first true high-rise dwellings were not built until the seventeenth century.

The significance of the Tower of Babel as a model for architects began to increase as soon as they recognized its potential as a self-contained miniature city, a vertical city within the city. Its famed depictions in paintings of the sixteenth and seventeenth centuries — in 1563 by Pieter Bruegel the Elder (1520–69), by Lucas van Valckenborch (1535–97), and in 1679 by Athanasius Kircher (1602–80) — probably contributed much to this realization. The tops of Bruegel's and Kircher's towers even pierced the clouds, indicating the arrogance and absurdity of the project. While all of the towers in these paintings already had an urban character, Bruegel and Valckenborch apparently assumed such structures were fated to remain unfinished. Sections of the tower at various stages of completion or decay symbolized the entire undertaking as vain, for the work of human hands is not exempt from the eternal cycle. Kircher, trained as a Jesuit, brought a highly interesting qualitative leap into the history of

The Building of the Tower of Babel. Thirteenth-century mosaic, St. Mark's, Venice

Book of Hours of the Duke of Bedford. *The Building of the Tower of Babel*, ca. 1423

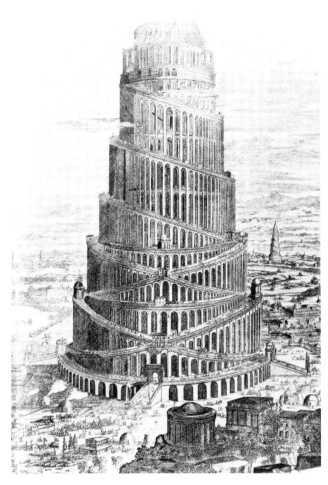

Athanasius Kircher, *Model of an Ideal City*, 1679

the interpretation of the Tower of Babel. He envisaged it as a basi-cally feasible ideal city, of the kind that had come into fashion with the authors of sixteenth- and seventeenth-century state novels ("*Staatsromane*"), who were on the trail of the Golden Age and hoped to contribute to bringing it into being. With Kircher's far-sightedness, the door was opened for the ideal designs of modern tall buildings.

From the Gothic period onwards, ecclesiastical architecture satis-fied urban religious prestige with ever-higher church towers to the glory of God and as a symbol of his City. Competition to build the highest church tower soon set in. The 466-foot-tall tower of Stras-bourg Cathedral held the record for a full 450 years, until it was sur-passed in 1880 by the 515 feet of Cologne Cathedral and in 1890 by the 528 feet of that in Ulm. Other religions, such as Buddhism and Islam, also recognized the myth-engendering function of the tower as a visible symbol of religious community, identity, and power. Considerations of utility naturally played a part as well. What the church bells were to one religion, the muezzin calling the faithful to prayer was to the other.

In the meantime, however, the literary tradition of the tower motif had brought forth a characteristic variant, in William Beck-ford's eighteenth-century novel, *Vathek*. Here, biblical sources, pop-

Robert Delauney, *The Eiffel Tower (The Red Tower)*.
Oil on canvas, 1911

ular legend, and Oriental fairy tales issued in a story of personal megalomania. It was no longer collective presumption but collective stupidity that submitted to the criminally sacrilegious thirst for knowledge and immeasurable conceit of the Caliph Vathek. Beckford's novel was, among other things, a satire, which lent the tradition of Babel a new aspect while including all the earlier ones. For by this time the sacred associations of the tower had long been supplemented by military, scholarly, and commercial, utilitarian functions, such as those of the lighthouse that guides ships past shallows and shoals to safe harbor. Architecturally, Vathek's tower, where he and his mother, Carathis, devoted themselves to occult sciences and monstrous crimes, was a veritably endless shaft with 11,000 steps, a psychologically swaggering phallus symbol with which Beckford compensated for the frustrations of his forbidden homosexuality. Yet at the same time, his tower anticipated the visions of modern architects, who since the 1950s have been dreaming of, and sometimes actually planning, tower projects of 3,000 or even 6,000 feet in height.

The nineteenth century brought considerable progress in the field of engineering, particularly in the glass and iron construction of bridges, crystal palaces, and towers, the most renowned of which, Gustave Eiffel's, was inaugurated in Paris in 1889. At 984 feet, the Eiffel Tower remained the tallest structure in the world until the 1930s, when the honor was taken over by the Empire State Building in New York City. Such towers became familiar landmarks, and often enough the pride of an entire nation. The construction of tall apartment and commercial buildings, on the other hand, had to wait for a number of technical inventions, especially the elevator — first the steam-powered one, patented by Elisha Graves Otis in 1861, followed by Werner von Siemens' electric lift of 1880. Another key

Maurits Cornelis Escher, *The Tower of Babel.* Woodcut, 1928

Erich Kettelhut, *Metropolis.* Film set, 1926

31

development was the steel and concrete skeleton structure. When, in 1883, the first modern high-rise building of eleven stories opened its doors in Chicago, a race for new height records began, and is still under way. But what interests us here is not so much an outline history of the skyscraper as its effects on architectural thinking and innovation,[9] because in many respects the skyscraper resembles the Formula I racing car — what stands the test of extreme conditions is often good for the assembly line.

Historically speaking the skyscraper, the dominant form of tower architecture for a hundred years now, having supplanted its ecclesiastical forerunners in terms of myth-forming vision as well, was indeed born old. Skyscraper architects have begged or borrowed whatever they could in the way of ennobling features from church and palace, in order to hide the fact that their designs frequently consist of little more than a vertical pile of stereotyped functional levels.

But it would be unfair to attach to skyscrapers only the negative aspects of the Babel myth: technological ambition, a striving for power and prestige or masculine potency, scientific presumption. The other side of the coin gives just as true a picture, for skyscrapers can be beautiful, exude optimism and a joy in life, represent a challenge to the arts of engineering, statics, and design. Louis H. Sullivan (1856–1924) and his successors, who made Chicago and New York into the cradles of the skyscraper, also introduced innovative leaps on a tremendous scale. For a very long time neither the Protestant nor the Jewish ethic of the American middle and upper-middle class had any difficulty in merging sacred and profane motives, God and money, to the point of indistinguishability. Every dollar bill still carries the motto, "In God We Trust." Success in the here and now promises success in the hereafter. The architectural embodiment of such thinking, justly termed "cathedrals of commerce" by the evangelist Dr. S. Parkes Cadman, were department stores and office buildings like the Singer Building (1908), the Woolworth Building (1913), and the many designs submitted to the Chicago Tribune competition of 1922. Like the neoclassical, art deco, modern and postmodern variants of later years, these structures were a perfect expression of twentieth-century commercial society. Their elegance, beauty, and style will outlast many a fashionable trapping and short-lived fad.

Top left:
Hugh Ferris, *The Mooring Mast,
An Airport of the Future.*
Drawing, ca. 1930

Top right:
Hugh Ferris, *The Convocation
Tower.* Drawing, ca. 1924

Bottom:
Matthäus Böblinger, *Ulm
Cathedral.* Sketch, 1377

32

The skyline, a haphazard growth that nevertheless exhibited rhythmical articulation, was a concept and visual symbol of the modern metropolis that emerged in New York City. Soaring above the horizontal layer of pulsating life in the streets, it formed, as it were, an abstract urban melody, with towers setting *forte* and *fortissimo* accents. Thinking, planning, seeing, and experiencing in terms of the skyline concept gradually spread from New York and Chicago to the other big cities of the North American subcontinent, and has since increasingly influenced the look of South American, Asian, and European cities.

The modern idea of the Tower of Babel, visualized by Renaissance artists as a largely self-sufficient city in a single building, took on

Howells and Hood, *Chicago Tribune Tower*. Competition entry, 1922 (1st prize)

Adolf Loos, *Chicago Tribune Tower*, perspective view. Competition entry, 1922

Hiroshi Hara, Umeda City 1993. Vision
of a twenty-first century high-rise building
capped by a futuristic arcade

concrete shape in such skyscrapers as the Rockefeller Center in New York and, more recently, in the Shim Umeda City project by the Tokyo architect Hiroshi Hara.

Before functionalist modernism (or, as the Americans say, the International Style) reduced tower architecture to the minimal point that in Mies van der Rohe's hands could still be high art but in those of his camp-followers produced functions in a box, neoclassicism, beaux arts, and art deco had brought forth richly ornamented towers that were aesthetic events. Then, in the 1960s and 1970s, there suddenly began to appear erections in steel and glass that unabashedly expressed the money-making mentality, such as Minoru Yamasaki's World Trade Center in New York.

It all began in the 1920s and 1930s, when Hugh Ferris, a true visionary of monumental architecture, supplied his lyrical drawings to a number of offices specializing in skyscrapers. The result was a great building boom among the financiers, who were asked to make huge loans available for the purpose. Skyscrapers had always been very expensive, as their long construction periods necessitated considerable interim financing and, when they topped fifteen floors, security regulations and technical problems raised costs to the point of seriously threatening their profitability. Under Ferris's hand, however, dreams became reality and reality a dream. He borrowed prolifically, from the Babel myth as much as from Greek and Roman temples, from the motifs of medieval architecture and from those of Mayan and Aztec cultures. Ferris managed to create an enthusiasm for building, working and living in tall buildings whose set-piece Mesopotamian, ancient Greek, and Latin American decor formed a kind of substrate for American dreams of the future.

When a narrative element returned to architecture under postmodern influence in the 1970s and 1980s, the smooth, generally mirror-finished shafts of tall buildings suddenly began to sprout decor: loggias, balustrades, parapets, projections, ramps, ramifications, multi-material facades. From historical quote to gags and surprises, anything that would lend skyscrapers color and interest again was back in demand. Out of a misunderstanding

34

about the American life-style and the role played by show business there — especially during the Reagan presidency — most European architectural critics reacted with moral indignation over the ostensible dishonesty of this latter-day historical revival. What they overlooked, as has now become apparent as the period draws to a close, was the infusion of architectural imagination it brought to a late modernism grown sterile.

Cases in point are Philip Johnson's AT&T Building in New York City with its Chippendale cabinet cornice (1979–84; today the Sony Building); the mirror-glazed Gothic turrets and battlements of the PPG corporate headquarters in Pittsburgh, Pennsylvania (1984); the terraced, pseudo-Flemish pointed pediments of Johnson's NCNB Center in Houston, Texas (1984); and the Hohenstauffen castle character of 33 Maiden Lane, New York (1986), to recall only a few of the old costume master's creations. The enormous, sky-shooting columnar structures of Kevin Roche's J.P. Morgan Bank Headquarters in New York City (1988) also deserve mention. William Pedersen's alternately classical, medieval, Renaissance or, more recently, technologically neo-modernistic facades all evoke urbane culture in their knowingly playful manipulation of architectural history. In a postmodern computerized age where architects have every style and stylistic blend at their fingertips, this attitude is certainly defendable. What is more, their juggling with decor tends to hide the fact that behind the glitzy facades of 1980s skyscrapers, effectiveness and functionality have risen 50–60% by comparison to earlier generations, thanks mainly to better ground plans and new technologies. Still, many and the most spectacular of such designs never left the drawing board, and were relegated to the twilight zone of "unbuilt architecture."[10] The term is a broad one, and covers designs matured to the point of building which, for whatever reason, could not be realized; rejected, but frequently highly progressive compe-

Philip Johnson, PPG Corporate Headquarters.
Pittsburgh, Pennsylvania, 1979–84

Helmut Jahn, Northwestern
Terminal Building. Chicago,
1979–87

tition entries; and studies whose utopian or futuristic character earmarked them from the beginning as thought-provoking, visionary designs.

The skyscraper boom of the 1980s also revived the intoxication with high places felt by all tower-builders, including Frank Lloyd Wright, who in 1956 dreamt of a One Mile Building. In the meantime, U.S. and Japanese architects consider structures of 6,000 feet in height quite feasible, compared to which the present world-record holders, the Sears Tower in Chicago (1974), at 1,453 feet, and the World Trade Center in New York City (1972–77), at 1,352, seem just as dwarfish as the highest television towers, Toronto's at 1,749 feet and Moscow's at 1,772. With the Miglin-Beitler Tower in Chicago (first design 1988), 125 stories and 1,995 feet in height, whose plans are finished and approved but whose building has been postponed due to the recession, Cesar Pelli has set out to beat the existing

Peter Cook, *Trickling Tower 1996*, 1978–79

Skidmore, Owings & Merrill, John Hancock Center. Chicago, 1969

Robert Gabriel, *Design for a 2000-meter High Tower City*, 1969

height record for a skyscraper by all of 542 feet. Dubbed the Sky-needle, the tower with its progressively recessed stories would indeed create a dramatic impression of soaring to the sky. According to the architect, however, it is still entirely uncertain at this point whether and when the project can be realized.

Another of Pelli's large-scale projects need not fear a similar fate. Its first construction phase has already begun, and its completion is scheduled for 1996. And though the 88 stories of the new Kuala Lumpur City Center in Malaysia will end a mere 1,476 feet above ground level, it will make Pelli the king of skyscraper builders nonetheless. This is a gigantic project of truly Babylonian proportions, a city in a building consisting of two twin towers with an office space of eight million square feet, intended for the headquarters of the Petrona Corporation. It also contains one and three-quarter million square feet of shopping, restaurant, and entertainment areas, an

Cesar Pelli, Miglin-Beitler Tower. Model, 1988

Opposite page:
Cesar Pelli, Kuala Lumpur City Center.
Model, first building phase 1993–96

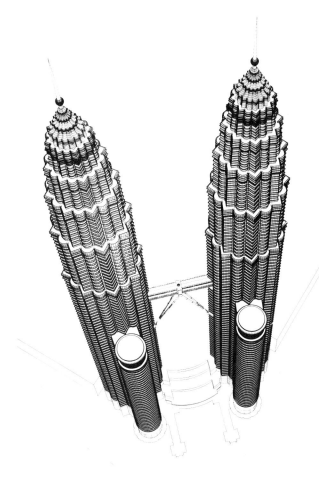

Cesar Pelli, *Kuala Lumpur City Center*. Isometric drawing and ground plan

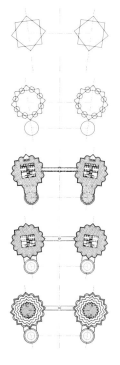

Helmut Jahn, *South West Center*, Houston. Competition entry, 1982

underground garage for 4,500 vehicles, a museum, a concert hall seating 1,000, and a multimedia conference center. This new landmark of Kuala Lumpur impressively emphasizes the shift currently taking place in the centers of world trade, which will naturally bring a growing influence and political clout in its wake.

The configuration of the two towers is based on the principles of Islamic geometry. Their ground plan consists of two rotated, superimposed quadrants which in turn are intersected and modified by a ring of smaller circles. This geometric system permits a flexible planning of the office space, and opens a panorama view from the windows on every side of the building.

However, the technical difficulties involved in construction increase with height. Without computers, sensor systems, and electronic control and supervision devices, the problems of energy utilization, utility lines, sufficient water pressure, fire and storm protection, the logistics of vertical traffic streams, climate control, and light regulation would be simply insoluble. When you consider that the 198 elevators in the World Trade Center carry 50,000 employees and 80,000 visitors daily, or that the Sears Tower express elevator takes only 72 seconds to reach the top of the building, you gain some

idea of the challenges faced by architects and engineers in designing and constructing today's tall buildings. And as the bomb attack on that very New York World Trade Center on 16 February 1993 showed in a glaring light for the first time, the security risks involved in the building of superskyscrapers are enormous, and explosions, bombings, and wars can have disastrous effects on life in the modern metropolis.

All of this suggests a number of arguments against the building of towers which deserve to be taken seriously. These extend from the religious and philosophical reasons associated with the ancient Babylonian hubris metaphor, to those involving considerations of ecology, transportation, and urban climate, and finally technological, humanitarian, and aesthetic arguments.

Still, the reasons in favor of building skyscrapers predominate. The trend to the megalopolis and increasing urban density will continue. How else can urban sprawl à la Los Angeles be prevented, if not by building vertically? If what American contract lawyers versed in the Japanese real-estate business tell me is true — that with the sum total of Tokyo's property prices you could buy the entire United States including Alaska — how can the cost of building land in big cities be kept under control except by resorting to skyscrapers?

The German artist Gerd Winner has been fascinated for decades now by urban structures and townscapes. One of the subjects he has done variation after variation on, recording its historical change and projecting its future, is Times Square in New York. Shooting upwards, turning and twisting, crumbling and falling, interpenetrating and superimposed, the architectural elements in Winner's paintings of Times Square symbolize the layered, developmental character of the big city. They evoke its unquenched vitality, and at the same time the danger of its falling prey to its own complexity, mobility, and unchecked acceleration of the city's vital processes. The color schemes and increasingly dynamic character of Winner's more recent paintings lend them an apocalyptic undertone. The day is not far when the great catastrophe, at least in this symbolically heightened imagery, will break over Times Square and with it over the modern Babylon.

The race to break the height record seemed to be over, when President Reagan's economic policy revealed its true core, namely a readiness to pile up astronomical debt that has logically resulted in a long and painful recession. The present oversupply of office space in skyscrapers around the country is considerable, and will probably last for years to come. Even in financially healthy Frankfurt, large tracts of Helmut Jahn's Messeturm, Europe's tallest office building at 842 feet, stand empty due to high rents. Not to mention the financial debacle in which Olympia and York, the largest financing company in the world, became involved when Canary Wharf in London turned out to be a flop.

The company's owners, the Reichman brothers of Toronto, had a

Gerd Winner, *Times Square*. Silkscreen print, 1987–88

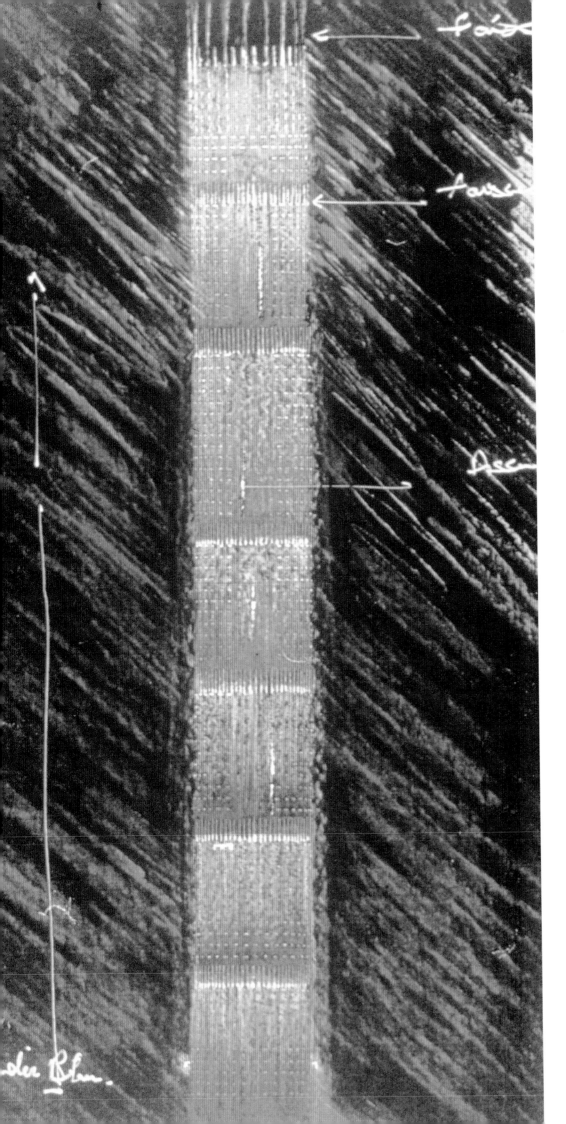

reputation for solidity and careful planning. Yet when you leaf through the glossy brochures from the planning stages and compare them with what has actually happened in London's Docklands, the necessity to continually temper architectural vision by reference to harsh reality becomes apparent. An offshoot of conservative Thatcherite economics, the project promised nothing less than an architectural squaring of the circle: a postmodern test-tube city of highrise and medium-height office and residential buildings, coexisting with an entirely refur-bished premodern Thames waterfront. When the Thatcher era came to an end, the bubble popped, leaving the old, organic city to emerge the winner.

Still, skyscrapers will continue to go up, and they will remain the urban landmarks of cities of the future, for their aesthetic appeal and engineering challenge cannot pale. It would seem, though, that their symbolism is increasingly shifting from an evocation of a specifically American outlook on life to that of a global, urban architectural language, in which regional accents nonetheless find a place. And as tall towers play such a highly visible role on the urban stage, creative imagination is especially crucial to their design. At present, the apparently irreducible, geometric containers for a given set of functions are occasionally mutating into urban chains of mountains, putting out lateral annexes, toying with new forms, geometries, materials, and medial elements. In an age of chaos research and computer simu-

Jean Nouvel and Yann Kersalé, *Tour de l'infini.*
Study, 1991

lation, organic configurations and fractals are coming to the fore. In recent skyscraper designs by Rogers and Foster, or by Pedersen and Zeidler, for instance, variously structured volumes emerge from one another like organic growths. It is no longer only visionary architects like Peter Cook, with his combinations of high-tech and ecological architectures, who are now experimenting in the field of skyscraper design in an attempt to find generally acceptable and humane solutions.

The original myth of the tower in its purest and, at the same time, its most compellingly poetic form, is represented by the *Tour de l'infini*, a tower of infinity, envisaged by Jean Nouvel in collaboration with the French artist-in-light, Yann Kersalé, for the experimental quarter La Défense in Paris. The project foresees, behind the Grande Arche, a cylindrical tower with an overall height of 1,511 feet, erected over a ground area of only 131 × 131 feet. At this 11.5 : 1 ratio of height to width, the structure would achieve an unprecedented degree of slenderness. Its coloring, beginning with a base of black granite, would pass through subtle gradations of gray and finally to complete transparency; the upper twelve stories (157 feet) are to consist entirely of glass, including their floors. During the night, changing lighting effects would be produced with the aid of a computer programmed to react to various parameters, such as the traffic flowing beneath La Défense and the number of visitors entering the tower. The illumination is designed to accentuate the impression of a progressive, irresistible upward motion, gradually changing from dark blue at the base to a pure, dispersed white at the top. There, the spotlights of Kersalé's light cannons would project vertical beams as far as 13,000 feet into the sky, further increasing the effect of an infinitesimal transition from earthbound materiality to the immateriality of light in space. As photons are simultaneously waves and particles, Kersalé sees his installation as symbolizing both the spiritual and physical character of poetic thought and philosophical systems.

The effects are to be created by means of sixteen light cannons installed in the foundations, supplemented by light-sensitive pixels on the skin of the building's facade. These will receive light from 96 motorized parabolic mirrors mounted on six different floors, at vertical intervals of 151 feet. Also, prisms connected to generators by fiber-optic cables will be distributed over the facades, to refract and intensify the light, and contribute to the play of luminous color over the skin of the tower.

Kersalé is a magician, a crusader in light who takes up the challenge of the powers of darkness, wrests their secrets from them, creates new ones, and submits the realm of obscurity to the metamorphoses of light. As he has shown with the Grand Palais or the Opera de la Bastille, he is capable of divesting architecture of its mass, making it appear to hover weightness. With the aid of powerful projectors Kersalé accentuates key architectural passages of

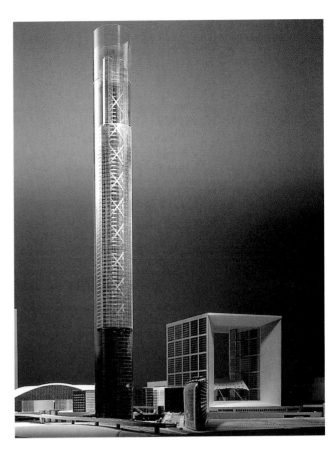

Montage with *Tour de l'infini* and Grande Arche, La Défense, Paris

Jean Nouvel and Yann Kersalé, *Tour de l'infini*, foyer Study, 1991

43

buildings and lets them glow in festive brilliance. And, as he says, the signs and messages he projects out into the night and into nature have mythical and mystical overtones.

The plans for the tower are finished, the building permit approved, and a construction firm has even been found. Yet whether the ambitious project will ever become a reality remains to be seen. France is no exception in having been hit hard by the 1990s recession, which has led to a surplus of office space. Right now, returns on investments seem inadequate to justify a project of this scope. Then, too, a political epoch, the Mitterand era, is coming to an end. Like no other socialist president in the past, François Mitterrand linked up to the building traditions of the absolute monarchs, encouraging *grands projets* not so much with an eye to his own future fame as to the status of his country as an international cultural power, an aim probably best achieved by architecture. Thanks to its concentration of significant modern architecture, Paris remains one of the most attractive cities in the world. Nouvel and Kersalé's *Tour de l'infini*, which they alternatively call a *Tour sans fin*, embodiesan architectural vision that is a match for the ideal designs of Boullée and Ledoux. Now that the civil aviation authorities have dropped their objections, the realization of the tower at least has become imaginable, though the new political era on the horizon promises to relegate it to the distant future, if not entirely to the realm of architectural fantasy. If the tower were indeed built, Paris would have gained yet another unique architectural landmark.

Jean Nouvel and Yann Kersalé. *Tour de l'infini*. Model

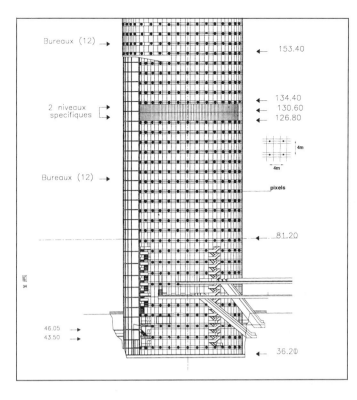

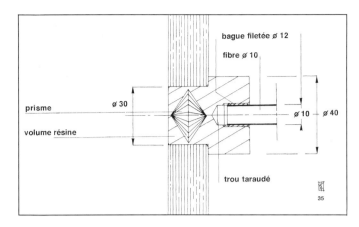

Left: *Tour de l'infini*. Side view of pixel wall
Right: *Tour de l'infini*. Detail of light installation with
glass fiber cables, generators, and prisms

Yann Kersalé, representation of light effects in the *Tour de l'infini*

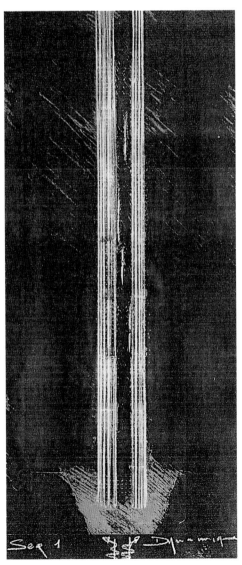

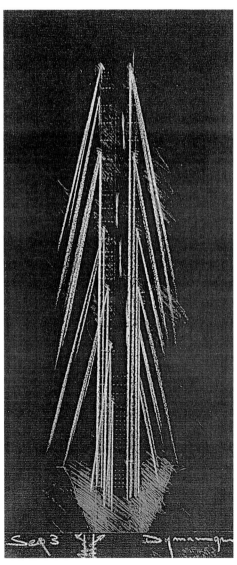

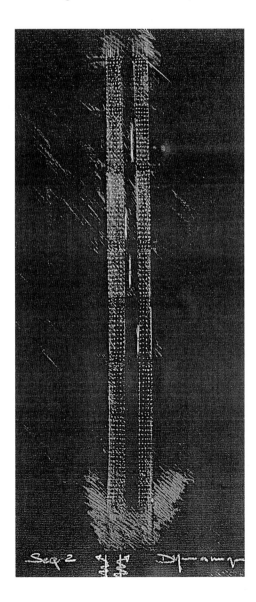

Consciousness Goes Modern:
Giovanni Battista Piranesi
and His Successors

Giovanni Battista Piranesi, *Le Carceri.* First plate, 1760

As eighteenth-century European monarchs were laying out their residences and palace parks in accordance with geometrically harmonious ideal plans, a Roman architect, draughtsman, and engraver projected the visions of his troubled mind onto copper plates in a way that made him seem, to later Romantic artists, a congenial spirit who had anticipated their own world view. Today he is understood as the first visual artist to capture what his contemporary, Laurence Sterne, had captured in language: the traumatic experiences of an anxious ego that had become just as aware of its psychologically precarious position as of the societal compulsions to which it was subject. In this respect, Sterne and Piranesi were the legitimate predecessors of James Joyce and many other twentieth-century artists.

The official architecture of the period was a different matter entirely. It was a time of late Baroque abundance and ostentation, insouciant Rococo ornamentation on churches, palaces, and pleasure seats, followed by neoclassical temples and facades that were bright and friendly but determined by a strict order reflecting the intactness of a class society and the stability of its rulers' tastes. Piranesi was at cross-purposes with his era, and not surprisingly, his *Invenzioni Capric di Carceri* (1745, second state 1761) — commonly known as *Le Carceri* (The Prisons) — on which his present-day fame rests, met with bafflement and rejection when it was published. His contemporaries valued him for other imaginary architectural views, like the series *Antichità Romane,* the *Vedute di Roma,* or *Il Campo Marzio dell'antica Roma,* for the simple reason that they were based on actual, existing architecture. The distortions in perspective, proportions, or dimensions may have bothered Piranesi's viewers, his manneristic flourishes and details may have seemed ridiculous, or the gulfs that opened over an urban underworld rather disquieting — nevertheless, the mastery of his engraving technique could not be gainsaid. But the *Carceri…*

Not only the Romantic Period but also the immediate present has come to rely on Piranesi as on an Atlas of visionary architectural drawing, whose shoulders have been made to bear a continually growing flock of adepts toying with the bright or sinister side of the utopias his work evokes. Piranesi has also become the progenitor of a now flourishing, now stagnating genre of architectural renderings with which specialist galleries have made a market for themselves. And none of the innumerable exhibitions of visionary or utopian architecture, past or present, would be imaginable without a reference to Piranesi. Genuine shows of his own work, too, remain unflaggingly popular.

So it is time to suggest that apart from stimulating the mind and filling the museum, Piranesi's art has had a direct influence on working architects, such as Aldo Rossi, or such as the late Charles Moore, even if this influence blends with many others. As the architect Günter Krawinkel notes:

Critics have remarked certain traits in the postmodern — or, as Charles Jencks has recently termed it, the "late modern" architecture of our day which also can be detected in Piranesi's drawings: a tendency to the monumental, a distortion of scale, a play with symmetry, a preference for diagonals, a use of historical quotes, a deployment of building elements as set-pieces to the point of ironical exaggeration, and not least, the ambivalence of many statements (buildable/not buildable, inside/outside, light/darkness, construction/destruction).[11]

Giovanni Battista Piranesi, *Le Carceri*. Seventh plate, 1760

There are various reasons for Piranesi's popularity, including the insecurity of our era and the resulting feelings of anxiety and tendency to introspection, and also the renewed intensive research and expertise that have been devoted to Piranesi's oeuvre since the 1970s. Postmodern detachment and irony with respect to architectural vision and design have also played a role.

Literature, especially English literature, was quick to absorb what Piranesi provided in the way of architectural metaphor. Yet art history, which sometimes tends to avoid an involvement with the work by concentrating on its developmental context, long overlooked the fact that Piranesi's effect has been a largely literary one. His influence on English literature and on French Romanticism has been described by a number of authors. It is a tradition that must be taken into account by anyone who sets out to investigate the interplay between built and projected architecture, or between architecture in literature and painting. And if it results in abbreviating Piranesi largely to his *Carceri*, the reasons are to be found in the literary movement that emerged shortly after the publication of the second, revised version of that portfolio — the Gothic novel.

The effects of Piranesi's views of Rome have been lasting as well, motivating generations of European travellers to complete their education with a Roman tour, and invoking like no other depictions before them the ambivalent, fantastic atmosphere of the city. Piranesi treats Rome as a special case, *the* city per se, telescoping two millennia of building history into a single, compelling image. A print like *Ideal View of the Via Appia* shows a grotesque agglomeration of monuments, Babylonian, Graeco-Roman, Renaissance, and exotic inventions concatenated. The result cannot help but speak to the postmodern sensibility. Rome, as the architectural museum it doubtless is, exhibits itself here, and with disbelieving gestures the tourists point out its sights to one another. The scene has something incredibly theatrical about it, like Ludovico Ottavio Burnacini's opera sets of the late seventeenth century. Awe gives way to laughter, laughter to horror as the traumatic experiences which massed brick and stone can also elicit begin to surface, when, in other prints, the city itself seems prostrated by fever, dreaming a dream that turns into a nightmare, of a bottomless pit from the depths of which subterranean terrors spring, where decay spreads everywhere, in all directions and human reliance on plans and rules dissolves in a pro-

Giovanni Battista Piranesi, *Le Carceri.* Third plate, 1760

Giovanni Battista Piranesi, *Le Carceri.* Eighth plate, 1760

liferating chaos. In its mixture of the sublime, the cruel, and the ironically funny this aesthetic of the grotesque is, moreover, beautiful, which lends Piranesi's imagery its timeless and perennially modern character.

The *Carceri* can deny their relationship with the architecture of Roman baths as little as their reliance on contemporaneous stage sets. They derive their aesthetic effect from the device known as paradox: a simultaneity of opposites, such as hall and dungeon, light and darkness, inside and out, palace and ruin, yawning spaces populated by tiny, deindividualized figures, flight after flight of stairs offering escape only to collide with a wall from which instruments of torture appear to dangle. Piranesi's visionary architecture is like the setting of a dream blown up to gigantic scale, and it recalls the latter-day dreams in semi-sleep which played such an important part in Surrealism. Thanks to Piranesi's vision, the aesthetic canon of the period was expanded by the concepts of anxiety and fear as preconditions for the effect of the sublime. This is why Norbert Miller entitled his detailed, scrupulous, and ingenious study on Piranesi *Archäologie des Traums* (Archaeology of the Dream).[12]

Edmund Burke's *Philosophical Enquiry into the Origin of Our Ideas of the Sublime and Beautiful*, a philosophical study of the sublime in which the concept was divorced from previous notions of beauty, was published in 1756, almost concurrently with the second edition of the *Carceri*. As this fact indicates, quite independently of time, place, and social position, a reorientation in aesthetics took place in the latter half of the eighteenth century, towards "the aspect of a provocation of the sensibilities in a liberating breaking down of the bounds of reality by means of a depiction of the infinite."[13]

In England, Horace Walpole was the first to give Piranesi his aesthetic due and moreover to attempt to translate Piranesi's imagery into literary practice. Initially, in his *Anecdotes of Painting in England* (1762–80), Walpole advised artists to study Piranesi, saying he piled palaces on bridges and temples on palaces, striving to reach the heavens over mountains of architecture. Yet for all their daring, Walpole went on, Piranesi's drawings revealed an impeccable taste, a grand dignity of design, and a prolific imagination expressed in fluently yet carefully rendered details.[14]

Then, with *The Castle of Otranto* (1764), Walpole published the first novel to use Piranesi's new aesthetic and impressions of architectural space in a programmatic way. "Written without a sense of the uncanny," noted Miller, the story "introduced the uncanny into the novel genre, in fact even into the thinking and ideas of the eighteenth century."[15] Walpole was a distinguished connoisseur and art critic, but not a particularly talented author. The joints and hinges of his novel tend to squeak rather amateurishly, despite the fact that it already contains almost the entire list of "haunted house" attributes: a castle equipped with a labyrinth of dark corridors, underground passageways and vaults, creaking doors, eerie noises, halls plunged in semi-obscurity, vague light sources, flights of stairs, drawbridges, secret entrances, and dungeons. These are supplemented by other, more affective motifs such as young innocence persecuted, a family curse, incest, trial by torture, inquisition, a convent, a cave, an abyss, mountains, a demoniacal protagonist — in short, an iconography that can be described as a semiotics of violence, oppression, sublimated sexuality, sadism, domination and demise, the reverse of which is individual loneliness, isolation, abandonment. And, as never before in the history of literature, novels of this type derived their mood and atmosphere from emotionally charged architectural motifs. Awkward as its style may be, *The Castle of Otranto* deserves recognition as having provided the stock in trade for an entire genre. That Walpole was influenced by Piranesi is without a doubt; in one of his letters, to the Reverend William Cole, he described a dream in which a great, gauntleted hand rested on the balustrade of a Gothic stairway — a clear reference to the *Carceri*.

Giovanni Battista Piranesi, *Parte di ampio magnifico Porto. Opere varie,* 1750

A more congenial soul was William Beckford, to whom toying with horror was a source of pleasure from childhood on and for whom a spinning out of Piranesi's dungeon fantasies provided compensatory sensual satisfaction. Not only did Beckford embody a rare combination of megalomania, infantility, and an exquisite aesthetic sensibility, but he possessed the financial means to put his caprices into practice. The design of Fonthill Abbey, begun by James Wyatt in a fantastic Gothic style in 1797, surely went back to Piranesi's monumental architectural views. The central tower was over 320 feet tall, and the hall over 320 feet long and 80 feet high. The famous Christmas celebration of 1781, at which Beckford gathered around him his married mistress, his underage mistress, and various comrades, was an orgiastic attempt to combine stylized Satanism with imaginary Orientalism. The exquisite decor was provided by Philip James de Loutherbourg, a prominent scene-painter. For Beckford the titillation of the affair essentially lay in holding a party in surroundings à la Piranesi as if his *Carceri* had been dedicated to deliciously blasphemous orgies. It was a conscious challenge to the banality of the era, to which Beckford opposed an artificial and art-

Giovanni Battista Piranesi, *Antichità Romane.* Vol. 2, second frontispiece, *Ideal View of Via Appia*

Arnold Böcklin, *The Island of the Dead.* Oil on wood, 1883

ful fantasy world. From this same spirit, in 1786, issued the novelist's major work, *Vathek* (originally written in French). It is the story of an oriental Faust, whose addiction to pleasure, search for happiness and knowledge, love of power, and overweening sensitivity to beauty finally drove him to ruin. From the "Palace of the Five Senses" through the "Magic Tower" already mentioned to the subterranean chambers of the master of the spirits, Eblis, all of the decisive stations in Vathek's life were couched in architectural metaphors. Eblis's realm was especially indebted to the *Carceri.* Watchtowers, ruins, colossal figures, flights of stairs, immense vaulted halls, and perspectives as draperies of an incarceration in beauty formed an architectural iconography in which Vathek, his mistress Nouronihar, and other guilt-laden souls aimlessly wandered, their hearts burning with icy fire, their lips sealed by hate. Naturally there was also a great deal of de Sade in the scene — the delicious torments of combining pleasure with pain, the apotheosis and fall, the quest for enlightenment that leads to damnation, all cast in a grandiose architectural vision.

The cult of ruins that flourished during a large part of the eighteenth century and was continued by the international Romantic Movement to the extent that it reached into the nineteenth doubtless belongs in the same context. It is an ambiguous, titillating, decadent fascination that suffuses the period's innumerable paintings of ruins, not only Piranesi's but those of Carl Blechen, Georg Blendinger, and Georg August Wallis, to name only a few. Their message was the transience of power, the beauty of decay, and a toying with the idea of the decline of civilization that represented a sensitive indicator of social change. Even the best paintings of Arnold Böcklin, done late in the nineteenth century, still exude a mystical longing for death, as in a tragedy where the velvet-gowned heroine dies of arsenic-laced meringue, a melodramatic veil cast over the ubiquitous presence of death in nature.

The English Piranesi tradition was continued by other eighteenth- and early nineteenth-century authors. Ann Radcliffe's Gothic novels relied heavily on descriptions of interiors, with landscapes serving to supplement or to set off architectural visions by contrast. Her books abound with gloomily twilit halls, gigantic gate towers, stairways, huge vaults, colonnades receding into the obscurity, constricting chambers and corridors — a cell-like space enclosed by stone in which the exits lead nowhere, and the imprisoned human beings are transformed into helplessly submissive creatures. Scenes of pursuit through corridors and up stairways, through heavy gates and vaulted rooms, finally lead to a complete loss of orientation and an entanglement in a web of psychotic fears. Radcliffe's novels veritably cry out for psychological interpretation, as she obviously uses the labyrinth as a metaphor for the relationship between self and society.

Giovanni Battista Piranesi, *Gruppo di Scale*, ca. 1750

The case is similar with other novels of the genre, such as Matthew Gregory Lewis's *The Monk* (1796), Charles Robert Maturin's *Melmoth the Wanderer* (1820), and above all William Godwin's political thriller, *Things as They Are or The Adventures of Caleb Williams* (1794), in which the Piranesi metaphor is applied to an entire society. Late-eighteenth-century England at the time of the French Revolution is made to seem a total and unqualified penitentiary, in which humans are subjected to torments only darkly alluded to in Piranesi's *Carceri*.

The key English intermediary between the literature of his own country and that of French Romanticism was Thomas De Quincey. In his *Confessions of an English Opium Eater* (1821), De Quincey established a reciprocal relationship between architectural metaphor and the salient aesthetic, ethical, and psychological ideas of the period. De Quincey was an opium addict, like Samuel Taylor Coleridge, the greatest poetic talent of English Romanticism. Let us, with Norbert Miller, quote that passage from his book in which the architectural visions of Piranesi seem to corroborate "the dangerous alteration of consciousness effected by drugs." Under their influence the author has the feeling of floating free, of losing physical and emotional contact with reality, and in his mind arises a vision of Piranesi:

Many years ago, when I was looking over Piranesi's "Antiquities of Rome,"
Coleridge, then standing by, described to me a set of plates from that artist,
called his "Dreams," and which record the scenery of his own visions during
the delirium of a fever. Some of these (I describe back from memory of Col-

51

Giovanni Battista Piranesi, *Le Carceri*. Eleventh plate, 1760

Maurits Cornelis Escher, *House of Stairs*. Lithograph, 1951

eridge's account) represented vast Gothic Halls; on the floor of which stood mighty engines and machinery, wheels, cables, catapults, & c., expressive of enormous power put forth, or resistance overcome. Creeping along the sides of the walls, you perceived a staircase; and upon this, groping his way upwards, was Piranesi himself. Follow the stairs a little farther, and you perceive them reaching an abrupt termination, without any balustrade, and allowing no step onwards to him who should reach the extremity, except into the depths below. Whatever is to become of poor Piranesi, at least you suppose that his labours must now in some way terminate. But raise your eyes, and behold a second flight of stairs still higher, on which again Piranesi is perceived, by this time standing on the very brink of the abyss. Once again elevate your eye, and a still more aerial flight of stairs is descried; and there, again, is the delirious Piranesi; busy on his aspiring labours: and so on, until the unfinished stairs and the hopeless Piranesi both are lost in the upper gloom of the hall. With the same power of endless growth and self-reproduction did my architecture proceed in dreams.[16]

In France, Charles Nodier, Victor Hugo, Théophile Gautier and Charles Baudelaire became the literary torchbearers of Piranesi. They recast the motif of the stairway to redemption into a treadmill metaphor, evocative of the eternal return of the same, the vain quest of the artist for glory, the rat race of life, its nausea and ennui — as it was to be illustrated in our own century, fantastically and not without irony, by M. C. Escher. Gautier, an opium-smoker like Coleridge and De Quincey, used reminiscences of the *Carceri* in his novella *La Pipe d'opium* (1838) with a vividness that recalls today's computer-animation and cyberspace effects:

In the meantime I had reached the landing of the stairs and tried to descend them. They lay half in darkness, and in the fantasies of my dream, they took on cyclopean and gigantic dimensions. The two ends obscured by shadow appeared to plunge into heaven and into the underworld, two boundless

Master of the Barberini
Panels, *Presentation
of the Virgin in the
Temple,* fifteenth century

abysses. When I raised my head I perceived, vaguely and in a confusing perspective, countless superimposed stairways, landings, and ladders, as if one could climb them to the top of the tower of Lylacq. And when I lowered my eyes again, I sensed beneath me deep caverns, whirling spiral stairs, and the scintillation of vertiginous revolutions.[17]

Victor Hugo celebrated Piranesi as the architect of a New Babylon and a sorcerer of the imagination. At the same period, official, built architecture revelled in buildings that looked like domesticated Piranesis, their oppressive character lurking behind a thin veneer. Piranesi's motifs were employed to more original effect by an author who combined the influences of German and French Romanticism with the English tradition, an American whose books are still best-sellers today — Edgar Allan Poe.

Giuseppe Galli-Bibiena, *Visionary Palace, with David Appearing before Saul.* Oil on canvas, ca. 1740

Poe's *Philosophy of Composition* (1846) reads like a construction handbook for architects, and it has in fact been included in architectural anthologies. In his short stories the psychology of Gothic space plays a key role, for Poe is a master of the description and analysis of the structures of dreams and anxieties. These frequently find expression in the metaphors of Gothic vaults and dungeons, but also in an interplay of nature with architecture, as in the famous story of *The Fall of the House of Usher*.

Under the surface, the architecture of uterine vaults and the overwrought human sensibility that leads to incest and morbidity finds a continuation here. And the proximity of Piranesi-inspired architecture to stage decor becomes evident in the operatic demise of the House of Usher, accompanied by lighting effects whose accentuation is nothing less than cinematic.

In fact, not only have Poe's short stories provided the visual material for any number of feature films, but Piranesi's architectural fantasies have proven perfectly adapted to the needs of film set designers. Working in a field that combines painting, stage design, and actual architecture, they can employ all the tricks of perspective and lighting to create structures that in practice would be precluded by the laws of statics, practicability, and the properties of materials. Film architects can build visionary architecture. And Piranesi has not only supplied the models for the series of English *Frankenstein* movies of the early 1960s, but he is invariably referred to whenever a filmmaker wishes to create an effect of terror, evoke an ambivalent psychological mood, or produce a vision of incarceration or apocalypse in a monumental architectural setting.

A salient example is Peter Greenaway, one of the most artistically gifted directors of the late twentieth century. In *Prospero's Books* (1991), his technically pioneering film of Shakespeare's *The Tempest*,

Michele Marieschi, *Fashionable Party by a Lakeside*. Oil on canvas, ca. 1736

Greenaway covered Prospero's island with architecture à la Piranesi. The semi-permanent architectural vision of the film was based on a collage of drawings by Michelangelo, Piranesi, and other Romantic and Classical architects. Prospero's bath house and palace were actual, built Piranesis, and the possible objection that Piranesi was not born until 110 years after Shakespeare wrote his play seems carping in light of the result.[18]

What better justification of architectural vision could be found than the fact that it has been integrated in the most significant artistic invention of the twentieth century, moving pictures, where it continues to stimulate the imagination through our optic nerves and brains and thus to encourage that fascinating play of materiality and immateriality which is not only one of the key traits of visionary architecture but is rapidly becoming essential to art itself?

Revolutionary Architecture in France and Russia

Two revolutions in the modern age caused worldwide reverberations the aftershocks of which are still felt today: the French Revolution of 1789 and the Russian Revolution of 1917. The term "revolutionary architecture" to describe the designs made in their historical and political orbit was first used in a substantiated way by Emil Kaufmann, who in 1929 applied it to French architecture in lieu of the rather inappropriate practice of naming styles for kings. Yet this term, too, does not really apply to the two French protagonists of the movement, Etienne-Louis Boullée (1728–99) and Claude-Nicolas Ledoux (1736–1806), both of whom were shocked by the revolution and escaped into utopian dreams.[19]

Ledoux, in fact, was an outspoken advocate of the *Ancien Régime*. Having been employed more than any other architect of the period by the rich and powerful, he lost all of his clients after the fall of the monarchy. As he was quite wealthy and kept three servants, he was declared a suspicious person and imprisoned. While in jail he talked and dreamed about nothing but columns of a 5/12 diameter, reported a fellow prisoner. After his release, no longer in demand as a practicing architect, Ledoux wrote *L'Architecture*, which has survived all of his buildings.[20]

The term revolutionary architecture is much more apt in connection with the post-revolutionary Russian Constructivists, El Lissitzky, Melnikov, Tatlin, Chernikov, the Vesnin brothers, and others, many of whom were influenced by Futurism and its engineering aesthetic. All of these men supported the ideology and ideals of the new regime, and all of them fell into disgrace in the latter half of the 1930s. Socialist Realism became the party line, and it became evident that Stalinism, popular art, and democracy were mutually exclusive terms. A democratically oriented modernism apparently could not be made palatable to the Russian people, who preferred a hierarchical, lavishly ornamented traditional architecture to an uncompromisingly progressive style that had set out to overcome the old architectural hierarchies and insignia of power for good.

It is at this point that French and Russian revolutionary architects can be seen to have shared much in common, despite all the differences between their eras and revolutions, and in terms of individual approach. Evidently the spirit of uprising and violent change bears within it a two-pronged thrust: to level all distinctions of rank on the one hand, and on the other to strive

Etienne-Louis Boullée, *Cenotaph for Sir Isaac Newton.* Pen-and-wash drawing, 1784

Etienne-Louis Boullée, *Project for a Temple of Nature*, section.
Pen-and-wash drawing, 1793

for lucid rules, an elementary formal idiom, technical innovation, a universal architectural language, the grand gesture, and communal buildings as a secular surrogate for religious ones. In such periods, in short, architects attempt to set signposts for the age. Whether they be called Temples of Reason, of the Virtues, or of Nature, or Cathedrals of Socialism, People's Buildings, or Palaces of Culture, such public edifices, despite the dreams of their makers about creating a better world through better architecture, generally tend to serve the needs of those in power. It would seem just as difficult to infuse them with the spirit of democracy as it is to interest a democratically governed populace in an architecture that is much better than mediocre.

Like all true artists, however, good architects possess a seismographic sensitivity to tremors of their era. In the case of Boullée and Ledoux, this meant following up on the anti-Baroque tendencies within neoclassicism and dropping all camouflage and decor. Boullée built little, and what he did build evinces little of the radicalism of his utopian designs. These, in contrast, proved eminently important as visions, giving food for thought to generations of architects and encouraging them to experiment with unconventional points of view. Boullée's Tower of Babel (1785), for instance, became a beacon fire and symbol of an egalitarian society, and his cenotaph for Sir Isaac Newton (1784), a grandiose gesture of mourning, was seen to embody not only Newton's universal science but the perfection of the cosmos, eternity and infinity. The gigantic cupola of his project for a Temple of

Etienne-Louis Boullée, *Design for a Conical Cenotaph*, n. d.

Claude-Nicolas Ledoux, *Field-Guard's House*, 1792

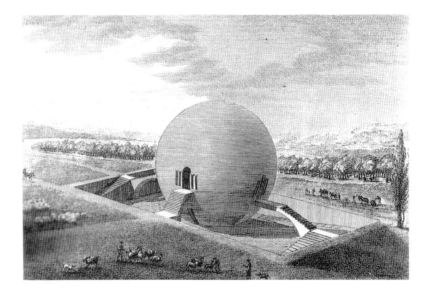

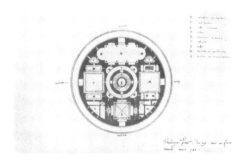

Laurent Vaudoyer, *Project for a Spherical House*, 1784

Nature (1793), inspired by the veneration of nature which the revolution had installed as a quasi-divine authority, was to manifest the polarities of earth and heavens, chaos and order, matter and mind, in a lasting architectural image.

Whether or not Boullée's spherical structures were inspired by the domes of Turkish baths or the huge globes of the period, the vision of these projects has continued to preoccupy the modern movement down to this day, and even to spark such attempts at realization as Richard Buckminster Fuller's geodesic domes, various exhibition structures, and sports arenas like the Houston Astrodome.

To Boullée's way of thinking, architectural designs should engender a sense of the sublime, emanate poetry. This caused him to reject residential buildings as being prosaic. That such buildings could indeed take on a monumental, ideal character was demonstrated by his rival, Ledoux. Ledoux managed to infuse country houses, commercial buildings such as a saltworks, the house of the river authority, even a field-guard's bungalow with timeless rhetoric, dignity, and style. When the distant rumbling of the Revolution made itself heard to sensitive ears, Ledoux, hoping to be ennobled and already using an earl's coat of arms, drew the massed rhetorical fire of his

Claude-Nicolas Ledoux, *The Graveyard at Chaux*, 1783

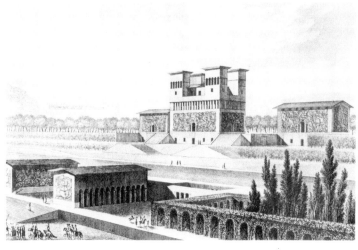

Top left: Claude-Nicolas Ledoux, *Rendez-vous de Chasse*, 1778

Top right: Claude-Louis Chatelet, *Maupertuis Palace,*
built by Claude-Nicolas Ledoux in 1763. Oil on canvas, 1767

Center: Claude-Nicolas Ledoux, *Hotel Thélusson.* Artist unknown,
watercolor

Bottom: Claude-Nicolas Ledoux, *House of the River Authority*, after
1780

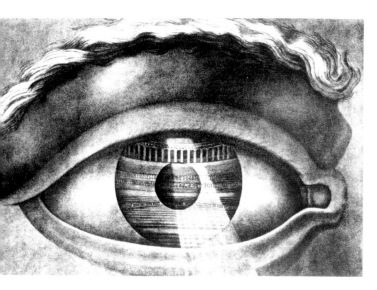

Claude-Nicolas Ledoux, *The Eye*, reflecting the auditorium and colonnade of Besançon Theater, ca. 1775

Claude-Nicolas Ledoux, *The Saltworks, Director's House*, longitudinal section, ca. 1775

academic opponents, who among other things managed to prevent him from building the new gates of Paris. "Monsieur Ledoux, you are a terrible architect," exclaimed one Sébastien Mercier in 1787,[21] and there ensued for the architect of so many prototypical palaces, villas, and official buildings a period of decline and obscurity.

In 1773 Ledoux began having everything he built or dreamed of building recorded in copperplates. This graphic oeuvre was revised again and again until 1789. As the revisions indicate, Ledoux's visionary tendency informed even the projects that had come to fruition, their graphic translations diverging increasingly from the reality and assuming a utopian character.

Subsequently, with his project for the town of Chaux, begun in 1773 and developed through various stages to 1789, Ledoux became the founder of a modern ideal city that differed considerably from those of the Renaissance. Ledoux's vision, which can be traced in philosophic terms back to Plato's *Republic*, was unprecedentedly precise with respect to economics and trade, education and recreation, justice and culture, and moreover was painstakingly illustrated. After numerous delays caused by the revolutionary troubles, *L'Architecture* was finally published in 1804. Ledoux's friend, Dellile, remarked about his conception of Chaux:

> He incessantly improved his plans for an imaginary city in which all the buildings which were of use to the inhabitants and which served their edification were united and put in the best possible relationship to one another: temples, palaces, academies, factories, theaters, public baths....It was truly an architectural utopia, and the project might have been intended for Plato's Republic. In order to put it into practice, several billions [of francs] and a few centuries of peace would have been necessary, and generation after generation would have had to labor at it assiduously.[22]

In his designs Ledoux invariably combined a fanatic concern for detail with a tendency to the universal, linking garden-city ideas with the infinity of the cosmos. He was an architect in body and soul, and considered his craft akin to that of a demiurge. His statements about the architectural profession ran accordingly: "Is there anything at all an architect does not need to know, he who is as old as the sun?"[23] he asked, and then later answered his own question: "To be a good architect, one must be at home in the immeasurable domain of human sensibilities."[24]

The contribution of Russian revolutionary architecture to the modern movement was, for political and ideological reasons, long played down, or even denied, in the Western world.[25] Not until the late 1980s were the Russian Constructivists exposed on a wide basis in France, the United States, and Germany, revealing the fact that there was indeed a Europe undivided by an Iron Curtain in the 1920s, and that she enjoyed multifarious and reciprocal cultural exchanges of the kind we are again becoming used to in the 1990s. Russian revolutionary architecture was initially marked by a strongly academic tradition (Sholtovski, Ilin). Then, in the early 1920s, representatives of modernism were temporarily able to set the tone. Individualists like Kasimir Malevich (1878–1935), whose Suprematism — a radical reduction and abstraction of art to basic elements and free sculptural-architectural compositions — exerted a considerable influence on young architects, never kowtowed to the reigning political ideology. For him, the freedom of art took first priority. Others, such as Konstantin Stepanovitch, Vladimir Tatlin, and the brothers Alexander, Victor, and Leonid Vesnin, supported the goals of the revolution with whole-hearted idealism.

Konstantin Melnikov (1890–1974) was the first of them to achieve an international reputation, based on his daring pavilion for the *Exposition internationale des arts décoratifs et industriels modernes*, held in 1925 in Paris. The dynamic character of his designs, his unusual ground plans and technical innovations remained without imitators for years. Melnikov's Rusakov Workers' Clubhouse in Moscow surely helped stimulate Coop Himmelblau's *Merzschule*, one of the first deconstructivist projects ever, designed for Stuttgart in 1981 but prevented at the last minute from being built by the objections of concerned parents. At the time, the Vienna group spoke of the "dissolution and alteration of a house into a confident, bold, open system"[26] and of their structure's resemblance to a bird, both statements that would surely have found Melnikov's approval.

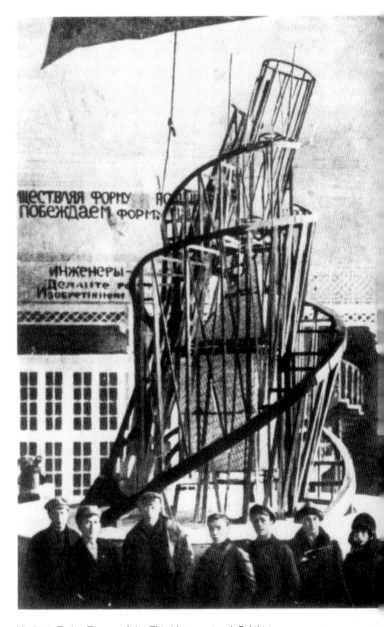

Vladimir Tatlin, Tower of the Third International. Exhibition model, Moscow, 1929

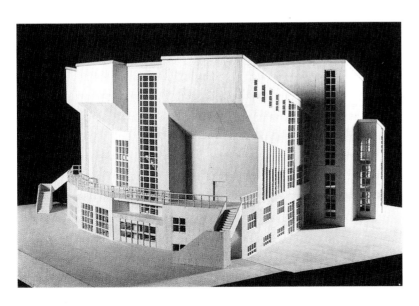

Konstantin Melnikov, Rusakov Workers' Clubhouse. Moscow, 1927–28

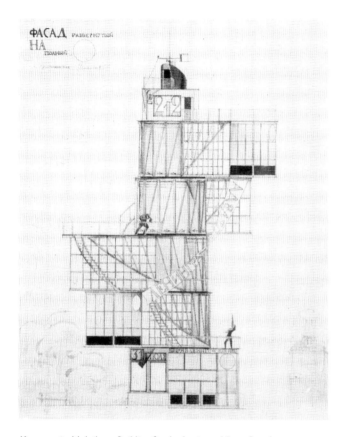

Konstantin Melnikov, *Building for the Leningradskaya Pravda*.
Competition project, 1924

Vladimir Tatlin (1885–1953), with his monument to the Third International of 1920, created one of the principal icons of Russian Constructivism. It was an architectural vision of such intensity that even today, almost everyone interested in architecture still holds an image of it in his mind. In September 1993 a great Tatlin retrospective was held in the Kunsthalle, Düsseldorf, and travelled via Baden to Moscow and St. Petersburg. This show, with the catalogue-book edited by Anatolij Strigalev and Jürgen Harten, introduced Tatlin's work to a wide audience for the first time. It also revealed previously little-known facets of it, such as the stage sets and costumes Tatlin designed for over thirty plays and operas.[27] Very rarely does an architect's fame rest on a single, not to mention unbuilt, project. Yet behind the Tower for the Third International, once again, the shadowy outlines of the Tower of Babel can be discerned. Tatlin considered the Futurist-related technological metaphor he employed to be an aesthetic equivalent to the social renewal introduced by the 1917 October Revolution. The spiral of the steel framework symbolized the rise of the people under the revolutionary impulse. Three crystalline volumes were incorporated in the structure: a cube at the bottom, a tetrahedron in the middle, and at the top, a hemisphere above a cylinder. These were to house, respectively, the legislature, the executive, and the propaganda ministry of the Comintern. The government offices were planned to revolve around their own axis at various speeds, the cube once a year, the tetrahedron once a month, and the hemisphere and cylinder once a day. Contributing to the cosmic symbolism was the angle of inclination of the tower, which corresponded to that of the earth's axis. At some 1,300 feet in height, Tatlin's structure was to overtop the Eiffel Tower, to certain structural elements of which his model moreover alluded.

A similarly magnetic icon of Russian revolutionary architecture was produced by El Lissitzky (1890–1941), whose *Wolkenbügel* (Cloud Link) has been seen as an aesthetic challenge by many recent architects, including, again, Coop Himmelblau. Conceived in 1924 in

El Lissitzky, *Wolkenbügel* (Cloud Link),
1924–25

the course of an exchange of ideas with Mart Stam in Minusio, near Locarno, the Cloud Link represents a Russian, indeed a European reply to the American skyscraper. With its horizontal structure rising above the vertical shaft, the design activates the horizontal airspace above the street. Hovering as if divorced from the dictates of matter, the Cloud Link is indeed more than an architectural landmark. In the conventionally grim urban context of high-density cities it would shine out in terms of structural daring and architectural novelty. In the meantime, elements of this horizontal sky-city have been taken up by the "skywalks" of North American and Canadian cities like Minneapolis and Calgary, where cruel winters truly make it sensible to build covered walkways and streets connecting tall buildings high above the ground. But as far as skyscraper design is concerned, the American tower has proved just as victorious over the Russian skylink as American capitalism has over Russian socialism. The tower is more practical, more efficient, more cost-effective, and perhaps even aesthetically more satisfying than that architectural feat of a horizontal super-symbol whose useful space did not begin until 150 feet above ground level.

Coop Himmelblau, *Wolkenbügel.* Model for a hotel in Vienna, 1990

Like the Russian Revolution itself and especially the Stalinism that ensued, many Constructivists — Melnikov, Tatlin, the Vesnin brothers — exhibited a tendency to gigantomania. Doubtless the Vesnins designed and built several examples of lucid, objective, and aesthetically convincing modernism; but their unrealized design for the Lenin Library (1928) and their four projects for the Palace of Soviets (1930–34) already began to prompt those ambiguous feelings which Stalinist architecture triggered at first sight. On the one hand they evinced a respect for grandeur and an aesthetic mastery of large-scale projects arising

Coop Himmelblau, model of *Merzschule*, Stuttgart.
Project for the school extension, 1981

from an attempt to express community spirit; on the other, such projects evoked a sinking feeling at the degradation of the individual within a mass society and the concomitant personality cult around tyrannical dictators, regardless of whether the dictator be called Mussolini, Hitler, or Stalin.

By now it has been largely forgotten that the early Constructivists had good reasons for employing the machine metaphor. First, their revolutionary aesthetic entailed a revaluation of things previously considered beyond the pale of art, and second, they were euphoric about the liberation of mankind from manual and slave labor thanks to the economic and technological progress which machinery indeed promised. One of the architects who used this metaphor most intensively — and whose significance has been longest underrated in the Western world — was Jakov Chernikov (1859–1951).[28]

Within a very few years, Chernikov had over fifty constructed buildings to his credit, and in the mid-1920s he rapidly became one of Leningrad's most respected teachers of architecture. Still, he continued to consider his visionary projects the more important part of his oeuvre. In 1935, when doctrinaire Socialist Realism took over, Chernikov began to feel the effects of official disapproval. He was permitted neither to teach nor to build, all of his books were banned from Russian libraries, and he was prohibited from publishing more.

The eagle's wings had been clipped. Frustrated and humiliated, Chernikov finally sat down at his desk on 11 April 1938 and wrote a letter to "Dear Josif Vissarionovich Stalin." He objected to the fact that he, a man who had devoted his life to architectural research and design in the service of the glorious Stalinist Era, had been prohibited to work, and merely because he possessed a highly developed imagination. And this gift he wished to place in the service of Stalinism as well, but was prevented from doing so. Reading this letter, one can well imagine the narrow-minded bureaucrats and red-tapers who enjoyed nothing better than placing obstacles in the way of a dynamic, futurist spirit.

Predicated on technological realities, Chernikov went on to write, he had used the powers of his imagination to further the development of society in accordance with the ideals of Stalinism, but had been deprived of the bases of his career due to his alleged formalism and obstinate advocacy of pure fantasy (*fantastischnost*). Chernikov asked

Alexander and Victor Vesnin, competition design for the Palace of Soviets, Moscow. First design, 1934

Jakov Chernikov, *Design for a Factory*, 1993

Jakov Chernikov, *Architectural Fantasy*, 1930

Opposite page:
Jakov Chernikov, *Architectural Fantasy*, 1933. Axonometric drawing

to be reinstated in his position, in order to be able to continue his work as an architect and teacher.[29]

Dear Josif Vissarionovich did not reply; he probably never set eyes on the letter at all. But what the affair illustrates is one of the reasons the communist system eventually proved unviable: the chasm it created between visionary ambition and the philistine, small-minded attitudes of its decision-makers.

In a sense, the accusation of formalism placed at Chernikov's door was justified, if for the wrong reasons. Chernikov was an architect who concerned himself with the basic principles of the trade, the grammar of the art of building, and who tried to instill these into his students in the name of a well-founded education. His was an analytical mind that set out to plumb, illuminate, and question stylistic categories like Constructivism in order to fill them with life, which certainly would have been good for architecture. His great visual symbol in all this was the machine, which in fact did lead him in the early years, like the French revolutionary architects, to overstrain such symbolism and fall into the ever-present trap of all-too facile architectural imagery, an *architecture parlante*. Yet in the long run the accusation could not hold water, especially as Chernikov made a point of distinguishing between actual practice and architectural visions, whose necessity for the creative process he nevertheless emphasized.

Official Constructivism, represented at the time by Moisei Ginzburg and the brothers Vesnin, looked askance at Chernikov, because he defined the style much less abstractly than they did. Chernikov advocated a synthetic process of design in which harmony, symbolism, and beauty would come together to elicit a sense of well-being in people, who, after all, were the users of architecture. From the functional whole of the machine, which undeniably exhibited certain aesthetic norms and laws, Chernikov extrapolated his version of Constructivist principles: a mutual interpenetration of elements in which they would grip, surround, frame one another, interweave, interlock in relationships of tension, and finally produce an integral whole. What emerged from Chernikov's drawing board in the way of architectural visions between 1920 and 1935 were designs, some more realistic, some more extravagant and futuristic, of industrial, office, and cultural buildings that were characterized by freshness of approach, vitality, dynamics, and lucidity of conception. Chernikov employed disk and arch elements in an innovative way, and experimented with referential signs and a great range of colors, forms, and styles, always with an eye to suffusing his architectural compositions with a musical rhythm.

Chernikov was probably also the first architect ever to write a book entitled *Architectural Fantasies*, which was published in 1933. In this book he not only championed imagination in architecture but postulated its necessity for the creative architect, who would find his way back to the solid ground of facts and serious questions of detail

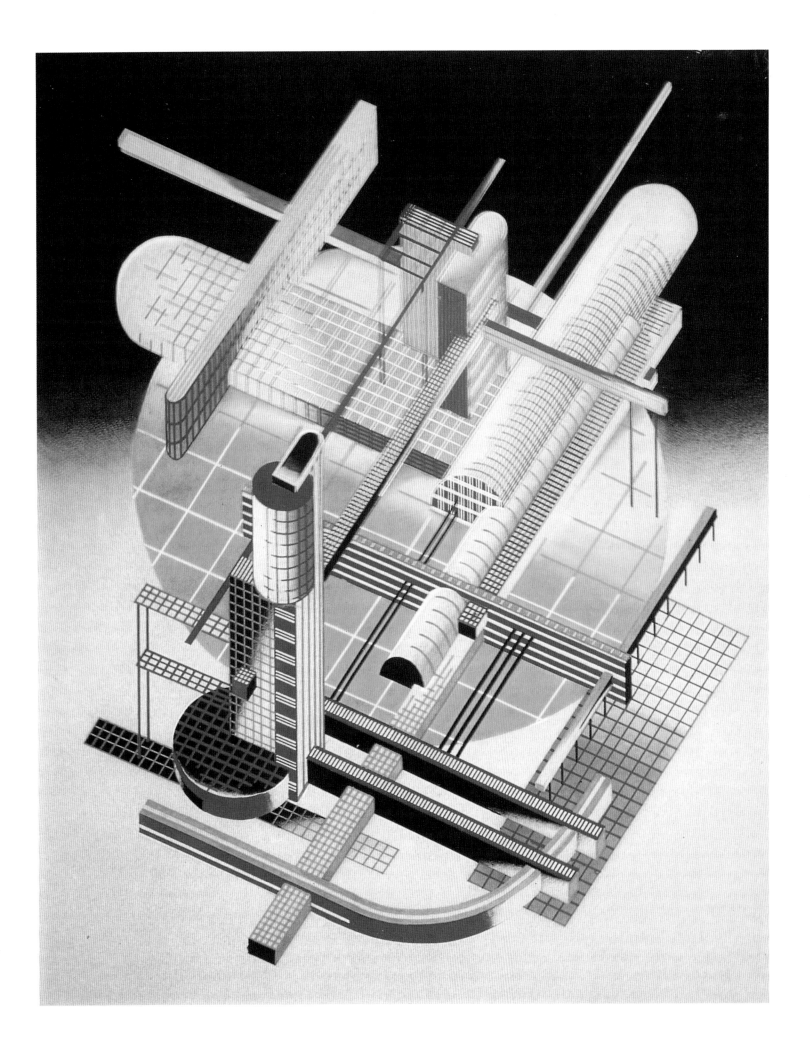

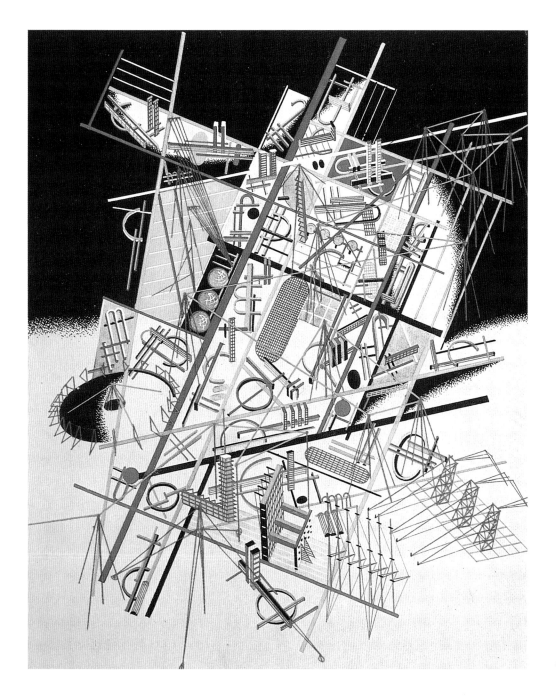

Jakov Chernikov, *Musical Composition, Architectural Fantasy No. 87*, 1933

soon enough as it was. But first, said Chernikov, he should train his imagination. This training should be an integral part of an architect's education, for it would enable him, for instance, to recognize basic structures, and to treat volumes in a rhythmical, aesthetic manner. Both monolithic and dynamic properties of architectural elements could be better assessed by means of such training, and it would further the ability to evaluate harmonies of form and color, and to combine constructional elements.

"Architectural fantasies," Chernikov went on, "show us new compositional processes, new modes of depicting; they nurture a feeling for form and colour; they are a training ground for the imagination; they excite creative impulses; they draw out further new creativity and ideas; they help in finding solutions for new architectural intentions, and much more."[30]

Chernikov reached a conclusion that might stand as a motto for the present book, namely that "great thinkers of all times accorded vast importance to fantasy, as being the forerunner of any kind of progress. To look one-sidedly at the idea of fantasy (as merely fantastic), and not to consider its positive role in all fields of culture and art — this means to make a great mistake."[31]

Chernikov has proved right, and courageous as well. But it was the tragic error of his life to have publicly advocated, indeed to have insisted on, the importance of imagination in architecture. His claim to his creative birthright cost him his career. In the end, though, it was hardly a mistake, because Chernikov's stance had a great deal to do with the dignity of man and of the artist.

The fact that dream structures are frequently found in architectural visions, that fleeting, subconscious imagery readily assumes the apparent solidity of imaginary architecture, became evident at the latest with Piranesi. It also became evident that such visions can represent an extrapolation of the dreams and nightmares of an era. In a later era, De Quincey told Coleridge about the palatial visions of his opium reveries; Coleridge, in turn, inspired De Quincey to his influential interpretation of Piranesi. Coleridge's *Kubla Khan* (1816) rapidly advanced to one of the key poems not only of the English but of the international Romantic Movement. In keeping with our present topic, I shall limit my discussion to the architectural aspects of the poem.[32] *Kubla Khan*, then, is one man's architectural vision in verse:

Carl Blechen, *Palm House on the Pfaueninsel*, Potsdam. Oil on canvas, 1832–34

> *In Xanadu did Kubla Khan*
> *A stately pleasure-dome decree:*
> *Where Alph, the sacred river, ran*
> *Through caverns measureless to man*
>   *Down to a sunless sea.*
> *So twice five miles of fertile ground*
> *With walls and towers were girdled round:*
> *And there were gardens bright with*
>   *sinuous rills,*
> *Where blossomed many an incense-*
>   *bearing tree;*
> *And here were forests ancient as the hills,*
> *Enfolding sunny spots of greenery....*

Kubla Khan, Marco Polo, and Xanadu — or Xamdu, as it is called in the source of Coleridge's dream, *Purchas, his Pilgrimage* (by Samuel Purchase, 1613) — were quite familiar to his contemporaries. The stock-in-trade of early-nineteenth-century Orientalism included palaces, Elysian gardens, caverns, rivers, waterfalls — all of which Coleridge evokes in melodic and vivid language. The Orient fired the imagination of the time, and the magic charm of the exotic led, above all in England, then in Germany and with qualifications in France, to entire waves of imitation oriental architecture and interior decoration, which caught up the rising middle class as well as the declining aristocracy.

As if synaesthetically, the term "plea-

Julius Hoffmann, *Design for a Byzantine Castle*, 1885

sure-dome" combines ecclesiastical and secular architecture, palace and religious dome structure, whereby the dome figures as a symbol of harmony per se. Dimensions are not given; on the contrary, the caverns through which the Alph flows are "measureless to man." And then the cultivated soil, "twice five miles," is protected by walls and towers, cut out and isolated from nature like Cosmos from Chaos in Milton's *Paradise Lost*.[33] The oriental and vaguely sacred associations are supplemented by medieval ones, like those for example of the Duc de Berry's books of hours. The architecture of the whole is fantastic and paradisal, but it is a paradise in jeopardy:

> And 'mid this tumult Kubla heard from far
> Ancestral voices prophesying war!

Panciatichi, Castello di Lammezzano at Rignano sull'Arno, rebuilt 1843–73

Twice more in the course of the poem the architecture is invoked as a symbol of beauty, perfection, and culture itself:

> The shadow of the dome of pleasure
> Floated midway on the waves;
> Where was heard the mingled measure
> From the fountain and the caves.
> It was a miracle of rare device,
> A sunny pleasure-dome with caves of ice!

Paradoxes are conjoined; sun and ice produce the precarious harmony, the unstable stability of visionary architecture. Kubla Khan's personality is not established except in terms of his creation. After the first, relatively concrete description, Coleridge heightens the fantastic aspect of the pleasure-dome in lines that have the transient character of a dream, saying its shadow "Floated midway on the waves." And after having stood on the cultivated soil of Xanadu and then been reflected in the river's holy waves, the palace materializes again, this time as a truly synaesthetic image in sound and aerial form:

> That with music loud and long,
> I would build that dome in air,
> That sunny dome! those caves of ice!

70

Yet at this third mention, and in the poet's imagination, the creation of fantastic architecture has become subject to the conditional mood: "Could I...,I would..." Light and shimmering as a reflection in a soap bubble, the poet's architectural vision floats before the reader's eyes, its fragmentary character serving to stimulate his imagination all the more.

Coleridge the citizen composed his dream-palace out of influences and elements both Oriental and Occidental. Similarly, the citizens of Western Europe in the nineteenth century erected actual Xanadus, in the shape of palm gardens and crystal palaces built for exhibitions,

Humphrey Repton, *Project for the Reconstruction of the Royal Pavilion, Brighton*, 1868

particularly the various World Fairs held in Paris and London. Modern building materials, glass and steel employed in imaginative designs, entered a symbiosis with exotic plants and landscaping and an upper-middle-class plush-and-velvet interior decoration, which after years of general disfavor has since the 1980s again captured the interest of architects and their clients.

To leap to the twentieth century and the new medium of film, Orson Welles recreated Xanadu once again in *Citizen Kane* (1941). Widely considered one of the best movies in cinema history, it is packed with all of the reverberating symbolism which the tradition had since acquired. The title itself contains a bipolar tension, between Citizen and Kane, with the family name in turn splitting into three divergent connotations: ordinary name, the biblical Cain, and Kubla Khan. Then there is the additional tension between Citizen and Xanadu, a quasi-mythical imperial palace which is created by an ordinary man running for president in a democratic country. Kane's character oscillates among all of these trains of association. His residence itself, Xanadu, figures as a further main protagonist in the film. It was based on San Simeon, the hypertrophic dream-palace of newspaper czar William Randolph Hearst (1863–1951). This combination of Mediterranean villa and oriental palace furnished in neo-Renaissance style, built in Southern California on the edge of what until recently was the Wild West, was a compelling embodiment of wish-dream and hubris. But to interpret the film, one need go no farther than its title and the name Xanadu. Every victory of Kane's turns into a defeat as soon as he holds the spoils in his hands. And his vision of Xanadu, as soon as it becomes real, torments him and melts away like Coleridge's mirage — and quite logically so, for this is in the nature of architectural fancies.

Alexandre Marcel, *Le Tour du Monde, Paris*, 1900

Maurits Cornelis Escher, *Different World.*
Wood engraving and woodcut, 1947

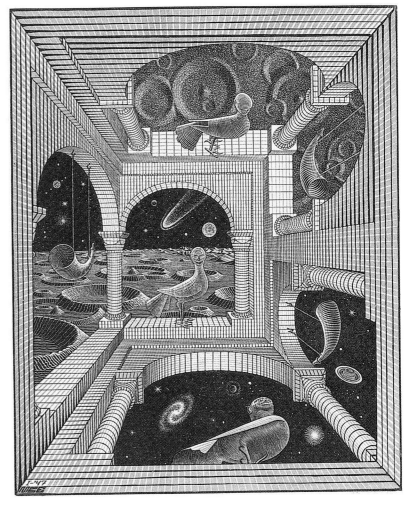

Neuschwanstein Castle, northern stair tower with palm columns

A KING'S DREAM: NEUSCHWANSTEIN

When one enters a travel agency in the United States or a department store that offers trips to Europe, chances are the big glossy posters on the wall will include one of Neuschwanstein Castle in Bavaria. Neuschwanstein outranks even Heidelberg, or the beautiful Pfalzgrafenstein, a toll fortress in the middle of the Rhine near Kaub. It is the most commercially exploited, and emotionally and aesthetically the most intensely charged symbol of Germany and "the Old Country." And quite correctly so. A commodity-oriented society must sell surrogates, cater to consumers' romantic yearnings by offering *the* architectural dream become stone par excellence. But how many realize that Neuschwanstein took on surrogate character the moment it was finished? It has served as the wedding-cake model for all the larger and smaller Disneyland-style castles ever erected in the United States and Europe, scaled down to fit private lots, the Legoland castles of latter-day entrepreneurs.

The dubious thing about the process is the tendency surrogates have to supplant reality. This was apparently the case even for Neuschwanstein's builder and owner, Ludwig II of Bavaria. When they yanked him out of bed in the middle of the night on 12 June 1886, when reality exacted its cruel due and Ludwig was declared insane, the shock was too much for him to stand, and had fatal consequences. Thirty-six hours later the king, known kindly and slightly condescendingly to his most faithful supporters, the Americans, as "mad King Ludwig," was dead, drowned — under exactly what circumstances no one has ever found out.

Neuschwanstein raises a crucial problem of architectural visions and visionary architecture. As soon as a project of this type is built, it often tends to seem unconvincing, escapist, corny, especially if it is built not by the dreamer of Xanadu him-

King Ludwig's bedroom at Neuschwanstein

Neuschwanstein Castle, built 1879–86

First design for Falkenstein Castle, Christian Jank, 1883

self but by someone else. Here lies the key difference between Neuschwanstein and Cheval's Palais Idéal, Gaudí's Sagrada Familia, or the bizarre, waterborne dwellings of the eccentric individualists of Sausalito, California.

It was not only a reaction against his era, an era of industrial barons, railway magnates, stock-market millionaires, and founders of empires, that led a provincial king to seek an ideal counterworld in a pseudo-medieval knight's castle and a conception of royalty that defined it as a kind of weightless state of aesthetic bliss. What Ludwig yearned for was basically a life like a perfectly staged play. But he did not possess the artistic gift to direct the play, merely to serve as its producer, whose skills consisted in the ability to select and harmoniously arrange a number of cultural and dramatic set pieces.

Ludwig, in a word, did not direct *Parsifal*, *Lohengrin* and *Tannhäuser* himself. He commissioned in 1868 the theater-set painter Christian Jank to draw up the designs for Neuschwanstein, based on stage sets. The built result, for all its grandeur, had an over-facile look — too stiff, too impersonal, too off-the-rack. And when anyone involved in the construction suggested alterations, the king refused to permit the slightest personal touch. The interior of Neuschwanstein conforms to its exterior style to the letter. But why shouldn't a man put up a castle "in the authentic style of the old German knights' castles," as Ludwig wrote to Richard Wagner on 13 May 1868? Indeed, why not? The Löwenburg in Kassel, another pseudo-medieval princely toybox, provided a long-standing example. But prefabricated parts are not the stuff that dreams are made of. Medieval castles derive their character not least from their angles and corners and irregularities, their rough-hewn stone, their craggy look. In the facades of Neuschwanstein harmony and regularity of measure and great smooth surfaces flip over into kitsch, which of course does not prevent grateful tourists from finding it sublime.

Despite its look of a dream setting for a backward-looking utopia, Neuschwanstein is enormously popular. Although the castle can handle no more than 11,000 visitors a day, in the high season about twice that many line up before it hoping to assuage their curiosity and their genuine need for a little romance. Ironically, the conservative king inadvertently fulfilled precisely that need for mass-produced sentimentality which was such anathema to him.

A POSTMAN'S DREAM: THE PALAIS IDEAL

At the age of forty-three, in the best years of his life, Ferdinand Cheval, country postman in southern France, could no longer contain his dream. The stones he had collected on his delivery routes, rough, gnarled, fantastically shaped rocks that had weighed down his mailbag, had to be built into walls, they positively called out for it.

So he finally gave his visions free rein, and in 1879 began building

Opposite page:
Ferdinand Cheval, Palais Idéal, 1879–1922. The Three Giants

Ferdinand Cheval, Palais Idéal, detail

Ferdinand Cheval, Palais Idéal, detail

his personal Xanadu, feverishly, with his own hands. When over forty years later his major work was at last completed, in 1922, Cheval decided it was time to begin work on his own grave, which he erected in the same dream-association style as his Palais Idéal, until death intervened.

In a superb essay Peter Weiss has described Cheval's structure and retranslated an architectural dream made real into poetically evocative language.[34] At the same time Weiss managed to achieve something no author before him had done — to shed light on the essence of dream architecture without subjecting it to the kind of dissecting analysis that destroys the delicate tissues of the ideas and obsessions that underlie it:

The undefinable, at first sight amorphous mass down there, in the garden on a slope. A towering termite nest, as if cemented together with secretions. Stones, seashells, roots, mosses. Poured over with gray dough, kneaded, dug into with the hands whose presence is everywhere felt, the hands that assembled these scraps. Scraps as if permeated with saliva. One initially comprehends the whole, this confusing configuration, only suspecting the secret rules that guided the movements of [Cheval's] hands. The eye feels its way over the tortuous shapes, discovers faces, figures, limbs, animals, but at first only as suggestions. The basic clay of dreams. The first confrontation. Something is emerging here. A world of thought. A murmuring, a monologue with voices from dreams. Words. Dream words, incised in a flux, words hardly understandable, shattered, tattered. The reality of an ego in the course of formation. My ego, which means my imagination. I am dreaming. Out of impulses, ideas, I shape forms. All interwoven, confused, overladen with impressions from the world of day. Illustrations from old dog-eared magazines, oriental architectures, Indian or Balinese temples, Pre-Columbian sculptures, African jungles.

It is necessary to quote a comparatively long passage to show the intensity with which Weiss enters into the mind of the creator of Palais Idéal and sheds light on the links between language and architecture. For the syntax and grammar of Cheval's architectural idiom must remain a closed book to anyone unwilling to empathize with him, which also entails descending into the labyrinth of one's own ego and id:

Everywhere forms revolve, descend and ascend, proliferate into ornaments, growths, fruits, have eyes, extend limbs, protrude, draw me deeper and deeper into passageways, mine shafts, alcoves, at first still inducing memories of stalactite caves, garden grottoes, Etruscan sepulchers, aquariums, then suddenly transforming into something unique, incomparable. I am inside a dream.

A frequent feature of fantastic architecture is its tendency to externalize an inward vision, to put everything into the facade leaving the interior empty, for the simple reason that the vision demands to be

76

manifested in outward shape. Yet Cheval turned his vision both outward and inward, let the shapes of the stones, pieces of lava, fossils, and boulders he found suggest affinities with the architecture of many countries and stylistic periods. As Weiss points out, the Palais Idéal is not a work of art but the expression of a psyche, the labyrinth of a soul, a subterranean cache of feelings and thoughts. When one enters into a piece of built architecture, Weiss states, one enters also into the imagination of the person who created it.

Cheval had no literary outlet; he was compelled to build, obsessively, to lend shape to his vision, much as Ludwig, laughed at by Wagner for his building mania, was compelled to build Neuschwanstein. The king retired to his study to work on designs, pored over book after book that served his purposes; Cheval ceased communicating with other people almost entirely, murmuring to himself as his pent-up obsessions emerged:

All of his anal, obscene drives are contained in this dream. In the dream the inside of his intestines appears, he digs into masses of excrement, kneads the heavy clumps of excrement, everything flows with excrement, twists and snakes, and finally congeals into pregnant columns, ledges, spirals, pendants. And out of these project great phallic mushrooms, curved, protruding, wanton. And in long rows, female breasts, swollen, tempting, with tenderly twirled tips. And incised in the soft mass of the elemental material, the slits of wombs, with rounded lips, the wombs of all goddesses of the earth, frightfully fecund, surrounded by heads of horned animals. But all of this still in a state of transformation.

Cheval's Palais Idéal reveals much of the traumatic force inherent in dreams. "Everything is architecture," Hans Hollein once said, and Cheval took this view more literally than anyone before him. One of the most baffling insights to be gained from a visit to Hauterives, where in 1969 the Palais Idéal, an "example unique au monde d'architecture naïve," was declared a historical monument, is the conclusion that it was not the work of a visionary amateur at all, but that of a brilliant architect who followed an inner calling. The overall composition of the structure is so convincing, the eclecticisms are so perfectly integrated in a superordinate style, that the observer can only

Ferdinand Cheval, Palais Idéal, detail

gaze in admiration. As a built architectural fancy the Palais Idéal is a unique monument, and symbol of the shaping power of inward vision.

The opulence of Cheval's style admittedly had parallels in turn-of-the-century architecture, in which the colonial nations of Western Europe took up impulses from subject peoples around the world. Still, Cheval was alone in the unmatched persistence with which he realized a visionary *spectaculum mundi*, and unlike Gaudí, who, recurring to a great Moorish tradition, was a rational, engineering genius by comparison, Cheval retained the evocative, dreamlike power of amorphousness while at the same time lending it sculptural and architectural form.

A DREAMER'S DREAM: THE INVISIBLE CITIES

In 1972 one of the most beautiful, poetic, and profound books ever written about cities appeared, Italo Calvino's novel *The Invisible Cities*. The fifty-five city portraits — or rather, prose poems — which Marco Polo projects in conversation with Kublai Khan in the book amount to a virtually endless list of the states and potentials of urban life. The novel is clearly a piece of postmodernist literature. Instead of following a linear plot, the narrative is based on groups of five subtexts the elements of which are interrelated in a complex weave, a tapestry depicting the imaginary stories of imaginary cities and at the same time describing highly real architectures and ways of life, vividly evoked by allusions that spark the reader's imagination.

Interspersed are imaginary conversations between Marco Polo and Kublai Khan. Having spent seventeen years, from 1275 to 1292, in the Khan empire, Marco Polo tells of the cities he saw, their past and present, in a way that blends present and past and makes them one. Calvino's approach reflects a sensibility that has become increasingly important for our contemporary understanding of reality, a sensibility for the historical stratification of urban architecture. The key mark of postmodernism, an ability to bring multiple viewpoints into historical perspective and focus, is expressed here with a combination of playful insouciance and philosophical profundity. Under the narrator's magnifying glass the presence of the past becomes incredibly vivid, it suffuses the present and tinges the future; we glimpse potentials that might have been realized, if only…

The vignettes, the puzzles of which Calvino's urban portraits consist call up a multifariousness of facets — both architectural and relating to human life and activity — the sum total of which is the city. This is a book about love for cities, and also a book about fear of them. Their heady perfume and their smell, their harmonies and cacophony, their aesthetic and unaesthetic aspects are all brought to life with a tenderness that makes any attempt at analysis seem a brutal incursion on this linguistic web of dreams.

Alfred Kubin, *The Premonition*. Distemper on cardboard, 1906

The invisible cities take visible shape before the reader's eyes out of allusions, accents of color, the music and magic of language, much as the delicate strokes of Peter Kubovsky's pen breathe life into his poetic images of cities. If in Kubovsky's case it is often Venice or Prague that embodies the city per se, Calvino's sketches focus again and again on Marco Polo's home town, Venice. The book, then, is a history of the rise, heyday, decline, and fall of the great Italian port as well.

And still, "No one, wise Kublai, knows better than you that the city must never be confused with the words that describe it. And yet between the one and the other there is a connection."[35] Every city sketch, every dialogue between Marco Polo and Kublai Khan is at the same time an offer to the reader to participate in the conversation, an offer that will strike each reader differently and elicit a different reply. Calvino's book also possesses considerable allegorical qualities. When in the second half the city portraits gradually grow darker, when their previously distinct configurations blur into amorphous masses surrounded by festering waste dumps, it becomes increasingly obvious that we are reading a disillusioned if lyrically melancholy description of the state of modern big cities. Love for the city gradually gives way to the feeling that it is turning into a prison, for Marco Polo as for Kublai Khan, and for their author, Calvino.

Yet the bizarre aspects of the city, he feels, still hold great and creative surprises in store. This is why his novel, for all its dark presentiments, has an optimistic, even utopian undertone, making a quiet but incredibly insistent appeal to the reader's imagination. Calvino would have us love cities nevertheless, and by living creatively and imaginatively make them places worth living in:

If I tell you that the city toward which my journey tends is discontinuous in space and time, now scattered, now more condensed, you must not believe the search for it can stop (p. 164).

Dream architectures have existed at least since Piranesi, we said, but we must now add that they probably go back much further. If any author has ever succeeded in capturing the architecture of dreams and the life played out in it, it was Italo Calvino:

With cities, it is as with dreams: everything imaginable can be dreamed, but even the most unexpected dream is a rebus that conceals a desire, or, its reverse, a fear. Cities, like dreams, are made of desires and fears, even if the thread of their discourse is secret, their rules are absurd, their perspectives deceitful, and everything conceals something else (p. 44).

Peter Kubovsky, *Fondamenta della Sensa.* Pen-and-ink drawing, 1984

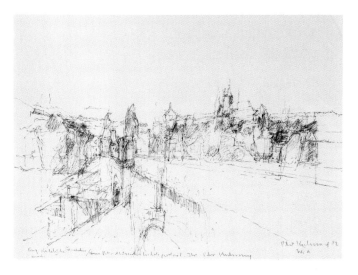

Peter Kubovsky, *Praque, Charles Bridge with Hradcany Castle in the Background.* Pen-and-ink drawing, 1982

Leon Krier, *Royal Mint Square Housing.* London, 1974

Crystalline Architecture and Organic Sculpture

Wenzel August Hablik, *Cathedral Interior: Festival Hall, Gondola Canal, Fountains, and Glass Globe Gaslights.* Oil on canvas, 1921

When the genocide, suffering, attrition of men in the First World War finally came to an end, many artists and architects of republican or socialist leanings, influenced by the revolutionary events in Russia and the German rising of November 1918, were gripped by a yearning for peace and a determination to make a new start. Young architects short of commissions in the first postwar years began to reflect on their craft, draw, and write instead. The idiom they chose was that of Expressionism, which had already emerged full blown in the poetry of the war and prewar years.

On 24 November 1919 Bruno Taut sent a letter to Carl Krayl, Paul Gösch, Hans Scharoun, Walter Gropius, Adolf Behne, Jakobus Göttel, Hans Hansen, Wenzel August Hablik, Max Taut, Wilhelm Brückmann, Hermann Finsterlin, and Wassili and Hans Luckhardt, suggesting that "…each of us will draw or write down at regular intervals those of his ideas that he wants to share with our circle, and will then send a copy to each member. In this way an exchange of ideas, questions, answers, and criticism will be established. Above each contribution will be a pseudonym."[36] With the exception of the critic Adolf Behne, all of the addressees took up Taut's suggestion, though there were a few passive members like Gropius who participated in the exchange without submitting written or graphic contributions. What resulted and was to last for just over a year, until December 1920, was dubbed *Die gläserne Kette* (The Crystal Chain) by Alfred Brust, a correspondent who joined the group later.

This informal gathering of architects and artists with quite diverse intentions, styles, and talents has been called "probably the most significant exchange of theoretical ideas on architecture this century."[37] Given that other theorists hardly exchanged ideas at all, this statement has a certain truth. But it is certainly not valid when individual theoretical contributions on an international level are taken into account. Whatever the case, the writings and drawings of the Gläserne Kette, especially those of Bruno Taut, Finsterlin, Hablik, Scharoun, and Wassili Luckhardt, have continued to stimulate architectural thinking and practice to this day. Much of what was long considered absolutely utopian and visionary has since entered the realm of the feasible thanks to new computer technologies and materials. Reality has long since surpassed utopia in many areas.

While the drawings of the Gläserne Kette have retained their immediacy, the written productions are marred for a contemporary reader by a great deal of bombast and flights of would-be poetic fancy. Yet if one takes the trouble to penetrate to the essence of what is being said, one is often rewarded by acute insights, many of them amazingly prophetic. The group had a literary predecessor, Paul Scheerbart, author of profuse, if qualitatively highly uneven, fantastic texts. Some of these were published posthumously by his friend, Bruno Taut, in the journal *Frühlicht*, which succeeded the Gläserne Kette. In phonetic poems, novels, and short stories full of bizarre inventiveness Scheerbart again and again invoked a theme that had preoccupied the European mind ever since Sir Joseph Paxton's Crystal Palace of 1851 — glass architecture. For Scheerbart, it took on a veritably cosmic significance, for, as he wrote in his *Glasarchitektur*, published in 1914:

Hans Scharoun, *Principles of Architecture*, ca. 1919

Bruno Taut, *The Crystal Mountain*. Pen-and-ink drawing, 1918

81

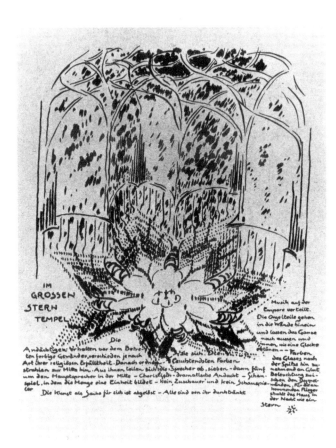

Bruno Taut, *In the Great Starry Temple*, 1920

In his story "Der Architektenkongress" (The Architectural Convention), Scheerbart has the great architect Privy Councillor Krummbach exclaim:

The potential disadvantage of total transparency, total surveillance, was soon to be experienced by countless artists in Russia. In Evgeniy Zamyatin's novel *We* (1920), the totalitarian practices of Stalinism were prophetically foreshadowed. At the same time as Scheerbart and members of the Gläserne Kette were dreaming of utopian cities of glass, Zamyatin described how the denizens of the glass buildings of his millennial unified state were deprived of all will-power and "healed" by destroying the imaginative center of their brains with X-rays. Bruno Taut, Wenzel Hablik, and Hans Scharoun in particular had no inkling of such dystopias. Scheerbart's evocations of the veritably weightless nature of glass architecture, of crystal columns and walls and floors of colored glass fascinated Bruno Taut, whose assumed name in the group was actually "Glass," to the point of obsession for many years.

Even before the end of the war, in 1917, Taut began work on his first "glass fantasies." By 1918 they had grown into a portfolio of thirty drawings, which was published the following year under the title *Alpine Architektur*. In these wonderfully lyrical renderings crystalline configurations spread over entire mountain valleys and chains. Here glass was no longer merely a thin, water-clear skin that helped dematerialize architecture or integrate interior and exterior; it was crystalline, cut like gems, shone with noble brilliance, and was charged with all the symbolism of a romantic medievalism. This included a yearning for a Holy Grail influenced by Wagner and Nietzsche, which put the Expressionists at the end of a tradition stretching from the idealized Middle Ages down to the twentieth century. The Grail, a crystal chalice symbolic of divine mercy, had been the object of all the Arthurian knights' quest. Whoever caught sight of it would enter a state of complete bliss that corresponded to a oneness with God. Crystal was thought to have powers of healing and regeneration, and it also stood for innocence, purity, peace of mind, closeness to nature, and the ability to start one's life anew. In this vein, the Expressionists adopted the reflections and refractions of crystal as embodying the optimism and dynamics of a new architecture. Taut dedicated his *Glashaus* pavilion at the 1914 Werkbund Exhibition in Cologne to Paul Scheerbart, whose name lived on in the projects of the *Arbeitsrat für Kunst* (Workers' Council for Art) and, exalted to cosmic dimensions, in Taut's *Der Weltbaumeister* (1920). This architectural drama was first performed — in sets designed by the Viennese group Coop Himmelblau — in Graz, Austria, in 1993.

With the exception of Hermann Finsterlin and Paul Gösch, all the other group members also contributed architectural visions in crystal. The emphasis, apart from megastructures bridging entire mountain valleys and landscapes, lay on buildings designed to further community spirit — theaters, concert halls, museums, community centers, cathedrals of socialism. These hopeful if rather vague and romantically populist conceptions by such ingrained pacifists as Bruno Taut differed fundamentally from the belligerent and back-

Wenzel August Hablik, *Architecture: Temporary Buildings*, 1925

Wenzel August Hablik, original sketch of the interior of an exhibition palace, 1914

Artist unknown, colored sketch for the main hall
of Farbwerke Höchst AG, by Peter Behrens, ca. 1920

ward-looking sentimentality, the racism and militarism, which the National Socialists distilled from Nietzsche's and Wagner's ideas.

Seeking to find an architectural embodiment for a "religion of art," Wenzel Hablik devoted his life to projecting a Museum in the High Mountains, as well as to collecting crystals. His former residence in Itzehoe, Germany, still contains a lovingly cared-for and extensive collection that attests to his passion. To Hablik, crystals provided an answer to his questions concerning the purity and original source of human existence.

Hablik's crystalline architectural designs were highly diverse in terms of approach and character. They ranged from examples of a naively romantic nostalgia for medieval castles to a lucid modernity that recalled Vesnin, Chernikov, and de Stijl, and to crystalline urban utopias along New Jerusalem lines. Like many others at the end of the First World War, Hablik believed that a new era in human history was imminent. In a manifesto addressed to the peoples of the world he first reminded them of their common origins: "All of you represent humanity, a single great family of the same origin, and all equally transient. In the beginning the earth was your garden, a dwelling in which all of you held equal rights — Paradise." The main thrust of the manifesto was the creation of "A new architecture, the basis for a new religion and philosophy, the confederation of the nations of the earth."[40]

As he hoped that even the very thought of war could be forever expunged from people's minds, the triumph of Nazism in Germany would have been the most bitter experience in Hablik's life. Perhaps it was a blessing that he died in 1934, of complications after an operation for a small tumor in his right eye. Besides gardens of Eden and crystal cities in Alpine chasms, Hablik's utopian projects included even airships and urban settlements in the stratosphere. Hence among his other merits, he was one of the pioneers of extraterrestrial architecture.

The members of the Gläserne Kette not only sparked new developments in architectural theory but attempted to humanize building by lending the interrelationship between body and soul visible architectural form, as the two mystics of the crystal, Taut and Hablik, endeavored to do. Taut's later achievements in urban planning are beyond the range of our topic. But other group members like

Wassili Luckhardt and Hans Scharoun, while sharing Taut and Hablik's romantically mystical beliefs about the symbolism of crystals and a new religiosity, were also quite practice-oriented. Scharoun's colored drawings, for instance, burst with vitality and movement, elegance and musicality, apart from exhibiting a fine sense of form and color. As Wolfgang Pehnt has pointed out, the "crystalline architects" were imbued with the ancient belief in the affinity of architecture with music. But architecture may be "frozen music," Hans Poelzig is reported to have quipped, with reference to Schopenhauer's famous aphorism, "bei Taut, da taut's" (With Taut, it thaws). In keeping with Expressionist intentions, Poelzig explained, Taut was capable of making architecture a vehicle of deep feelings that would cause icebound (i.e. rigid, ossified) positions and conditions to melt away.[41] With respect to Scharoun, Poelzig noted how in his designs of the Gläserne Kette period the sheaves of form licked like flames, and sheaves of crystals projected out of the earth or burst like exotic fruit. "The streamlined shapes of the somewhat later drawings, like strange creatures made of some unknown kind of protoplasm, rush as if from afar into the rectangle of the paper."[42] The highly musical aspect of these architectural visions had its source in the reciprocal relationships among mathematics, music, and architecture, which were even more strongly emphasized in the crystalline architectures of the Gläserne Kette.

One of the group's protagonists, however, Hermann Finsterlin, remained unexcited by crystals. In early 1919 he had read Walter Gropius's appeal to young unknown architects to participate in an exhibition of the same name. Finsterlin sent a few designs to Berlin; the selection committee found them so good that they asked him for more, which sent him into a creative frenzy. In his memoirs Finsterlin recalls having submitted over one hundred drawings to the show. While this cannot be corroborated, a full third of the available exhibition space was in fact devoted to Finsterlin's work.

It was the first public recognition the thirty-two-year-old architect had had. Finsterlin dabbled in chemistry, medicine, philosophy, and Indology, and also tried his hand at various arts, such as painting and sculpture, poetry and essays, play writing, and musical composition. Yet like many multitalented self-taught people, Finsterlin could not manage to concentrate on and develop any one of his abilities to the point of reaching excellence in a particular scientific or artistic field. As his independence was ensured by a family fortune that dwindled but did not disappear in the postwar inflation, Finsterlin was never forced to earn his living or make compromises.

Wenzel August Hablik, *Way of the Genius.* Oil on canvas, 1918

Wassili Luckhardt, project for a sacred building in concrete and colored glass, 1919

Hermann Finsterlin, *Formal Study for Casa Nova,* 1920

Also, he was exempted from military service due to a riding accident. Lacking in self-criticism, Finsterlin considered himself a genius, an all-around, universally gifted artist who moreover enjoyed the blessings of divine inspiration. As late as 1970 he could still write, to Louise Mendelsohn,

> *My patience, my voluntary waiting, are not mystical attributes in my eyes. It is a matter of simple knowledge of the law of maturation of the highest differentiations. The lioness gestates for weeks; the human being for months. Zeus bore Hercules in his thigh for years, and how long Athena slumbered in his head, no myth writer of antiquity was ever able to determine. This insight cannot detract from the indispensable importance of the great grade and bridge-builders who span an arch over the gigantic abysses of time. And perhaps a certain intrinsic duality plays a role…. And so we, Erich [Mendelsohn] and I, were perhaps the most significant inaugurators of a future architecture, a true Janus, the double-headed god of the era.*[43]

In retrospect it is not surprising that Finsterlin avidly took up Bruno Taut's suggestion to participate in the planned exchange of ideas, assumed the name Prometheus, and mailed out the longest, most numerous, and most emphatic contributions of the group. For him the Gläserne Kette was like a dam breaking after a great storm contained. As his biographer, Reinhard Döhl, puts it, Finsterlin blew all his fuses when he at long last found a hearing for his ideas. In the context of the Gläserne Kette, his writings stand out for their enthusiastic tone and fondness for superlatives, but to a present-day reader they also seem swollen, verbose, and marred by cloyingly sentimental purple passages. Still, they occasionally shine with brilliantly formulated insights on new approaches to architecture, on the relationship between architecture and the environment, and on organic building and thinking.

Finsterlin's historical significance has since come to rest almost exclusively on the drawings he produced between 1918 and the end of the 1920s. These mark him as the absolute antipode to "classical" modernism and its rationality. As Finsterlin himself rightly judged in this case, to the coolness of functionalist modernism he opposed "the Tropics of Prometheus," their sultriness, their organic and erotic entanglements.

In one of his often witty and sarcastic aphorisms Finsterlin speaks of the existence of "fattened pigs and gazelles," leaving no doubt as to which species he belongs, just as when he declares that you "cannot lock a bird of paradise in a chicken coop."[44] His opposition to functionalist modernism is precisely stated, if without naming names, in his short autobiography. After marrying during the First World War, Finsterlin moved with his wife from Munich to Berchtesgaden, where the mountain environment, and love, made him into a new man:

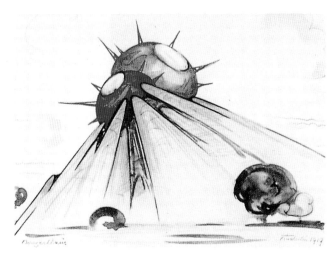

Hermann Finsterlin, *Concert Hall*, 1919

> At just that time [when Gropius's advertisement appeared] a very strange and inexplicable distaste for living in cubes, for flat surfaces and right-angled corners, for household crates alias furniture, had arisen in me. On awakening or when daydreaming my eye no longer desired to ricochet off vertical or horizontal walls, but yearned, as in dreams of magnificent caverns or gigantic organs, to caress complicated configurations, a rich, vital, and exciting environment of the kind presented by the only apparently amorphous kaleidoscope of the grand mountain realm we saw daily on our many walks. In keeping with this, the Baroque — or at most High Gothic or the temples of India — seemed the only congenial architecture to me.
>
> I now began to design dream houses in which I imagined myself living. Mad configurations, inside and out; but even here, despite the most audacious dynamics, always retaining static equilibrium.[45]

Finsterlin's designs were based on organic and natural forms, having neither right angles nor any other attribute of Euclidian geometry. Abounding in unusually shaped walls and windows, his residential, theater, and concert-hall projects resembled sculpture more than traditional architecture. When Jørn Utzon designed his famous opera house in Sydney, he surely had not only the sailboats in the harbor in mind but Finsterlin's drawings as well. These evoke colorful buds, mushrooms, phallic shapes, sea urchins, coral formations, shells, tentacled underwater creatures, erotic couplings from which emerge bizarre thorns, zigzags, and rays — but they also sometimes have an embarrassing touch of Snow White and the Seven Dwarfs about them. When Willi Wolfradt spoke in *Die Weltbühne* of "dream villas in the candy-box mode,"[46] he was right with respect to many of Finsterlin's designs, but after all they have continued to divide critical opinion to this day.

Hermann Finsterlin, *The Red House*, 1921

What makes Finsterlin so exciting to many contemporary architects is his insight that the right angle was perhaps not the greatest

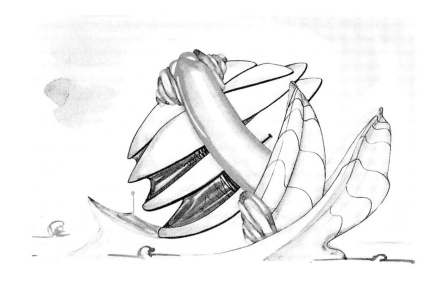

I. M. Pei, Louvre Pyramid, 1989. Interior with structural scaffolding and lighting

invention of human civilization after all. With an increasing use of fractals and experimental organic configurations employing materials both old and new — stone, glass, concrete, plastics, textiles — architects are beginning to invent flexible architectural volumes which, as Finsterlin envisaged, are capable of growing like tropical fruit. Finsterlin dreamed of the ideal interior space as being a human space instead of merely the hollow inside of a geometric solid. In this regard, Johannes Langner notes:

> With "elementary geometric bodies" Finsterlin jettisoned the entire book of rules that had previously governed the shape of a building's volume and the space enclosed by it: the axiomatic nature of horizontals and verticals, the obligation to employ straight lines, right angles, and arc segments, and the primary two-dimensional and three-dimensional forms defined by these. He rejected the products of their sterile dictates in every field, whether ecclesiastical or secular architecture, as being "God cages" and "object coffins." Instead Finsterlin advocated an organic mobility of form in which geological and zoomorphic patterns would merge."[47]

The crystalline designs of the Gläserne Kette have continued to stimulate architects down to the present day, including such otherwise diverse men as Frank Lloyd Wright, Bruce Goff, Gordon Bunshaft, and Walter Netsch. Their influence is also apparent in Buckminster Fuller's geodetic domes and Konrad Wachsmann's studies of space-enclosing structures, but more often actual practice falls far behind the vision. Finsterlin's ideas have tended to remain the province of outsiders, the eccentric Southern Californian and Brazilian builders of homes intended to be just as organic as the lush environment in which they are set. Recent years, however, have brought remarkable developments in terms of both crystalline architecture and organic sculpture. Examples of the former are I. M. Pei's pyramid at the Louvre in Paris (1989) and Moshe Safdie's Canadian National Gallery,

I. M. Pei,
pyramid entrance
to the Louvre.
Nocturnal
view past the
Arc de Triomphe and
Champs-Elysées to the
Grande Arche
de La Défense

Top: Moshe Safdie, Canadian National Gallery, Ottawa, 1988
Left: Moshe Safdie, Canadian National Gallery, Ottawa. Domed hall

Ottawa (1988); and of the latter, Douglas Cardinal's Canadian Museum of Civilization, also in Ottawa (1989).

Pei's glass pyramid represents a provocative, and long hotly debated, contrast to the old Louvre. With its timeless, minimal form, both highly modern and associated with diverse historical phases and world cultures, the pyramid confronts the hallowed architecture of the Western European Renaissance, challenging it to enter a dialogue and thus infusing new tension into the historical style.

Safdie employs large-scale crystalline configurations to an extent unprecedented in contemporary architecture. The corner points of his Canadian National Gallery are dominated by three glass domes of different size. Between them extends the gradual slope of a colonnaded ramp leading to the main entrance, from which one has an open view of Parliament Hill. At the end of the ramp one enters the Great Hall, which with its soaring 138-foot-high ceiling communicates an overwhelming sense of space. Safdie has translated into reality for the first time what Hablik, Scharoun, and Taut dreamed of in their crystalline designs. And here, too, an experience of space is described in terms of a musical analogy: "In walking through this building," Safdie says, people will "experience a variety and range of emotions comparable to the enjoyment of a symphony."[48]

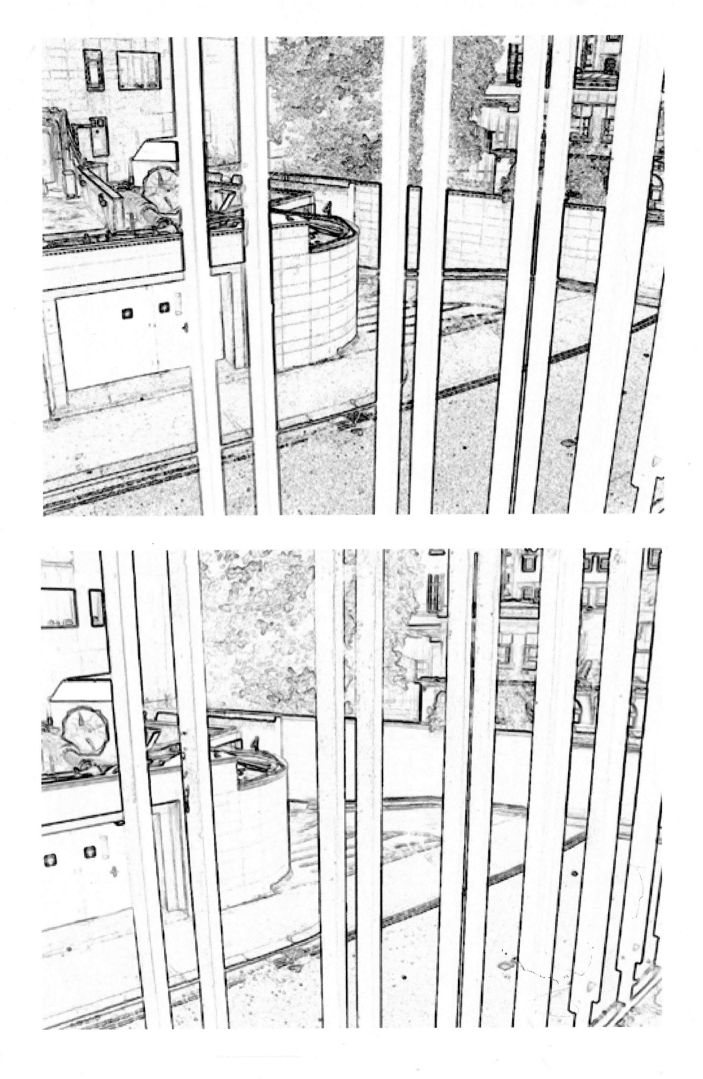

On the opposite bank of the Ottawa River, the Canadian Indian architect Douglas Cardinal has ignored the architectural idioms of recent Western civilization. Like Finsterlin, he mainly feels an obligation to Baroque traditions, for apart from indigenous Indian forms he alludes directly to the Baroque, to Bernini and Borromini, as well as to Gaudí and Finsterlin. Above all he relies on the computer, which, Cardinal says, offers the ideal opportunity to produce elliptical and curved surfaces and to take continually changing lighting conditions into account in designing a building.

All three architects — Pei, Safdie, and Cardinal — have brought ideas from the visionary architecture of the Gläserne Kette to fruition in prestigious public buildings. Ottawa is the only city in the world where its two main alternatives — crystalline form and organic sculpture — come together with the neoclassicism of the buildings on Parliament Hill to produce a grandiose architectural triangle evocative of the cultural tensions of a young nation torn between the Old and the New World, between European and native American traditions.

Douglas Cardinal, Canadian Museum of Civilization, Ottawa. Detail

Douglas Cardinal, Canadian Museum of Civilization, Ottawa. In the background, Parliament Hill

"To Seeing Born, To Scanning Called": Watchtowers, Lighthouses, Ivory Towers

DEEP NIGHT
LYNCEUS, the keeper on the watchtower
of the palace, singing
LYNCEUS To seeing born,
To scanning called,
To the watchtower sworn,
I relish the world.
Sighting the far,
Espying the near,
Moon-disc and star,
Forest and deer.
In all I behold
Ever-comely design,
As its virtues unfold,
I take pleasure in mine.
You fortunate eyes,
All you ever did see,
Whatever its guise,
Was so lovely to me!

[Pause.]

Not for pleasure, though, my master
Placed me on this lofty stand;
What a hideous disaster
Threatens from the darkened land!
Spattering sparks are winking, glaring
Through the linden's double gloom,
Fanned by rushing air, the flaring
Burrows deeper and gains rooms.
(Goethe, Faust II, 11288–11311)[10]

Valencia de Don Juan,
a castle in the province
of Leon, Spain.
Fifteenth century

The Marksburg, Braubach on the Rhine. Begun in the thirteenth century

Goethe's keeper on the watchtower is right when he says he is "sworn" to the watchtower, bound by it, dependent on it. One sees more from a tower, raised above one's fellow men, closer to the gods. Yet at the same time, the life of a keeper is a solitary life, apart from the mass. This prompts him not only to see, but to "scan," to comprehend. And if seeing is innate, comprehending must be learned; it is a vocation, to which one is brought by others, or by oneself. From the vantage point of a tower one sees more than most, not only of the countryside below but of one's own inward state. Towers encourage introspection as well.

The tower is an archetypical image, and the keeper represents an archetypical human state. Not only is the range of his eyes extended by the tower, but it raises him in the eyes of others, brings him status, and brings others protection and power. From a higher vantage point, he sees imminent good or evil approaching sooner. Hence the keeper's duty to give warning, sound the alarm, think of courses of action as long as there is still time. Nowadays, however, "sighting the far" has been largely supplanted by "television," a basically passive occupation that leaves little room for true vision.

Towers spark the imagination — that of their builders, who attempt to make them ever higher and more imposing; and that of their viewers from below or their occupants within, astronomers or astrologers who look to the skies or watchmen or thinkers who gaze down upon the world. The Tower of Babel was only three hundred feet high, yet the Jews in the plains believed its builders were at-

Keep of Steinheim Castle, on the Main River

tempting to reach heaven, a sacrilegious undertaking. Or they wished to believe it, and to convince others:

> *And he cried: My lord, I stand continually upon the watchtower in the daytime, and I am set in my ward whole nights: And, behold, here cometh a chariot of men, with a couple of horsemen. And he answered and said, Babylon is fallen, is fallen; and all the graven images of her gods he hath broken unto the ground (Isaiah 21.8–9).*

The Bible is full of towers and full of their praise, especially the towers of Jerusalem. When Homer's Odysseus neared a city, he generally described its towers and palaces first. Then there were the towers of Troy, and Dido seated in her watchtower in Carthage, looking for a sign of Aeneas. The Romans were considered the best tower builders in the ancient world. No wonder, as they had the most talented engineers and masons, and the most slaves to do the labor.

Towers are landmarks and emblems of cities. What would cities be without towers? Gate towers, church towers, bridge towers, dwelling towers, debtors' towers. Jerusalem, Babylon, Samarkand, Carthage, Rome, Bologna, Florence, Padua, Vicenza, Pisa. No matter if the tower happens to lean; all the better for the city's image.

Towers are also the salient marks of castles and palaces. The turret was a symbol of indomitable defense. In sieges the highest tower of a castle often witnessed its last stand, being defended story by story, stair by stair. This is why the spiral staircases in towers always turn to the right; this permitted defenders backing up the stairs to hold to the central column or banister with their left hand, and have space to wield a sword with their right hand.

The mirror image of the medieval tower was its dungeon, a tower dug into the earth, a negative tower, as it were. The hierarchy of towers was quite simple and obvious: those upstairs held power, and those downstairs were pitiful.

Until the twelfth century, apart from evocations of the Tower of Babel, hardly any significant literary descriptions of towers are found. An exception is a story called "The Tower of Crescentia" in the *Kaiserchronik* (V. 11518ff.).[50] Men are interested in only one thing, we may conclude from the tale, but women think twice. Crescentia, on the point of being seduced by her brother-in-law, convinces him first to build a solid, secure tower where they can meet:

> *ainen turn vil waehe*
> *den solt dû wurchen aller êrist....*
> *hôhen unde wîten —*
>
> A tower full strong
> Shalt thou first of all erect....
> High and wide —

King Alfred's Tower, Stourhead Garden, Wiltshire. Designed by Henry Flitcroft, built 1765–72

At Crescentia's behest heavy locks are forged and great stocks of provisions laid away in the tower. Finally, the *heiltuom* (sanctuary) is carried to the lady's chamber. There follows a detailed description of how the faithless brother-in-law is tricked into entering a cell and locked away within the invincible walls of his intended trysting place.

The watchtower very rapidly became a tower watched. The best chambers were occupied by ladies-in-waiting, while the lord of the manor was out on a crusade, the key to his wife's chastity belt in his pocket. If he did not return, she was in trouble — unless she knew a good locksmith. And she was in worse trouble still if he returned after all.

In the Orient, entire towers were reserved for women, the harem towers. The ladies were kept there in luxury, were permitted a chaste glance from the windows, and spent much of their time intriguing, often enough against their own men. There is a description, dating from about 1220, of the ladies' tower in which Blancheflur was kept captive in Konrad Fleck's *Flore und Blanscheflur* (V. 4162ff.). It was a fantastic tower, a hundred fathoms high and eighty fathoms wide, with three stories connected by stairways. The stories had vaulted ceilings, and contained seventy chambers in which the loveliest harem women lived. Floors and ceilings of the chambers were encrusted with gold and lapis lazuli and crystals, "as if in Paradise," for they contained nothing that displeased the eye. Instead of a roof, the tower was capped by a huge golden dome:

View of a Harem Garden, Faiz Allah, ca. 1765

der knopf ist sô hel,
so diu sunne shinet vaste,
daz ir von sime glaste
swüerent wol er brunne —

The cupola is so bright
That when the sun's rays are strong
You would swear from its glow
That it was ablaze —

Frank Thiel, Berlin-Hohenschönhausen, 1991

Anonymous reconstruction of the Pharos of Alexandria

From the peak of the dome emerged a golden rod set with a garnet that, at night, shone bright as the moon and illuminated all the streets of the city. The tower chambers were supplied with water by an exquisite system of silver pipes, installed in a hollow pilaster:

daz der brunne rinne	*That the well might run*
durch daz silber alsô klâr	*Through silver and stay clear*
und kalt belibe über jâr	*And cold the entire year,*
und auch deste schoener sî;	*And be better for it, too;*
anders war der nôch von blî —	*Elsewhere it was still of lead —*

The pilaster is described as being cut from a single piece of marble, and the water as rising to a high point in the conduit, then running back down from story to story. This watchtower was not only guarded but so heavily armed that not even the massed Roman legions could capture it.

Another watchtower watched was the one without stairs in the fairytale where the witch held Rapunzel captive. When she wanted to visit her, the witch called out "Rapunzel, Rapunzel, let down your hair," and used the girl's hair in lieu of a ladder. The prince said the same thing, but with more intimate overtones: "Baby, let your hair down." The two had lots of time to talk. This resulted in twins. When after seven years and considerable suffering they finally found each other again, they all lived happily together for ever after. But they apparently forgot to wall the witch into the tower as she deserved. Either their love was very great or the witch's magic very powerful, perhaps so powerful that masonry would not have fazed her. As one can see, towers provide food for thought, trigger associations — "To seeing born / To scanning called...."

In our own day, most watchtowers have metamorphosed into outlook towers. Everyman his own watchman — a democratic development. Yet again there is a dark side to the outlook tower, the modern watchtowers that, serving as guardposts on national borders or in prisons, concentration camps, or labor camps, play probably the most inglorious role in the history of tower architecture. Gun slits, machine-gun nests, alarm systems are accoutrements that underscore the kinship between this architecture of oppression and the medieval castle turret.

If the watchtower is a type of tower that is primarily receptive to signals, the lighthouse is one that transmits signals as well. It, too, is a tower in a prominent position which must fulfil its function of warding off dangers, and this, as in the case of the watchtower, stimulates the imagination. The imagination of the builders of lighthouses who must design them to suit diverse geographical and meteorological conditions; the imagination of those who perform solitary service there; and the imagination of those who see or visit lighthouses and consider what they mean.

The first known lighthouse has remained the most famous of all times: the Pharos of Alexandria, which has even lent its name to the science of lighthouses, pharology. It was a tower of superlatives. Begun in about 300 B.C. by order of Ptolemy II, it is thought to have been completed in the year 285, and to have cost 800 talents. Its builder's name has come down to us: Sostratus of Cnidus. Estimates of the height of the lighthouse vary between 430 and 560 feet, which is considerable even by today's standards. Located on the island of that name, the Pharos guided ships into Alexandria harbor. It continued to serve this purpose for a thousand years, then stood for another five hundred, until it was destroyed in an earthquake. The ancients declared the Pharos one of the Seven Wonders of the World, another of which, the Colossus of Rhodes, possibly also served as a lighthouse. Its beacon fire, according to Pliny, was visible from a distance of 300 stadia. That is over thirty nautical miles, a feat which, if true, was not achieved in Western Europe until the invention of nineteenth-century technology.

While the descriptions of the Roman historians were scanty, the English novelist E. M. Forster collected all the information available on the Pharos of Alexandria and prepared a detailed report. Forster too believes that never in history was a secular building so revered or preoccupied men's imagination so strongly. It was constructed, he says, of local sandstone or marble and granite from Aswan, with purplish-red veins. Encompassed by a colonnaded yard, the Pharos had four stories, the first of which was 230 feet high, with numerous windows, and about 300 rooms, where the mechanics and lighthouse keeper lived. Access to the top was provided by a spiral staircase, perhaps a double spiral. Conceivably the Pharos was even fitted with hydraulic equipment to transport oil

Lighthouse in Chesapeake Bay, Virginia, ca. 1870

Halfway Rock Lighthouse in Casco Bay, Maine, 1869–71

Etienne-Louis Boullée, *Lighthouse*, ca. 1785

for the beacon to the top. In addition to the beacon fire, Forster reports, the topmost platform may also have housed sensitive scientific instruments for astronomical calculations, and an astonishingly large mirror, perhaps of polished steel, whose purpose remains unclear. It may have been a reflector or an apparatus to record solar irradiation.

There were at least thirty lighthouses in the Roman Empire, the most renowned of which was the "Tower of Hercules" in Corunna. Their beacon fires generally also served as early-warning systems in case of invasion; all of them were harbor lights. The Pharos remained without real rival until 1584, when the French built the almost 230-foot-tall Cordouan Lighthouse at the mouth of the Gironde. Yet in terms of candlepower, lighthouses were destined to remain highly inefficient until the late eighteenth century. And as they frequently had no roof, the platform was inundated by smoke whenever it rained.

As a replacement for oil fire, wax candles were tried, but not even thirty massed together in a single stand produced sufficient luminosity. It devolved upon William Hutchinson of Liverpool, who once

Detail of a navigational light, lamp with reflector.
Cape Lookout, North Carolina

Navigational light of Sombrero Key Lighthouse, Florida

Right: Lighthouse on the horn of Cape Chat,
Saint Lawrence River, Quebec

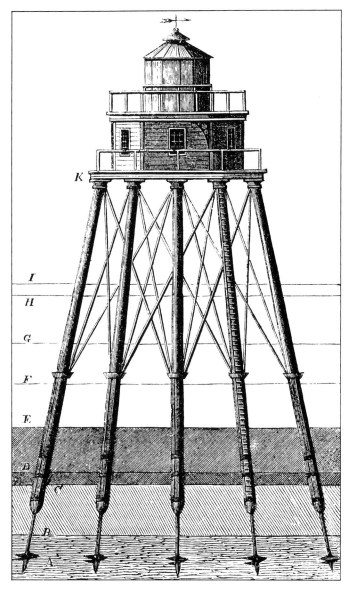

Lighthouse of Port Fleetwood,
northern England

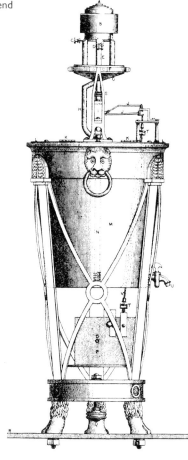

The navigational lights of Aimé Argend
were converted to oil in the
mid-nineteenth century

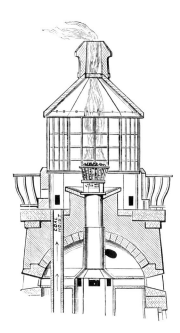

Coal-powered navigational light,
late eighteenth century

Right:
Cordouan Lighthouse at the
mouth of the Gironde, ca. 1770

had drawn the shortest straw among his shipwrecked comrades and faced a cannibals' pot when a ship saved them, to arrive, in 1763, at the idea of the reflector. After coal fire, tallow candles, and oil lamps the development of the beacon took another quantum leap when Augustin Fresnel conceived of lenses to be placed before the reflector, which considerably increased light intensity. In 1780 the argon lamp was invented, and in the course of the nineteenth century the French perfected a system of rotating lamps and beams. It was also a Frenchman who, shortly before the Revolution, envisaged lighthouses as symbolic beacons of visionary architecture: Etienne-Louis Boullée. Like Claude-Nicolas Ledoux, Boullée searched for a universal language of building forms, and he turned to the Tower of Babel as a model. Yet he completely transformed its meaning, making it over into a symbol of unity. A procession of figures, hand in hand, rises in a spiral up the conical tower of Boullée's design, evoking an egalitarian human society striving towards the light. After electricity was introduced into lighthouses, their beacons were gradually integrated into what today is a system of nautical signals understandable worldwide.

So much for a very incomplete crash-course in the history of lighthouses. Let us return to their more literary aspects. The American continent is encompassed today by a great number of lighthouses. Their seed, as it were, was planted by an entry made in the logbook of the *Santa Maria*. One October night in 1492, as Columbus stood watch on the upper deck of his flagship, he suddenly saw a light glimmering in the distance, and summoned crew members over to confirm his observation: "He saw the light once or twice, and it was like a wax candle rising and falling. It seemed to few to be an indication of land; but the Admiral made certain that land was close."[51]

The Pilgrim Fathers began building lighthouses soon after their arrival in America. It sheds an indicative light on their attitude that the puritanical Bostonians, despite the uncanny regularity with which lightning struck there, refused to fit their lighthouse with a lightning rod. For it would have been "vanity and irreligion for the arm of flesh to avert the stroke of Heaven."[52] O blessed innocence!

Stories and poems about lighthouses abound in children's literature especially. Also, authors as different as Jules Verne, in *The Lighthouse at the End of the World*, and Virginia Woolf, in her masterpiece *To the Lighthouse*, have felt attracted by the romance and symbolic richness of the motif. Not even prosaic engineers have proved immune to the poetry of lighthouses. Take Alan Stevenson's description of a beacon, which reads like a hymn to technology:

> *Nothing can be more beautiful than an entire apparatus for a fixed light of*
> *the first order. It consists of a central belt of refractors, forming a hollow cy-*
> *linder of six feet in diameter and thirty inches high; below it are six triangu-*
> *lar rings of glass, ranged in a cylindrical form and above a crown of thirteen*

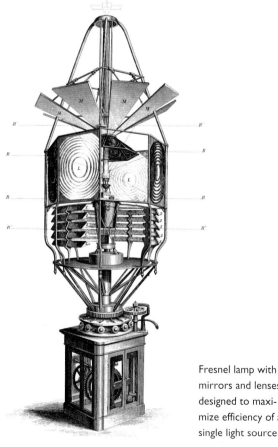

Fresnel lamp with mirrors and lenses, designed to maximize efficiency of a single light source

Large tower reliquary, Cologne, ca. 1200

rings of glass, forming by their union a hollow cage composed of polished glass ten feet high and six feet in diameter. I know of no work of art more beautifully creditable to the boldness, ardor, intelligence and zeal of the artist.

Lighthouses are solid and weather-resistant; they defy the raging elements; and they broadcast their own, strange signals:

Attention, now transmitting the scream of the laughing gull
Calling all sea-captains
Calling the men in the crow's nests
We're the new crew of the lighthouse
We're broadcasting the lighthouse news
Attention....

runs a poem titled "Seltsamer Funkspruch" by Günter Bruno Fuchs.

Ivory towers, by contrast, are made of much more fragile stuff, to a different design, and their denizens tend first to look inward before broadcasting any sort of message. Not elves but elephants provide the building material for ivory towers, and they will fortunately still exist long after the last elephant has been hunted down. (Always assuming, of course, that humankind manages not to catapult itself out of evolution first.) Compared to every other type of architecture, ivory towers have the advantage of remaining invisible if their creators so wish. This generally protects them from razing, urban improvement, and property speculation.[53] Their building blocks mainly

Robert Garcet, Eben-Ezer Tower. Eben-Emael, Belgium, 1964

consist of sheets of paper, stacked to various thicknesses between two covers.

Like the towers themselves, their inhabitants are of a very special breed. Many are not even aware of the fact that they live in an ivory tower, though others continually point it out. Some people enter voluntarily and call it "inner emigration." But as Walter Grasskamp warns, "People who live in ivory towers had better come out with their hands up — the building is surrounded."[54]

As with other forms of tower, the history of this "unpublic housing," as Grasskamp calls it, begins with the Bible. The first mention of the ivory tower bears connotations entirely unlike those we now tend to associate with it. In the otherwise so anti-carnal Bible, one book stands out for its lilting, poetic sensuality: The Song of Solomon.

Return, return, O Shulamite; return, return, that we may look upon thee… Thy belly is like an heap of wheat set about with lilies. Thy two breasts are like two young roes that are twins. Thy neck is as a tower of ivory; thine eyes like the fishpools in Heshbon, by the gate of Bath-rabbim: thy nose is as the tower of Lebanon which looketh toward Damascus (The Song of Solomon 6.13; 7.2–4).

The association of the ivory tower with the demureness, slenderness, and unapproachability of a beautiful girl continued to hold for centuries, until like so many other concepts it was torn from its context in the Romantic era and profaned.

This deed is attributed to Charles-Augustin Sainte-Beuve, who in his 1837 *Penseés d'Août* wrote of Alfred de Vigny: "…et Vigny, plus secret comme en sa tour d'ivoire avant midi retrait." The new meaning attached to the ivory tower is even more obvious in Gérard de Nerval's story "Sylvie: Souvenirs de Valois," which was published in 1857. Here the ivory tower of the poet is characterized as an exclusive place, far from the madding crowd and its banal concerns. Intoxicated by the pure air of solitude, immersed in poetry and dreams of love, the narrator concedes:

We are not at the age of ambition, and the greedy howling of the pack for the distribution of honors or positions kept us away from all possible spheres of activity. The only asylum left to us was the ivory tower of the poets, which we climbed higher and higher, to gain isolation from the crowd. At the elevated points to which our masters led us we breathed at last the pure air of solitude, we quaffed oblivion in the golden cup of fable and were drunk with poetry and love.[55]

Subsequently the ivory tower was generally inhabited by intellectuals, artists, and scientists, many because outside pressure forced them to sequester themselves, some voluntarily, under the banner of art for art's sake. Life in the ivory tower was indeed an ambivalent affair. When one "escaped inwards and upwards," as Montaigne called it, one came to breathe an exquisite, rarified air, enriched by

Renate Reimers, *A Man in Himself Is a City*, 1979–81

Ribart, *Triumphant Elephant.* Design for a monument on the Champs-Elysées, Paris, 1758

Valentin Bolz, *Tower of Grammar*

the perfume of high aesthetic standards. Still, most denizens of the ivory tower did not lead an irresponsible life of pleasure, as might appear from outside. As is shown by one of the most prominent examples, Oscar Wilde, the irreverence expressed in such maxims as "I love to play outdoor sports — dominoes!" did not prevent many of their number from being extraordinarily productive.

Ivory towers also were, and continue to be, occupied by outcasts, eccentrics, and fanatics, who doggedly or serenely pursue some ideal for which there is no place in a normative society. The pacifist anarcho-mystic Robert Garcet, to whom Jacques Lennep has devoted a delightful study, is one of the most impressive examples of the breed.[56] In decades of dedicated work, Garcet has erected a tower called Eben-Ezer, in Eben-Emael, Belgium. Based on a sophisticated numerology, the tower's rectangular ground plan, for instance, takes up that of the New Jerusalem, said to have measured 12,000 stadia on a side, and transposes it on a smaller scale to Eben-Ezer. Particularly compelling are the winged cherubim-monsters that, perched at its apex, guard the four corners of this unique ivory tower made of "living" flint: a lion, an eagle, a bull, and a man.

Among the classical ivory towers derived from the scholars' towers of the Middle Ages are institutions of higher education, from many of the colleges of Oxford and Cambridge to the American Ivy League colleges of Harvard, Princeton, and Yale. Here high-level research and exemption from quotidian concerns are combined with a far-reaching influence on society. Trinity College, Cambridge, for instance, has produced twenty Nobel Prize winners, more than the entire country of France.

As another built example of an ivory tower one might take Erich Mendelsohn's Einstein Tower in Potsdam (1917–21), an observatory and astrophysical laboratory, stylistically influenced by Art Nouveau and Futurism, that was intended as a home for typical scientific representatives of the ivory-tower breed. Yet what appeared to some a brilliant piece of Expressionist architecture woke in others, like the British architect Reginald Blomfield, threatening associations that recalled the belligerent history of watchtowers: "…that notorious Observatory at Potsdam, by Herr Eric Mendelsohn, which looks like the gun-turret of some nightmare battle-ship, with the lower part of it shaped like a ram, and windows designed to resemble the embrasure of eight-inch guns…."[57]

An effect on society at large is something not generally associated with ivory towers. Their inhabitants tend to be considered selfish escapists, unwilling to accept responsibility for anyone but themselves. Certainly allegations of this kind may sometimes be justified in my own country, Germany, perhaps more frequently than in the Anglo-American realm. Still, the works of literary denizens of the ivory tower in particular are often like signals, at first distant and barely discernible, then growing in intensity with time to finally suffuse our language and thought.

Think of Hölderlin's tower existence, or of the effects exerted by such solitaries as Marcel Proust, Franz Kafka, Elias Canetti, or Arno Schmidt. Friedrich Dürrenmatt's *The Physicists* describes the flight of scientists into an ivory tower as an act of desperation. Yet hardly have they settled in when it dawns on them that the commander of the tower is acting like one of those "wrecker gangs" among lighthouse crews who purposely send false signals that cause ships to run aground. Lively tales of such hoodlum heroism still circulate in places like Penzance, Cornwall.

Naturally it depends essentially on the individual ivory-tower dweller whether he or she is willing and able to combine an existence there with the responsibilities of the watchman, and moreover to send out effective light signals. If not, the fine ivory may suddenly prove mere bone, and the tower a charnelhouse for the bones of radiation victims. Seen in this light, even Faust's Olympian attitude would seem to be suffused by a dubious ambiguity:

Alex Wyse, *The Navy's Finest II*, 1982

> FAUST. [on the balcony, facing the
>   dunes]
> *Up on the keep, what crooning*
>   *whimper?*
> *The tone's outhurried by the fact:*
> *My watchman wails; my inmost*
>   *temper*
> *Is soured by the impatient act.*
> *But where the linden stand is wizened*
> *To piteous ruin, charred and stark,*
> *A look-out frame will soon have risen*
> *To sweep the world in boundless arc.*
> (Faust II, 11338–11345)[58]

The question remains what there is in infinity to "survey," and whether in the not-too-distant future anything worth looking at will be left.

In the Reagan era of the 1980s, watchtowers and lighthouses were spirited into the stratosphere or into outer space, and rechristened AWACS or spy or killer satellites. This madness, at least, has been stopped, or perhaps only postponed. It has been a long if logical path from ancient Greek teichoscopy and Goethe's watchman on his tower to orbiting cameras and multiple atomic warheads. The temptation is indeed great to escape to some ivory tower, to see nothing, hear nothing, and speak nothing — but who could stand it for very long?

Watchtowers and lighthouses are not immune to the trend to two-dimensionality, dematerialization, and virtualization, seen in other areas of architecture. Both are capable of being fully electronically automated and run by remote control, and ultimately their functions can be performed by satellites. Still, this is an order of immateriality quite different from that associated with the ivory tower.

Perhaps the only artist who has managed to blend the configurations and connotations of watchtower, lighthouse, and ivory tower is the Canadian Alex Wyse, with his strange box and tower objects — an eccentric but highly skilled craftsman who continually oscillates between dreamworld and reality. Let us conclude this chapter with his *The Navy's Finest* and *Angel Repair Shop*, an ivory lighthouse watchtower whose appearance is calculated to bring out the child in the man. Like some legendary ship in full regalia, it bristles with jibs, funnels, weather vanes, rainbows, life rings, fishing rods, pennants, signal flags, and periscopes, and it is manned by seagulls and human sailors. When you pour sand in at a certain point on top, the tower comes to life, beginning to rattle and clatter, emit gruff old seadog's commands, wave its pennants and sound its signal bells, until finally the over six-foot-high configuration turns out to be a three-minute egg timer. In this wonderfully clever bit of visionary architecture Wyse has combined sense and nonsense, integrated space with time. His watchman sounds no distressing alarm, sends no apocalyptic signals; with an ironic wink of his eye he settles comfortably into the same ivory tower in which a long line of British eccentrics from "my Uncle Toby" in Laurence Sterne's *Tristram Shandy* to the cartoonist Heath Robinson have pursued their delightful pastimes, recovering from the cuts and scrapes inflicted by a sharp-edged reality. The ivory tower, we may conclude, still presents alternatives of a kind that watchtowers and lighthouses have long ceased to offer.

Near Viterbo, Italy, there is an enchanted glade populated with strange carved figures that for centuries lay almost completely obscured by the mists of time. Not until the mid-1950s did it begin to attract the interest of artists and art historians, architects and architectural critics. This is the *Parco dei Mostri*, or park of monsters, the mysterious Sacro Bosco of Bomarzo (ca. 1525) located near the imposing 400-room villa of Duke Orsini. As Norbert Miller wrote in one of the first issues of the journal *Daidalos*, enthusiasts discovered here "an enchanted forest for a select circle of knights-errant of the imagination, who apply their power of fantasy to breaking its own bounds."[59]

The garden of Bomarzo is an enigmatic place. Neither its purpose nor the mental attitude behind it can be determined with any confidence today. Yet rather than being a site of philosophical contemplation, it probably witnessed fantastic discourses and equivocal orgies. Although the monsters have lost their terror for us today, with a little imagination, aided by historic knowledge, their manifold fascination can still be felt. Miller, for example, speaks of a transformation of the classical pleasure ground into a confusion of dark, bizarre visions. Arcadia, he says, was here reshaped into a wilderness of phantasmagorical wonders, where the outlines of the labyrinth become visible behind the masks of the Renaissance garden.

What seems to reign in Bomarzo is an enjoyment of fear. The park and its monsters are truly grotesque, both attractive and repellent, prompting a laugh that dies in one's throat. They confront us with classical, mythical, and literary allusions, but also with the carnival spirit of a very special brand of black humor cultivated in the late Middle Ages and the Renaissance. As Michail Bachtin writes, it was the extroverted, as it were cannibalistic spirit of a sensibility devoted to ingesting the world with all the senses, with every pore and orifice of the body, then digesting it and excreting it again. It was the domain of a Gargantuan, cruel, and cannibalistic eroticism. This is represented, on the one hand, by the giant known as Orlando, who possibly goes back to a scene in Ariosto's *Orlando furioso*, perhaps even to Ovid. The giant looks as if it were spreading the thighs of a woman to the point

The crooked house in the Garden of Bomarzo

Monster in the Garden of Bomarzo

of dislocation, then mentally eviscerating her with a mixture of sexual lust and cool anatomical curiosity. One is left uncertain whether rape or a good meal is foremost in his mind. On the other hand, there is a gigantic nymph in Bomarzo, reclining on a rock, surrounded by the remains of human lovers or playmates of both sexes, whom she appears to have devoured in an erotic frenzy.

The monster guarding the entrance provides a fitting introduction to this realm of extremes. Eyes, nostrils, and a huge mouth bristling with teeth agape, it engorges the world and its inhabitants, into a head which is evidently the seat not of rational intellect but of burning obsession, ecstatic frenzy. At the same time, the mouth evokes a uterine cavern, the Orco, entry to the underworld. The inscription *Ogni pensiero vo* recalls Dante's Gates of Hell, and the famous line from his *Divine Comedy*, *Lasciate ogni speranza voi ch'entrate!* (Abandon all hope, ye who enter!). A restorer, less imaginative, has completed but simplified the message to *Ogni pensiero vola* (All thought flies), which after all is quite an apt and fanciful simile.[60]

Inside the park we find stone benches and a bower. Is this where people met to begin a drinking bout, or to perform some initiation rite, and if so, devoted to what cult? Was it truly a cult of sensuality, a sensual derangement, a transgression of erotic boundaries induced by uninhibited architecture and sculpture? Every architectural fragment and sculpture in Bomarzo indeed bears an entire spectrum of meanings, and these are expressed as much through their structural elements as through ornamental, emblematic, or narrative aspects.

There is, for instance, the old penchant of the inhabitants of Etruria for monsters and chimeras, their willingness to enter the realm of dream and confront nightmares of anxiety. There is that cannibalistic sexuality that would overcome every human inhibition. There is the metamorphosis of humans into animals and vice versa. And, there is the classical beauty of the female figures, their sensual if cold and cruel smile. Passion is overshadowed by

Monster at the entrance to the Garden of Bomarzo

melancholy, that of the perpetual de Sade in men, an impression deepened by the fusion of the human element with the rank luxuriance of nature.

But the architectural climax of the park is surely its "crazy house," where all the laws of verticality and horizontality, gravity and equilibrium are turned upside down.[61] Looking through the windows, one sees slices of the life outside so unfamiliarly framed as to be completely disorienting. In a word, Bomarzo is dominated by a bizarre, deconstructivist approach that reveals the workings of an age-old, manneristic principle in art.

Ever since the Renaissance, bizarre architecture has continued to produce strange and beautiful offshoots. In our own century these have been numerous, because rationality, belief in science, and normative tendencies in every area of life have so strongly curtailed the free play of imagination that more and more people rebel. Normal people call these rebels dreamers, eccentrics, or worse. But at least they are capable of creating something, bizarre perhaps, but invariably unique. Psychology generally does play a key role here; many of these outsiders would be cases for the psychiatrist if they were not

Richard Henriquez, writer's studio in Banff, Alberta, Canada. The Elsie K., originally a salmon fishing boat from British Columbia, 1988

Abandoned ferryboat, Waldo Point, California

permitted to translate their life's dreams into built form. Some would indeed despair of life altogether. Their urge to build is so obsessive that they feel it not as a personal desire but as if something, some "it" were acting through them. So for them, the journey is the goal. Examples are the country postman Ferdinand Cheval, or Robert Garcet, who in the 1950s, in the Belgian town of Eben-Emael, began to erect his "Tower of the Apocalypse." In this symbol set against the chaos of the contemporary world, Garcet, a true mystagogue, relied on a complex numerology and the dimensions of the biblical Jerusalem.

This "setting of signs against something," whether it be modern technology, the big city, or the death of God, is characteristic of many examples of bizarre architecture. Buildings of this type are by no means without rules, but they do elude conventional, generally accepted rules and stylistic categories.[62]

The individualists and do-it-yourself architects who create these buildings often make a virtue of necessity and employ trash, recycling materials, old boards, glass bottles or fragments, bricks, ceramic tiles, clay, fieldstones, and many other objects that tend to lend the result a sculptural character. Interestingly this corresponds to a key tendency of twentieth-century art, the use of discarded things, objets trouvés, for aesthetic ends which in the final result ennoble them.

The builders of tree-houses and furnishers of caves work just as much along these lines as the captains of homemade houseboats or other mobile dwellings. And in the process something enters their creations that is otherwise rare in architecture: humor. Architecture may emanate a sense of gaiety, as in the Baroque or Rococo periods, but it seldom is actually funny. Some of the non-architects under discussion are veritable fountains of fun and irony. Or their buildings make an unintentionally humorous impression, which their creators generally bear with equanimity.

Clarence Schmidt, House of Mirrors. Destroyed by fire in 1968

Many of these structures express a very individual, occasionally labyrinthine philosophy. The houses of Clarence Schmidt of Woodstock, New York, are a case in point. After living for a few years in a cabin decorated with shards of glass, Schmidt began to build a "house of mirrors" that consisted of a huge agglomeration of trash and old window and door frames. The walls were covered in aluminum foil or painted with silver paint. The final result was a Kafkaesque castle seven stories high, resplendent with innumerable reflections. The house burned down in 1968, but Schmidt immediately began building a new one — only to see it, too, destroyed by fire three years later.

Many lovable eccentrics are found among the architects and inhabitants of houseboats, whether they live on the Seine, on Dutch canals, or in Sausalito Bay, where one of the world's largest houseboat colonies spreads out beneath you when you pass over the Golden Gate Bridge from San Francisco. Their creations, ranging from elegant waterborne villas to absolutely bizarre floating sculptures, combine great emotional commitment with aesthetic originality.

Whether by water, on land, or — one is tempted to add in view of brilliantly patterned balloons — in the air, the builders and embellishers of bizarre structures are frequently characterized by an inner urge to make manifest a very private universe of visual ideas. Another example is Marcel Dhièvre, who in twelve years of work transformed his small house on the village street of Saint-Dizier into a "Petit Paris," a world of flowers, plants, ornaments, and architectural monuments.

More often than any other architectural genre, the bizarre and grotesque exhibits a tendency to *architecture parlante*. In other words it tells a story by means of anthropomorphic, zoomorphic, or, as Charles Jencks has called them, "animalorph," references, that is,

Marcel Dhièvre, "Petit Paris." Residential building in Saint-Dizier, ca. 1965

Robert Venturi, *"I Am a Monument"*

Haus-Rucker-Co, *Street Noses*, 1974

more or less abstracted human and animal forms.[63] Surprisingly, however, this happens less frequently with eclectic do-it-yourselfers than with trained architects, some of them of high artistic talent. The motives behind "speaking architecture" may be predominantly commercial, as in the case of the elephant Horst Rellecke designed in 1984 for a garden show in Hamm, Germany. Or it may have been created just for fun, as in the case of French revolutionary architect Jean-Jacques Leqeu's silo for cattle, feed, hay and acorns.

Houses with a human face have repeatedly occurred in many and diverse world cultures. Unprecedented, however, are the degree and scale of anthropomorphism employed in an entrance to a great public building, the Indian mask of Douglas Cardinal's Canadian Museum of Civilization in Ottawa.[64] This architecture is less an example of bizarre eclecticism than of cultural and political calculation. On the bank of the Ottawa River opposite Moshe Safdie's Canadian National Gallery, which represents the European architectural heritage in Canada, Cardinal placed a mega-symbol of native Indian culture. The Grand Hall of the museum accordingly contains an exhibition on the folk art and everyday lives of the Indians of the Pacific northwest coast (see also p. 91).

The liberal and multicultural climate of Canada is evidently favorable to carefree architectural eccen-

Mobile dwelling, Venice Beach, California

tricity. An example is Canada Place, a combined luxury hotel, convention center, and exhibition building on the approach to Vancouver harbor, by the internationally known architect Eberhard Zeidler. In keeping with the genius loci, Zeidler suffused the complex with nautical references, which extend from tall clippers to freighters, ocean liners and cruise ships, and even, on the water side of his high-tech structure (1986), a Spanish galleon from the Age of Discovery.

Richard Henriquez, another Vancouver architect, not only possesses great aesthetic sensibility but loves a joke. To a competition for eight artists' studios in Banff, Henriquez submitted a West Coast salmon fishing boat which he had flown into the Rockies by helicopter and deposited at an altitude of six thousand feet. There it remains, a Noah's arc for writers in the midst of a colony of compo-

Robert Venturi, *Duckling*

Right: Eberhard Zeidler, Canada Place, Vancouver, 1986

Opposite page: Villa in Martinique, recalling a ship about to be launched

sers', painters', and sculptors' studios. The architect's own residence in Vancouver abounds with wild ideas with which he and his family, artists all, play tricks with conventional architecture. Yet such capers, like his design for a high-rise building in downtown Vancouver in the form of a Canova sculpture, remain accessories that in no way detract from the functionality of otherwise modern structures. The same holds true for the California architect Frank Gehry's buildings shaped like milk pitchers, binoculars, or fish. These are a far cry from the bizarre architecture of genuine eccentrics like Cheval, Garcet, or Simon Rodia (who built the Watts Towers in the early 1920s), the outward shape of which resulted from an intrinsic need, a mental universe which demanded expression.

Thus the range of bizarre architecture is especially great, extending from the highly sophisticated to the compulsive and naïve. An example of the first is Antoni Gaudí, who combined immense engineering and building talent with a fine sense of Catalonian, Moorish, and contemporary traditions, amalgamated in a melting pot of individual fantasy. The other extreme might be illustrated by the Long Island Duckling, a sales booth made famous by Robert Venturi, which he used to explain the symbolic form of a building-becoming-sculpture in contrast to the principle of the "decorated shed," where systems of space and structure are directly at the service of program, and ornament is applied independently of them.[65]

Perhaps the highest peak of bizarreness was reached by the Vienna-Düsseldorf group Haus-Rucker-Co, who in the wild 1970s projected a poetic Jacob's ladder piercing artificial clouds, framed actual landscapes at the 1972 Documenta in Kassel, built waterfalls that flowed upwards, or, in 1974, towed sham mountains titled *Street Noses* and *Alpine Hike* as non-architectures through downtown streets.

Advance to the Past — Return to the Future: Contemporary Visionary Architects

The twentieth century has produced more visionary architects than any comparable period in the past. Of course this is partly due to the increased number of architects all told; but it is also a result of the many crises of our era which, for architects, entailed a dearth of building commissions. Who can or wishes to build anything permanent when guns are firing and bombs are falling outside? Other factors that have influenced the visionary boom are the media and communication society, the worldwide distribution of architectural journals and books, a growing international exchange among schools of architecture, architects' avid borrowings from every conceivable context and period, and, in certain fields — such as hotels, airports, museum and university buildings, hospitals — the emergence of an international architectural idiom. The key trait of visionary or fantastic architecture, again, is that it has not been, or cannot be, built. Yet it nevertheless fulfils an eminently important function in the training and practice of architects. Frequently one also sees talented architects oscillating between utopia and reality, between the free play of daring, fantastic designs and the mundane job of making a living. But truly visionary architects generally insist that their drawings and designs be taken just as seriously as what they actually build.

Visionary architects are naturally free from a number of mundane compulsions, such as those of construction costs and materials, or the availability of lots. This allows them to concentrate on translating their daring and adventurous ideas into graphic terms, to take account of purely aesthetic or philosophical considerations, and to reflect on the potential links between architecture and any number of other fields. A key role in this regard is played by architectural aesthetics — the development of innovative ground plans, facade designs, and forms in general, as well as experimentation with light and shade effects, with color, and with materials both already available and yet to be invented. The process involves the introduction of poetic qualities and musical or rhythmical elements, but also an extrapolation of available and potential technologies — or, vice versa, it may entail a return to a vision of some Arcadian past, which the architect feels ought to be revived for future generations.

Visionary architecture indeed has a utopian aspect, which makes it especially conducive to thinking

Massimo Scolari, *Heliotherapeutic Baths in the Atlantic.* Watercolor, 1977

116

about the interrelationships between architecture and society, between architecture and ethics, politics, religion, power, and human community. Fundamentally, however, architectural fantasy tends to be oriented towards the future. This links it with science fiction and futurology, indeed with every farsighted and long-term trend and development, be it in the media, in environmental protection, in transportation, or in the employment of new technologies and their aesthetic.

Two basic thrusts can be distinguished, within which manifold differentiations may exist in the individual case. The first is represented by an architectural camp that tends to mistrust technological progress and industrial process, and would shape the future through a reconsideration of positive aspects of the past. The opposite camp tends to place all its hope in high tech, optimistically greeting every new idea and innovation in industry, science, and the arts.

Let us look at a few of the principal representatives of both groups, and briefly sketch their lives and works since the 1960s.

Massimo Scolari, *The Forgetting Machine, or History Liberated*. Watercolor, 1978

MASSIMO SCOLARI

The Italian architect Massimo Scolari belongs to the anti-technology camp. Since the late 1960s he has been painting, drawing, and designing ideal architectural prototypes which he frequently condenses, like Japanese *haikus*, into miniature formats.

A poet and visionary, Scolari has created his own personal architectural and artistic world. Although it contains allusions to Antonio Sant'Elia and shows the influence of Aldo Rossi, for whom Scolari worked as an assistant for a time, by and large it is a world in the classical Italian spirit. Ideal versions of Babylonian towers or the pyramids combine with abstract power plants, minimal house shapes, geometric bodies, stylized landscapes, sex symbols, and enigmatic flying objects, to produce a hermetic architectural cosmos. Here Scolari reigns like a demiurge, single-handedly laying down the law as to what architecture ought to be, and what not.

Scolari's world has a transfixing quality. It is a universe of pristine, soundless, cool beauty — cool even when he uses warm colors. This may be partly the result of a certain lack of human qualities in his architectural visions, which seem strangely incommunicative even in those cases where their scale is expressly related to the proportions of the human body.

His architectural depictions, repeatedly focusing on monuments and solitary structures, embody a discontent with modernity and postulate a timeless realm of ideal architectural form, in which things as banal and impure as everyday life and problems have no place. Scolari might be characterized as a resident in an ivory tower of pure architecture who disdains the daily round. His designs frequently pose riddles: What is the meaning of the Babylonian tower

Massimo Scolari, *Pyramid Landscape*. Watercolor, 1975

shaped like the French sculptor César's thumb-sculptures, but with a great aperture at the top? Or why do many of his structures hover in the air, or seem about to take off? And what do the strange, archaic, unmanned flying objects that jet through his imagery connote? Perhaps they are allusions to Daedalus, the great artificer, with whose aid the architect would spirit us into a post-human world of pure beauty.

LEON KRIER

Leon Krier of Luxembourg, the second contemporary visionary architect on our list, does not leave questions of this kind unanswered. He joins the fray, and based on a merciless analysis of the present, he uncompromisingly advocates a retrospective utopia. Krier is a mixture of radically conservative moralist and revolutionary. The only architecture that passes the test of his critical eye is classical architecture, in its Greek and Roman variants. Even the slightest taint of neoclassicism disgusts him. He is convinced that all the essential problems of architecture were already solved prior to the first industrial revolution, and that the worst thing one can do is attempt to industrialize architecture or advocate building with prefabricated parts.

Krier firmly believes that industrialization has been a scourge of humanity and has ruined architecture and urban planning. This belief leads him to mount a populistic attack on modern architecture of whatever stamp, which he says the majority of people do not understand, let alone like, while in classical architecture they feel comfortable, because they can identify with its human scale. The Modern Movement, he argues, was harmful and destructive to the highest degree.

Architecture has indeed existed, Krier states, but only in earlier

periods. Nothing being produced today deserves the name. His designs and urban planning theory reflect the influence of Camillo Sitte of Vienna, whose masterful craft is also detectable in Krier's work. His drawings are not only exceptionally beautiful, but they combine simplicity, balance of proportion, harmony, and symmetry with an obvious concern with utility and an aesthetic based on the classical canon and hierarchies of order. These are the means of expression he marshals against ubiquitous modernism. In his opinion, the myth of scientific and industrial progress has brought the highly industrialized nations to the brink of physical and cultural collapse, and destroyed the substance of almost every city that has developed organically over the centuries.[66] Long before the mass appearance of green movements and environmental parties, Krier was strictly opposed to the building of new city streets and expressways. Like many others, he thinks the American approach to city planning which has spread worldwide since the 1960s was absolutely wrong, because it destroyed urbanity by leading to a separation of the functions of living, working, education, recreation, shopping, and entertainment. The only meaningful remedy, Krier believes, would be to reintegrate these urban functions in neighborhoods entirely accessible on foot. These districts, if they were to work as cities within the city, should have no more than 15,000 inhabitants.[67]

Many of Krier's analyses sound convincing; some are certainly appealing; a few might even be feasible, which is probably what prompted Prince Charles in the 1980s to turn to Krier, and his protegé Quinlan Terry, as architectural advisors. Yet as correct as many of his culturally pessimistic arguments may be in detail, the conclusions Krier draws from them are fundamentally false and alienated from reality. In fact they are arch-reactionary, as are the architectural opinions of the Crown Prince and the sometimes considerable influence he exerts on urban planning and architecture in England, especially in London.

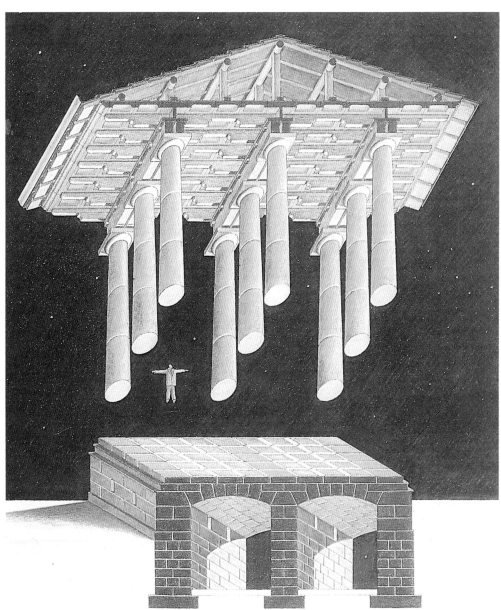

Leon Krier, *Market Building*. Berlin-Tegel, 1982

Leon Krier, *House for G. Mayer.* Bagnano, 1974

Krier's demand that industrial and postindustrial societies be reduced to the preindustrial condition of an — idealized — seventeenth or eighteenth century is simply illusory and, for all the classical humanism behind it, exhibits a contempt for the human situation. Any projected architecture that is rooted not in its own era but solely in the past is bound to be stillborn. The world population has almost tripled between 1960 and 1994, from about two billion to about five-and-a-half billion; to conform to Krier's ideal state, it would have to be reduced to about a tenth of its present size. His statement that there is only one architecture, classical architecture, that its problems have been solved, and that everything else may be "building" but never "architecture" is sheer nonsense. It denies evolution, and would like to see human and architectural development frozen in a static equilibrium, implying an unchanging classical canon valid for all time. The same would hold, logically, for all the other arts. There would be only one type of music, one type of painting, and so on; and into the bargain, we must add, probably only one type of government: dictatorship. In view of such prospects the approach of the American postmodernists seems like a breath of fresh air, for Michael Graves, Charles Moore, and Stanley Tigerman employ Krier's classical canon and many other historical forms with a wonderful insouciance to produce a colorfully eclectic and vital blend. Krier's architectural realm apparently has no place for the raw realities of life, its dirtiness and imperfections, an omission reflect-

Leon Krier, *Atlantis.* The Agora, 1988

ing his idealized conception of the old, traditional, unalienated crafts and trades.

More worthy of consideration are Krier's thoughts on decentralized city planning and an integration of urban functions. Yet as he himself realizes, these desiderata have been rendered impossible by a capitalist market regulation of property prices which makes the provision of downtown living space in the metropolis and megalopolis unprofitable.

Confronted with this harsh reality, Krier retreated in the 1980s into a series of ideal city plans. The best known of these, designed in collaboration with Hans-Jürgen Müller, is the *Atlantis* project.[68] Krier had always insisted that he could make architecture only because he did not build. Now, offered the chance to actually create, on Tenerife, a classical, ideal city in conformity with his ideas, he changed his mind. The result was an accumulation of Greek temples, palaces, colonnades, obelisks, a lighthouse, and an agora, all in a synthetic, watered-down classical style. Whether the project is conducive to solving the urban planning problems of the twenty-first century is open to doubt. When one imagines harassed managers and successful young entrepreneurs in flowing togas and laurel wreaths in their hair, gathered in *Atlantis* to discuss the philosophical and economic issues of our age, one feels slightly amused at the degree of escapism the project reveals.

Haus-Rucker-Co, *Oasis No. 7*. Documenta V, Kassel, 1972

THE POSTWAR VIENNESE AVANT-GARDE: HANS HOLLEIN, HAUS-RUCKER-CO, COOP HIMMELBLAU, RAIMUND ABRAHAM

The extremely creative architectural scene in postwar Vienna produced a number of vanguard architects of international rank. All of them — Hans Hollein, Raimund Abraham, Coop Himmelblau, Haus-Rucker-Co — have been prolific in the field of visionary architecture, if in highly different ways.[69] Before making a name for himself as a practicing architect, Hollein advanced such ironic and provocative projects as aircraft carriers high and dry in the landscape, railroad cars transformed into ceremonial architectural sarcophagi, tower pastiches, tree houses metamorphosed into stone, fortress-like country houses, and lyrical watercolor sketches of cities combining Indian pueblo with classical monumentality. Hollein's fundamental belief that architecture must be rooted in the cultic, sacred, and erotic, his opposition to functionalist modernism, his penchant for visual symbolism, fiction, and narration in architecture, all stem

Hans Hollein, *House*, 1961

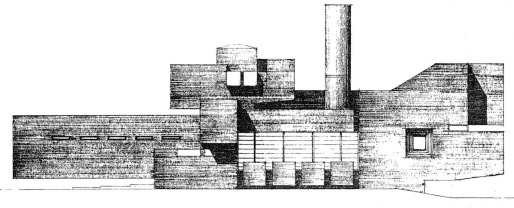

Hans Hollein, *Railroad Car Monument*, 1963

Raimund Abraham, *Church at the Wall*. Berlin, 1982–83

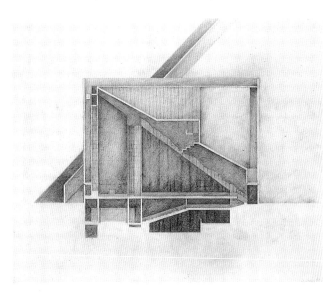

from this early phase of his career. What he learned from it, and still teaches others, is to see architecture from a fresh, unconventional vantage point, to discover the tectonic aspects of things generally considered unarchitectural, to charge them with emotion and dare to create symbols, metaphors, and images that can serve to enrich architecture. In a quite different way from Scolari and Krier, Hollein draws sustenance from the traditional contexts of history. Not in order to revive them as perpetually valid codes, but in order to integrate them in a vital continuum leading to the future.

The reputation of Haus-Rucker-Co rests on a series of witty architectural surprises and astonishingly original solutions for old and new tasks that continued into the late 1970s. The Coop Himmelblau group combines exhibition projects and design work with visionary architectural projects which, fundamentally feasible, serve as a catalyst for their day-to-day practice. With them, infusions of fantasy and imagination ensure that architecture will never fall into a routine.

Raimund Abraham remained true to his vision perhaps longer than any of the others, making a profession of it for almost a quarter century before succumbing to the fascination of actual building. In 1964 he went to the United States. After several years at the Rhode Island School of Art and Design, he became a professor in 1974 at The Cooper Union, New York, one of the country's most respected schools of architecture.

Abraham makes great demands on himself and on his students. Disdaining current fashions, he advocates an archetypical poetry of building, visionary architecture as poetically condensed metaphors for physical and mental sensations. In the 1970s and 1980s he raised architectural drawing to the rank of a self-sufficient, autonomous work of art.

Like Krier, Abraham is a radical conservative, but of a quite different stamp. He believes in a holistic architectural thinking, seeing, and experiencing which, in a rigorous reduction to elementary forms and types, practices architectural archaeology with an eye to transforming the past in order to make it useful to the future. He recalls the essential function of architecture as dwelling, and concentrates on its grammar and rhetoric in the attempt to create an immune system against mere fads and trends. For Abraham, architecture is a multisensory art, charged with cultural memory and linked with transcendental values. This lends even his smallest building designs a momentous character and universal significance that puts one in mind of Ledoux.

Abraham's visionary designs of the 1970s and 1980s, uncompromising, monastically beautiful and rigorous, earthbound and yet lyrical, influenced entire generations of students. But when, after winning a number of competitions, he set out to put his principles into practice, his designs unexpectedly lost much of their poetic charm. What in the masterful colored drawings appeared so weightless suddenly metamorphosed into harsh, aloof, severe volumes which, despite their undeniable sculptural quality, proved rather unfriendly to the users' needs. The apartment buildings Abraham designed for the Berlin IBA (International Building Exhibition, 1983–86) and his Traviatagasse development in Vienna drew acerbic criticism for this very reason. His most recent award-winning design, for the twenty-story Austrian Cultural Institute in New York (1992), projected for completion in 1995, likewise puts Abraham's long-held postulates into practice, if with a sculptural force that verges on the frightening. Its glazed facades, four staggered surfaces that seem to slip over one another at a sharp angle of incidence, call up sinister memories of the guillotine. In the axe-shaped tower of this multifunctional structure, three vertical elements are sandwiched: an external glass facade which Abraham terms a mask, a central core with concrete walls, and at the back a tower of exposed metal steps, the building's backbone, inspired by the fire escapes of Lower Manhattan lofts.

The moral of the story might be this: Visionary architecture can indeed fire the imagination and stimulate creativity, but when it is actually built, it often turns out to be a double-edged sword.

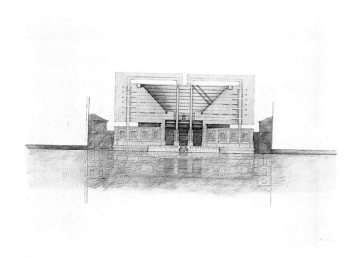

Raimund Abraham, *Ca' Venier dei Leoni*. Venice, 1985

Coop Himmelblau, *City with Pulsating Support System*, 1966

I JOŠ JEDAN S

Lebbeus Woods, *Zagreb Free Zone*, 1991–92

LEBBEUS WOODS

Since the mid-1980s a voice has been making itself increasingly heard in the international choir of visionary architects, that of a man whose graphic imaginations make him perhaps their major representative. He is like a contemporary Piranesi, who returns to premodern history in order to find a foothold from which to redefine the future: based on science, dominated by technology, and holistically including philosophy, architecture, art, and the entire range of engineering and natural sciences. He calls this interdisciplinary distillate "universcience," and his name is Lebbeus Woods. Born in 1940, Woods has taken the opposite path to his colleagues discussed above — from practicing architect to artist-architect, visionary architect, architectural philosopher. His friends, at least, have no doubt that someday he will begin building again. Film and exhibition architecture at first, perhaps; but then truly experimental creations informed by a new architectural aesthetic.

What emerged from Woods's drawing board in the 1980s, in a series of painstaking graphic renderings, was so strange, unusual, and fantastic that the conservative, commercially oriented American architectural establishment simply decided to ignore him. But if a prophet is not without honor save in his own country, success abroad usually remedies the omission. Woods is now recognized, even in New York. After the great success of his exhibitions and publications[70] in various European countries and Japan, and guest professor-

Lebbeus Woods, *Centricity Solo Tower with Livinglab*, 1987

ships at a number of architectural
schools, American museums and
institutes are taking a serious interest in the design sequences and
ideal city conceptions of this visionary.

Woods's graphic universe is indeed both enigmatic and strangely
familiar. It abounds with rough,
rocky projections, shooting out of
cliffs or penetrating into them, and
sometimes taking on the character
of metal, glass, or sculpted crystal.
Other forms recall domes, balloon-
like cupolas, spherical deep-sea research submarines, pyramids, or
airships like flying Noah's arcs, hovering and gliding, extra-terrestrial
architectural bodies that ignore the
familiar laws of geometry. Still
other elements bore into the earth
to form subterranean laboratories,
bulge out of the surface like buds,
or shoot off like rockets to explode
and scatter their payload of ideas.
These architectural visions rely on
an innovative aesthetic that dis-
obeys the established laws of proportion and symmetry. It is a rough
and ragged architecture, with aging
processes built in from the start. It
sets up extreme problems in statics

Lebbeus Woods, *Centricity, D-QUAD 190: Geothermal Livinglab,*
1987

and risky load-distributions, produces daring visual effects, suggests
enigmatic purposes, and evokes a new sense of time and space.
Woods's architectural designs are ideal city projects of a highly fic-
tional character, intended to help change reality, even to reinvent it
— well knowing that there is no such thing as "objective reality,"
that in our consciousness fiction and reality merge. Ideas and fantasies can indeed produce constructs of reality in our minds which
in turn exert an effect on external reality.

Woods is an altruistic communicator and organizer, who uses his
widespread international connections with kindred spirits to influence the thinking of younger generations of architects especially.
After his visionary projects of the 1980s, including *Underground
Berlin*, which predicted the city's reunification fourteen months before it actually occurred, Woods devoted himself to a review of architectural history. This led to a toning down of the wildly utopian
character of his designs, which have since come more into line with

125

Lebbeus Woods, *War and Architecture*, 1992

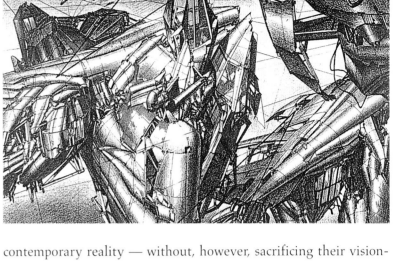

contemporary reality — without, however, sacrificing their visionary bite.

Due in part to changes in his personal life, Woods became involved in the situation in former Yugoslavia. Two projects resulted, *Zagreb Free Zone* (1991–92) and *War and Architecture* (1992).[71] As rampaging armies destroyed irreplaceable cultural treasures in Croatia and Bosnia, as mutual hate consumed the country house by house, village by village, city by city, Woods was already thinking about reconstruction, about the chance to create from the ruins architecture of a new kind. He spent November 1993 and March 1994 in Bosnia-Herzegovina, a sojourn that confirmed Woods in his vision of architecture as "a political act."

A parallel concern led him to investigate the simultaneous stratification characteristic of contemporary large cities. As a model, Woods took his native New York, a living architectural museum of the modern age. The most diverse architectural styles, population groups, economic and cultural processes interpenetrate and are superimposed on one another here. What interested Woods in this connection were the continual transformation processes to which the body of the city is subject, "heteropolis" conceptions of the interplay and improbable coexistence of contrasting architectural idioms, epochs, and approaches to form a stratified functional and cultural whole.

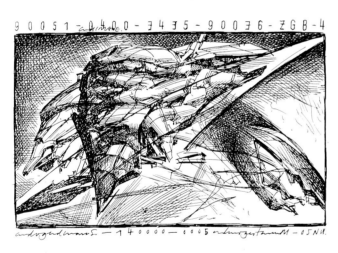

Lebbeus Woods, *Zagreb, 8. 27. 1991*

PETER COOK AND ARCHIGRAM

The most prolific and internationally most influential visionary architect of the postwar period is Peter Cook. After his appearance on the scene in 1961, apart from teaching at the London Architectural Association, Cook published, designed, organized, and held the *Archigram* group together for over a decade, until 1974, encouraging the production of continually new designs that irritated and shocked the architectural establishment.[72] By now, three decades later, it is

Opposite page:
Lebbeus Woods, *Aerial Paris. Photograph of a model, 1989*

126

Ron Herron and Peter Cook (Archigram), *Instant City,
Urban Action and Communication Rooms*. Collage, 1969

Ron Herron and Peter Cook (Archigram), *Instant City,
Urban Action and Communication Rooms*. Collage, 1969

difficult to imagine any student of architecture anywhere in the world who has not heard of Archigram or been influenced, at least subliminally, by the designs of the six British individualists Peter Cook, Warren Chalk, Dennis Crompton, David Greene, Ron Herron, and Mike Webb. This success owes much to the work of Cook, who considers it an obligation to bear the name of the famous circumnavigator of the globe whose successors established one of the largest travel agencies in existence. "P. Cook's tours around the world" is how this good-natured and untiringly unconventional architect refers to his jet-airline trips to teaching activities on seven continents.

The road to professor of architecture at Bartlett School of Architecture was no easy one. Beginning at the London Architectural Association, it led Cook through countless short-term teaching posts around the world. Then came a five-year sojourn as instructor of the architecture class at the Städel Museum, Frankfurt, where he endeavored to make the city a focus of the continental and intercontinental avant-garde. Back in his native London, Cook attacked the "calculated indifference" of the British architectural establishment to every innovation,[73] an insular arrogance that despite European Union and the Channel Tunnel has continued to prevent many an internationally known modern British architect from receiving sufficient work in his own land. What it has not been able to prevent, however, is the rising international reputation of architects like Foster and Rogers, the late James Stirling, Grimshaw and Herron, Future Systems, Zaha Hadid, and Peter Wilson. Archigram and Peter Cook played a material part in breaking the ground for all of them.

The 1960s was an era of farewell not only to one of the greatest empires in world history, but to Victorian prudery as well, as British mini-fashions, the Beatles and the Rolling Stones conquered the world. In this dissolution of hidebound attitudes and traditions Archigram, as Arata Isozaki aptly said, was the only architectural movement to question the repertoire of modernism that came on like a counterculture.[74] And not with theoretical manifestos, as surely would have been the case in Germany, but pragmatically and typically British, with an abundance of practical and flexible designs and ideas. The 1960s attack on conservative entrenchment, the decade's optimism, lust for life, love of technology, self-irony, ebullience, and pioneering new ideas, are all reflected in every Archigram project:

> *From a seemingly inexhaustible wealth of imaginative ideas, Archigram created rapturous utopian visions of a world of lattice frames, tubes, capsules, cells, spheres, balloons, robots, space suits, submarines, plastic and Coca-Cola bottles — of a society oriented toward high-technology recreation and leisure.[75]*

That the group sometimes overshot its goal, misjudged developments, and based its prognostications too heavily on technological progress and a society of surplus, cannot really be held against them, for they were not the only prophets of the day to have been proved wrong. Striking a self-critical note, Warren Chalk summed up the period as follows:

> *Nevertheless, Archigram in 1964 and long before that, seeking new directions, embraced this technology wholeheartedly and produced underwater cities, living capsules and the rest. David Greene, Spider Webb and I clamoured ecstatically over the rocket support structures at Cape Kennedy. I visited the NASA control centre at Houston and later witnessed the second Surveyor (manless) moon landing on the monitors at the Jet Propulsion Laboratories in Los Angeles, collecting small fragments of the moon surface. But it was an omen. The technician assigned to me, sitting in front of a bank of 39 closed-circuit TV monitors of lunar operation, was in fact watching the Johnnie Carson Show on the fortieth.*[76]

Still, the Archigram projects were always on the cutting edge, even in advance of their time, and this in a highly unconventional, exuberant, and irreverent way. Now, three decades later, many of the designs have become entirely topical and even technically feasible. An instance is *Plug-in City* (1962–64), built of prefabricated living capsules and access and supporting elements, and intended for integration in a larger urban megastructure. The project has been denounced as an inhumane production of twisted technological functionalism. Today every Central European community facing influxes of refugees would be overjoyed to have an infrastructure of this kind.

Another example of the Archigram panache is *Instant City* (1968–70), which exhibits an as yet unexploited potential for a flexible, culturally diverse city in a media-dominated age. It was the first project ever to seriously address the paradigm change from an analogue, material society to the digital, immaterial one in which we increasingly find ourselves, with no systematic ideas about how to meet the challenge architecturally. As I shall discuss in the final chapter, since the 1980s various suggestions have been advanced in

Peter Cook, *Real City Frankfurt*, 1986. Avenue Housing with Bushes, Villa Wall

129

Peter Cook, *Real City Frankfurt*, 1986

this regard, but all of them have met with acid criticism.

Or take the most praised, most ridiculed, and most widely publicized project of the group, *Walking Cities* (1964–66), made famous by Ron Herron's mobile urban monsters on stilts. These were inspired just as much by the rocket transport facilities at Cape Canaveral as by the Mars monsters in H. G. Wells's *The War of the Worlds*. Naturally Herron and the others enormously enjoyed the idea of high-tech mobile cities that could just saunter over to New York and show people what the future held in store. But projects like these were always very complex, and almost every member of the group contributed ideas. In this case Cook had the brilliant notion, based on tree houses, of a *Blow-out Village*, an inflatable mobile town that could be quickly transported and installed wherever it was needed, whether for a festival or in case of natural disaster or war.

It goes almost without saying that none of the many Archigram projects ever stood a chance of being put into practice. Still, the group held together for almost fourteen years, until a lack of commissions finally caused them to disband. To a greater extent than the others, Cook retained his drive as a visionary architect, probably because he realized that this was his true calling and because of his inspirational teaching skills in the field. Since the dissolution of Archigram in 1974, he alone, assisted by his partner, Christine Hawley, and changing student groups, has initiated, designed, and put into written form almost one hundred further futuristic projects.

Yet it is not the grand vision nor the grand theory that characterizes Cook's work, not the monomaniacal obsession of a Leon Krier nor the universalist, demiurgic system of a Lebbeus Woods. Cook is a man of less ambitious visions, of clever, pragmatic ideas, and of surprising aesthetic solutions. While these put him in advance of his times, it is not so far in advance that he can be written off as a dreamer. In his professional work Cook fills exactly the role Jakov Chernikov envisioned for architectural imagination within architectural practice, but was himself prevented from filling. Cook goes even farther, battling to realize certain projects, and that with increasing success. He has contributed to overcoming mental barriers to architectural vision and visionary architecture worldwide. Many

of his ideas, in one form or other, have since quietly become part of architectural common knowledge.

Cook is impelled by sheer, irrepressible enthusiasm. In the Archigram period it was for modules, circuitry, plug-in connections, mobile elements, capsules, pipelines, and variable steel-tube construction. In the early 1970s this technological romanticism made way for an intensive involvement with the topic of architecture and ecology. Long before the current environmental debate, Cook experimentally explored various aspects of the theme, and pointed the way to a new architectural aesthetic that envisions a relaxed, ambitious, optimistic, and energy-saving interplay among advanced technology, the environment, and the electronic media. His *Arcadia* projects (1976–78), in which innovative urban planning is reconciled with nature; the *Sponge* project (1975) for mountain structures of a kind Hans Hollein later took up in his suggestion for the Salzburg Guggenheim Museum in the Mönchsberg; the *Layer City* (1981), a model of urban stratification and stalactite towers marked by a pleasingly eclectic coexistence of styles; the glass architecture Cook designed for the Glass Museum in Langen, Germany (1986); and the hanging gardens of his various high-rise designs for Holland Park, London (1983) — all of these projects set accents in that new architectural aesthetic which is informed not by a sectarian urge to change the world but by British common sense, pragmatism, and a stringent analysis of what is required to meet the needs at hand.

Doubtless a number of charmingly eccentric projects have emerged from Cook's drawing board, such as *Bloch City* (1983). But why not design a high-rise town in the countryside, with structures arranged according to the notes of a violin concert? Mozart and Salzburg, Bloch City and Peter Cook — a cityscape based on the rhythms of great music, what a brilliant example of a combination of the arts! And here, as in the other projects mentioned, it is the eye-opening function of architectural imagination that conduces to inspire students and other practitioners, who are subject to enough dulling and enervating influences as it is.

Cook's designs of the early 1990s continue his Frankfurt experiments without transition. Still, his plans for Breitscheidplatz in Berlin, for Finchley Road in London, or for an exhibition building in Osaka, have come ever closer to the contemporary reality of building and to generally accepted notions of aesthetics. In collaboration with Christine Hawley, Cook in 1985 made his first assay into large-scale residential architecture at the International Building Exhibition in Berlin (IBA), submitting an apartment house design that was actually finished in 1990. Ever since, this dyed-in-the-wool visionary has suffered from a case of the feasibility flu.

At the great Archigram exhibition held from February to May 1994 at the Vienna Kunsthalle, not only were the multifarious facets of the group's work illustrated with unprecedented completeness, but models of all their key projects were built and presented, show-

Peter Cook, *Bloch City*, 1983

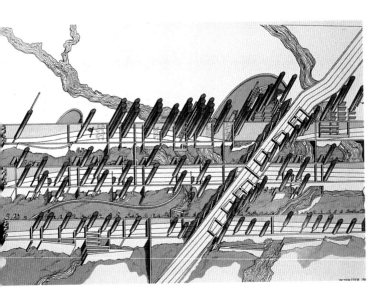

ing how eminently practicable many of them have since become. In addition, lines of development, especially in Peter Cook's and Ron Herron's oeuvres, were traced down to the early 1990s. It was a compelling demonstration of the transition from architectural vision to visionary architecture and functioning, experimental architecture. Also, the Vienna show included a multimedia installation in which the future potential of Archigram for a medialized architecture for public spaces, and for a genuine "media architecture," became strikingly evident.

Peter Cook, *Way Out West: Berlin*, 1988. Detail section at K, stage E

Deconstructive Designs and Built Architectural Visions

Deconstructivism in architecture is generally considered a reply to, and the antithesis of, postmodernism. Yet the two styles are closely related in terms of philosophy, deconstructivism being an offshoot of postmodern, post-structuralist thinking. In the United States especially, but beyond it as well, the emergence of postmodernist architecture coincided with the Reagan era. Brave new worlds, historical costumes and masquerade balls, pretty colors and pleasant jokes, offhand quotes and architectural play-acting, all came to the fore in a period when America's president was a man from Hollywood who strived to blur the borderlines between stage set and reality, between show business, art and commerce.

Of course this statement is much too broad to hold true for all postmodern architecture. Personal and regional differences evidently exist. At a certain level of abstraction, apart from style, one can only speak of good, middling, and bad architecture in any case. And with regard to a true revival of historical traditions, of metaphorical and narrative qualities, postmodernism has produced superb results. One need only consider Hollein and Stirling, Rossi and Portoghesi, Botta, Graves, and Tigerman.

Under the surface of this best of all possible worlds, however, rumors began to spread in the 1980s that the condition of the globe was less propitious than postmodern architects wished to believe. Religious conflicts, spreading poverty and environmental destruction, urban blight, the imminent collapse of the Soviet Union and the reverberations it has since set off — these politically and economically engendered shifts in the *Zeitgeist* had consequences for architecture as well. Not of course that wide sectors of the profession sat down and said, "It's time for some deconstructivism." Developments are not that simple; only beginners and camp-followers act in this way.

The architects discussed in this chapter are every one of them highly avant-garde, highly sensitive, and artistically gifted masters in their field. And in a period of stylistic pluralism, all of them were opponents of postmodernism, which, to use Zaha Hadid's words, was "kitsch" and an "intellectual catastrophe," or to quote Coop Himmelblau, was a "philistine, conformist kid's-show architecture."

When one seeks common traits that justify calling these highly diverse architects decon-

Antonio Trimarzo, Naples, 1990

Günter Behnisch, Hysolar Institute. Stuttgart University, 1986–87

structivists,[77] knowing full well that such labels always have something artificial about them (but also that human thinking cannot do without categories), the first that comes to mind is a development of Russian Constructivist principles. This involves an experimental continuation of the achievements of modernism, based on an awareness of the paradigm changes in postmodern consciousness. The architects under discussion deconstruct, that is, they reduce structures to their constituent parts in order to reassemble them in new, unfamiliar ways, for architecture is inconceivable without construction. Even apparently chaotic structures, as we saw in the chapter on bizarre architecture, obey certain individual, inherent structural laws. And deconstruction happens to be one of the oldest artistic principles there is. Composers and painters have always dealt with tradition in this way, as have poets, playwrights, and novelists. Shakespeare, for instance, was one of the greatest deconstructivists of all time. He showed what splendid results could be had by taking a literary language apart and composing from its elements, with personal additions, an entirely new language.

The process of architectural deconstructivism exhibits a certain potential for aggressiveness. It lies in ambush for the conventional, is willing to risk all, and is innovative and expressive. The approach manifests itself in a transgression of accepted principles and an irreverent use of materials, in a penchant for asymmetry, interpenetrations, piercings and incisions in solid walls, and interruptions of interior pathways and spaces. It involves an urge to overcome aesthetic borderlines and familiar structural principles, resulting in tilting walls and floors, inclined ramps, galleries, suspended elements

Günter Behnisch, University Library. Eichstätt, 1980–87

135

Zaha Hadid, *Victoria Peak*. Hong Kong, 1982–83

and floating platforms, interpenetrating rooms, sharp projections, acute angles — a combination of disparate effects that seemingly shows an acceptance of the ugly.

This last point brings us to the deconstructivists' demand for a change in visual habits, for the creation of a new aesthetic. In the late 1980s even an experienced and astute critic like Wolfgang Pehnt was led to term it a "disaster aesthetic," or an "aesthetic of violence, ugliness, offensiveness." Beauty, of course, is a highly subjective concept. Most people have since grown used to the fact that the deconstructivist aesthetic was one of provocation, daring, surprise, discovery — a poetry of harshness and dissection. And its shaky equilibrium truly seems better adapted to a world of threat, dissonance, and conflict than the pastel colors, petit fours, and cotton candy of postmodernism. Deconstructivism is characterized just as much by uncompromisingness and a claim to the absolute validity of its concepts, as it is by a devotion to craft, technique, and the technological aesthetic of engineering construction.

Let us outline some of the individual aspects of deconstructivism by reference to five of its main representatives. Then, to conclude this chapter, we shall look into the consequences and developments it can be expected to engender by the end of the decade, and, by implication, by the turn of a century and a millennium.

136

BERNARD TSCHUMI

Like all of the architects to be discussed in this section, Tschumi combines university teaching with professional work, and is thus very much at home in both theory and practice. Born in 1944, his career has seemingly followed a straight line, from Zurich by way of London and Paris to New York, where he is now dean of the Architectural Faculty at Columbia University. His conceptions are equally straight-lined, goal-oriented, and clear. To a greater extent than almost any other architect, Tschumi has been influenced by the cinema, photography, and the media; on the other hand, he is firmly rooted in the history of French ideas and philosophy in the twentieth century, represented by names like Artaud, Bataille, Foucault, Lacan, Derrida, and Baudrillard.

Tschumi is one of the breed of architectural internationalists who have grown ever more numerous since the early 1980s. They spend a considerable part of their working and creative life in airplanes, flying back and forth between lectures, selection committee meetings, client consultations, and building sites on various continents. This life-style requires a brand of thinking that comprehends diverse professions, levels of existence, and cultures, bringing them together if necessary, but valuing and empathizing with them individually as well. Tschumi has a view of reality and conception of architecture to correspond. One of his axioms is that contemporary life is basically disjunctive, dissociated, and discontinuous: that is, life takes place in leaps; there is no one reality but many; meaningful value judgements are no longer possible; history cannot be controlled; and nothing can be considered definite. Everything, Tschumi believes, is fragmented, multilayered, though it is nevertheless possible to correlate diverse levels and life experiences with one another.

In spite of various other successful designs like a second prize in the Tokyo Opera House competition, or another second prize for the Kansai International Airport, Tschumi's reputation still rests on the award, master planning, and construction of La Villette in Paris, which explored uncharted terrain as an entertainment, science, technology, and media center. Tschumi not only supervised its planning from start to finish but erected in a grid, at intervals of four hundred feet, a total of thirty-five pavilions, the Follies, steel-clad structures painted fire-engine red that articulate the site with a structural grid of entertainment facilities. As the last one was completed in 1992, we are in a position to ask whether Tschumi's conception has proved viable.

Bernard Tschumi, *La Villette*. Study, 1984

Bernard Tschumi, La Villette, Folly. Detail, 1991

Over La Villette he superimposed a layered structural network of points, lines, and planes: the points of the Follies, the lines of access ways inspired by film strips, and the planes of sport and recreation areas. Tschumi views such structural conceptions basically in terms of process; that is, in principle they have neither beginning nor end, and theoretically they could be extended to cover the entire world. Repetitions, distortions, superimpositions, interruptions, sudden breaks and fragmentations are taken into account as part of the process. If you will, these concepts bear an analogy to Tschumi's philosophy, outlined above. His Follies represent a conscious, anti-contextual contrast to the surrounding urban architecture.

What is relevant about them for our present context is the fact that they represent functional, visionary architecture put successfully into practice.[78] Tschumi himself describes the Follies as exploded parts of one of the largest buildings in the world. Based on a grid of 3.4 × 3.4 × 3.4 feet, any conceivable number of the red cubes could be piled over, next to, or behind one another. The important thing here is that closed and open, utile and completely free visionary architectures alternate within one and the same Folly. The utilization of the structure is variable, from café to kindergarten, from information stand to video pavilion. In its non-functional sections, allusive configurations like wheels, ladders, ramps, stairs, window mullions, and platforms project into the air, setting imaginative potential free. Inclined planes and walls, holes bored in the rigorous cubes, layerings, and superimpositions of function correspond to the deconstructivist premises discussed above. While an overtaxing of the public's mobility was initially feared, this apparently has not occurred,[79] though admittedly the operators have yet to exhaust the Follies' potential. Tschumi's architectural intercontextuality seems to work. In retrospect, this lends credence to his aesthetic of the disparate, whose combination of rectilinear rigor and associative fantasy serves to control and lend direction to chaos. Instead of postmodern, Tschumi has inscribed posthumanistic on his banner, and his unsentimental system has the advantage of great adaptability. Even if they were reduced to fantastic ruins, his Parisian Follies would be completely legitimate monuments to deconstructivism.

Tschumi's most recent designs of the late 1980s to the mid-1990s

Opposite page:
Bernard Tschumi, La Villette, Folly, 1991

138

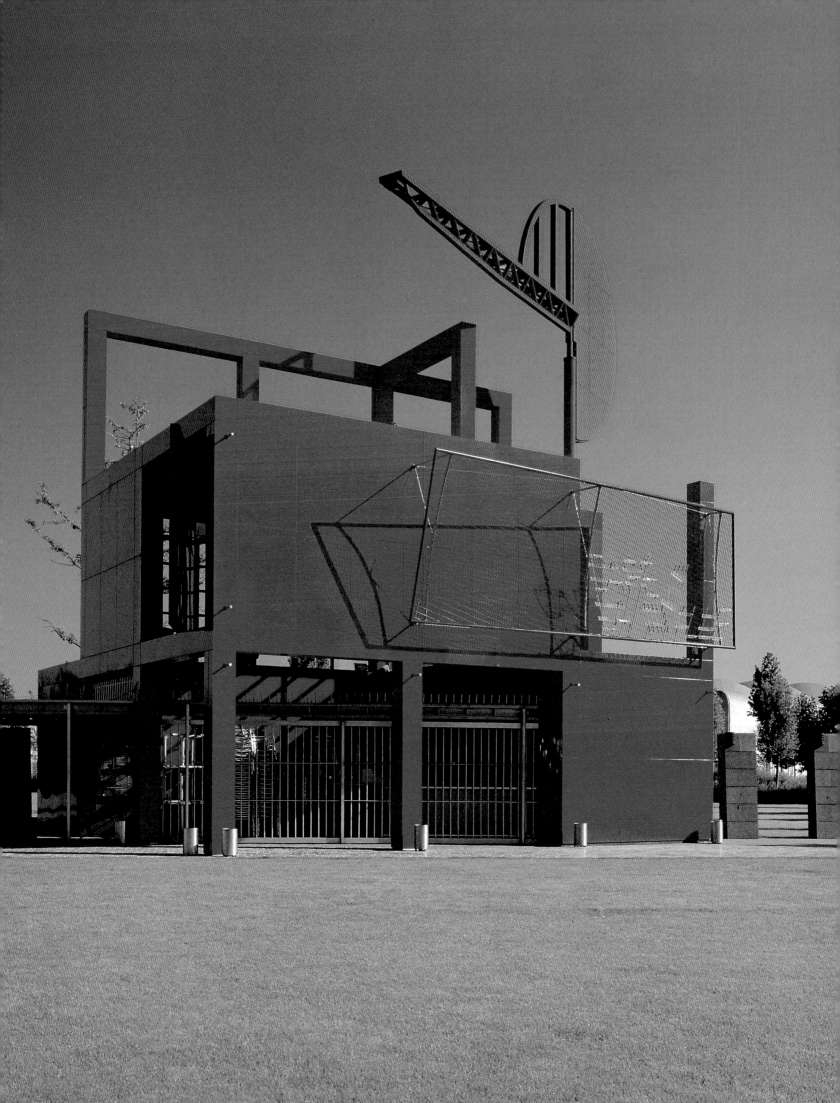

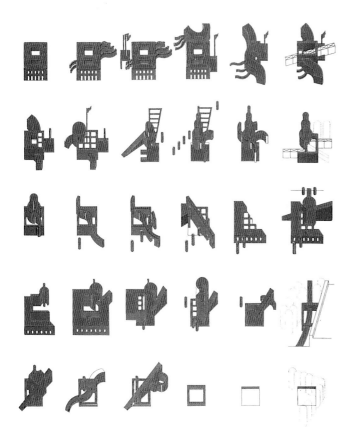

Bernard Tschumi, *Early Combination and Transformation Principles of the Follies of La Villette*, 1982

— for Kansai International Airport (1988), for the Karlsruhe ZKM (Center for Art and Media Technology, 1989), for the Amenagement du Centre du Quartier des Etats-Unis in Lyon (1991), or for the International School of Contemporary Art in Le Fresnay (1993) — represent logical continuations of this architectural and philosophical thinking. Tschumi is convinced that our lives will be increasingly and irrevocably influenced by developments in the media and electronic communications. Hence, from the earliest design stages on, he translates his cinematic experience of architectural spaces into what might be termed a five-dimensional aesthetic of media-produced, computer-simulated and animated architecture. The familiar dimensions of space and time are enriched in the process by musical and rhythmical elements, and by Tschumi's conception of layered, multipurpose, and open architectural spaces. This approach corresponds to the multiperspective perception and experience of a new generation that has come of age with the media, not merely with film and television but with video, fax, holograms, and lasers and, above all, with the computer as a multimedia instrument.

Tschumi therefore considers the process of deconstruction a positive challenge. One of the most profound thinkers in late-twentieth-century architecture, he developed the deconstructivism of the 1980s into a genuine media architecture, bringing the media into his designs not from the outside in, beginning with media facades, but from the inside out, beginning with experiences of space and functional processes. The vantage points from which his correspondingly photographed designs are seen already evoke those of a mobile viewer in a three-dimensionally animated cyberspace. Surpassing Piranesi and the one-point perspective of an observer fixed in space, this allows the viewer to take fluid and continually changing vantage points, and it also permits spaces and volumes to be conceived, and built to correspond.

ZAHA M. HADID

If Tschumi talks about the deconstructivist "big bang" of his Follies, the individual components of Zaha Hadid's designs seem to scatter into tiny particles. They fly past the viewer's ears like interstellar detritus, and one asks oneself how Hadid intends to retrieve them and reintegrate them in meaningful contexts of function, sequences of interior spaces, and facades.

By comparison to male representatives of the profession, there are still very few internationally known female architects. They include Gae Aulenti, Isuko Hasegawa, Ingeborg Kuhler, Karla Kowalski, and Laurinda Spear, but Zaha M. Hadid, born in 1950, is certainly the *enfant terrible*, the diva, a brilliant designer and scourge of contractors. The explosive temperament of the cosmopolitan Iraqi from London enters directly into her beautiful designs, whose cool, lacquer-like colors give the impression of computer graphics and yet are hand-composed with incredible care. In this case, first impressions are misleading. Hadid is a stickler for detail and order. She is an architect down to her fingertips and to the roots of her wild mane of hair, and the sharpness of her tongue has been felt by many a more wishy-washy colleague.

Her breakthrough in 1982–83 with a first prize in the great international competition for Victoria Peak in Hong Kong might never have occurred, if Arata Isozaki, with her trained and experienced eye, had not picked up Hadid's already rejected submission and brought it back to the selection committee's attention. Only Isozaki had realized that the displacements, obliques, and interpenetrations of its open spatial situations, its daring curves and arcs, its dynamically sensible planning of the extensive club grounds on the Peak were, first, feasible, and second, promised architectural experiences of a quite unusual intensity and richness.

Yet like so many of Hadid's designs, some developed to the point of construction, this one could not be realized, because the client decided that Hong Kong's uncertain political future made the investment too risky. Still, Hadid's success in the competition encouraged her and brought international recognition. Over the following years she learned to deal with setbacks, which true vanguard architects like her always face when clients are asked to put their money on unconventional designs. Hadid proved that nowadays an architect can achieve international renown without ever having had to pass the test of practice. Despite her undeniable artistic brilliance, this would not have been possible without the international architectural press, which is just as avid for novelty as any other branch of journalism. And every architectural department of the schools that can afford it occasionally likes to sun itself in the glow of some international architectural star.

Something else Hadid has proved is that one can have considerable influence on actual building practice without ever having built oneself. In the field of furniture design, this circumstance must drive her to distraction, because her designs for couches, chairs, and tables are continually plagiarized the minute they leave the drawing board.

Zaha Hadid, Moon Soon Bar, Sapporo, 1989–90. "Ice" restaurant on first floor

Zaha Hadid, Vitra Fire Station. Weil am Rhein, 1993

Hadid is absolutely serious when she attributes almost saintly status to Kasimir Malevich and his Suprematism. She was already
fighting for Malevich long before his international rediscovery.
What she appreciates about him is his pioneering, experimental
spirit, a modernity that in her eyes still has great unexploited potential. One of her earliest designs, for the summer residence of the
prime minister of Ireland (1979–80), is still one of her most beautiful in this respect. With compelling lucidity it demonstrates the geo-
metrical principles advanced by Malevich, while subjecting them to
a deconstructive development expressed in an interpenetration and
overlapping of access routes and building elements, a sensitive tectonic use of geometric symbols. It goes almost without saying that a
project of this type, which moreover envisioned the integration
of historical structures in the modern one, stood no chance of acceptance in conservative Ireland.

Disassembly, dissection of structures into parts that take off and fly, are recaptured and reassembled into new spatial situations without finite borders — this process is central to Hadid's approach. Representing in many ways the growing and increasingly influential internationally nomadic singles culture, she sees how new modes of living and working require new conceptions of architectural space, new perceptions of the stratified city, new conceptions of urbanity, and not the perpetuation of the suburban backyard-garden mentality of which she accused the initiators of the Berlin International Building Exhibition in the 1980s.

The Japanese bars and nightclubs Hadid has since completed in Tokyo and Sapporo exhibit a masterly sense of space, materials, and musical rhythms. The long-delayed fire station for the Vitra Chair Company in Weil am Rhein, whose enthusiasm for architecture had already led them to commission Frank Gehry with a chair museum marked by dynamic, elegantly curved volumes, was completed in 1993 and immediately became an architectural sensation. Zaha M. Hadid remains a brilliant pulsar in the architectural sky, whose strongest, most scintillating signals are surely still to come.

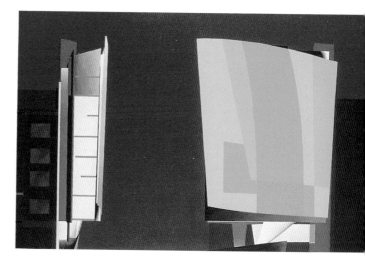

Zaha Hadid, Kurfürstendamm Project. Berlin, 1989

COOP HIMMELBLAU

It is no longer necessary to stand up for Coop Himmelblau, the Vienna office whose name implies a cooperative to shoot the blue sky. After years of bitter setbacks despite international publicity, Wolf Prix (born 1942) and Helmut Swiczinsky (born 1945) have made their way, and, apart from Frank Gehry, have probably contributed most to creating a climate of acceptance for the deconstructivist aesthetic. Ever since the group was founded in 1968, they have stood for aesthetic provocation, demonstrations, happenings, and an interest in new developments in the media and technology. Their aim has been not merely to shock the bourgeoisie, but to contribute to a vital urban culture. Disillusioned, plainspoken, temperamental, with an original viewpoint and a stupendous artistic talent, they have untiringly advocated an emancipated, self-determined, open-ended, unconventional, and aesthetically exciting architecture.

In 1990–91 Ettore Sottsass travelled around the world for *Terrazzo*, recording with his camera not new, freshly polished architectural creations but the ubiquitous tristesse, the wastelands, slums, and general destruction of urban habitats caused by traffic and overpopulation. This merciless documentation represents perhaps the most depressing evidence ever advanced for the failure of architecture, of political planning, of commercialism, and of middle-class aesthetics.[80] Coop Himmelblau had arrived at a similar analysis as early as 1978. The conclusions they drew were expressed in manifestos, such as "The Poetry of Desolation" and "The Future of the Splendid Desolation." To quote from the latter:

Coop Himmelblau, Groningen Video Folly, 1989

The architectures of the future have already been built. The solitude of squares, the desolation of the streets, the devastation of the buildings characterize the city of the present and will characterize the city of the future as well. Expressions like "safe and sound" are no longer applicable to architecture.[81]

Coop Himmelblau, Funder-Werk 3. St. Veit an der Glan, 1988–89

Bottom: Coop Himmelblau, Open House Project, Malibu. Model, 1983–91 (not realized)

Opposite page:
Coop Himmelblau, Jasmac Bar Building, Fukuoka, Japan, Model, 1989

In design terms, these texts marked the beginning of Coop Himmelblau's deconstructive phase, when they envisioned architecture that would "bleed, fag, puke, shine, rip, stab, tear, burn." Architecture that was carefully planned but, like the project *Hot Flat* (begun in 1978), was obviously destined to remain visionary.

Yet just imagine that somebody had had the courage to realize the idea of the great, transformable spatial structures of the *Hot Flat* loft, in which the building was to be pierced, deflowered by a massive steel beam extending through two stories and a flame-shaped glass roof was to cut through the upper-floor apartments. The result would have been an architectural beacon-light seen worldwide. The real light has a different shine. In Vienna, it is called the *Hundert-wasserhaus*, and its cloying alternative kitsch attracts hundreds of thousands of tourists annually.

Probably a project like the *Merzschule* in Stuttgart (begun in 1981) would no longer be rejected today. Inspired by Melnikov's Rusakov Workers' Clubhouse in Moscow (1927–28), it was Coop Himmelblau's first demonstration of their conception of inter-penetrating, interlocking, concentrated spaces. Everything in the structure seems on the verge of warping, twisting, and toppling, but this impression is counteracted by metaphorical allusions to take-off and flight. In the meantime, Behnisch, Gehry, Eisenman, Domenig, and not least Coop Himmelblau themselves have established this aesthetic, and the negative connotations of its metaphors have given way among critics and public to an understanding of the experimental spirit and new conception of architectural beauty embodied in the approach.

In an attic conversion for a law office on Falkestrasse in Vienna (1984–89) and in the Funder-Werk 3 in St. Veit an der Glan, Carinthia (1988–89), Prix and Swiczinsky employed superimpositions, intersections, shifts in perspective, projections, fissures, sudden breaks, and aggressively protruding frameworks to create an incredible range of innovative spatial effects. Their handling of this poetry of dissonances was so skillful that it made the entire architectural world sit up and take notice, and drew applause from the majority of its representatives.

The residential model developed from these projects, the Open House in Malibu (begun in 1983), was prevented from completion

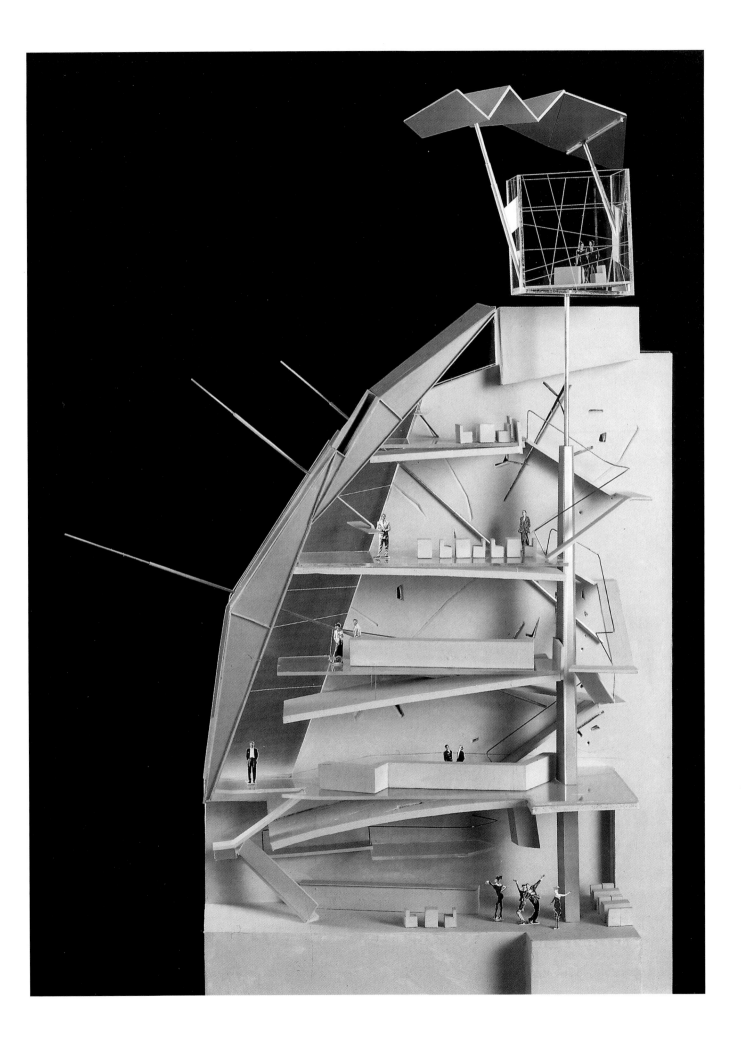

Coop Himmelblau, Exhibition Installation. Centre Pompidou, Paris, 1992–93

Coop Himmelblau, Melrose Avenue Project. Santa Monica, California, 1992

by its owner's death and subsequently the project, which could have resulted in an artistic monument, proved unsalable. Still, the house will remain a milestone of open, flexible, dynamic, and aesthetically challenging spatial design for a long time to come.

Despite the controversy attendant upon their first prize in the 1987 competition for the conversion of the Ronacher Theater in Vienna, directly opposite their office, the project promised to be Coop Himmelblau's first large-scale commission. It would have given them an opportunity to show that deconstructivist principles could indeed be applied to a model, multifunctional theater and media facility, which would have well behooved a city like Vienna, with its long and brilliant theater tradition. The project was foiled, in 1992, by a breach of contract on the part of the city fathers, who, saying it was too expensive, preferred to pay fines for nonperformance rather than risk criticism for sponsoring an unconventional building. Since then, the facade of the Ronacher has been prettified for André Heller's vaudeville circus. It well illustrates the prevailing mentality in political Vienna, that of intellectual dwarfs whose sycophantic populism goes hand in hand with artistic timidity. And so a city with an architectural past whose greatness is matched by its present insignificance has missed another chance.

Projects like the apartment and commercial building on Melrose Avenue in Santa Monica, California, the campus of de Jussieu in Paris, or such urban planning undertakings as in St. Pölten, Austria, and the new media architecture projects (see pp. 71–85) indicate

that, like other offices, Coop Himmelblau now views deconstructivism as a transitional phase. While retaining certain construction principles like the penetration of seemingly stronger elements by weaker ones, multiple perspectives, and reliance on high tech and engineering, they have since entered a new stylistic phase that is characterized by less agitated, more practical building volumes, cubes and box forms that nevertheless continue to be employed with experimental verve. These are accompanied by spatial layerings and media elements, for which Coop Himmelblau sees great chances for the future.

Their own future has already begun. It will be marked by a growing number of realized projects and by stylistic diversity. The Viennese group has written a chapter in twentieth-century architectural history; now everything will depend on their ability to retain their creativeness and their high standards of quality when it comes to translating ideas into reality.

GÜNTHER DOMENIG

In a country as small as Austria, someone who comes from Klagenfurt and Graz virtually comes from the Diaspora. If there is anything Günther Domenig (born 1934) has in common with his Coop Himmelblau friends, it is the metaphor of taking off and flying which manifests itself in the construction of his technologically decorative birdlike structures. He also shares with Prix and Swiczinsky a what-the-hell attitude whose genesis and symbolism, viewed psychoanalytically, would go far towards explaining Domenig's character.

Günther Domenig, *Central Savings Bank*, Vienna. Study, 1974

But unlike the two widely travelled big-city boys, Domenig is a lone wolf, a rough Austrian mountain man who draws his creative power from the region and belongs there with every fiber of his soul.

Domenig's deconstructivist phase began after the dissolution of his years-long partnership with Eilfried Huth, with the planning of the Central Savings Bank office in Favoritenstrasse, Vienna (1974; constructed 1976–79). With regard to the rational, architectural definition of the project, he wrote at the time:

The basic conception is predicated on taking up the linear and angular relationships of the existing urban neigh-

borhood and projecting these onto and into the structure. Every line and movement in space has its causal relationship to the location, be it functional or constructional. The roof landscape is a consciously formed and visible mountain chain that, in terms of sightline, does not appear the same from any of the possible vantage points in the urban surroundings.[52]

All this may be quite correct, but the resulting building is above all a highly personal masterpiece of organic deconstructivism, an architectural ego trip beyond compare that probably had to be undertaken if the architect was not to sacrifice his peace of mind. Like the later Stone House on Lake Ossiacher, near Klagenfurt, the project truly recalls Le Facteur Cheval (see pp. 74–78). It was fortunate for Domenig that a financial institute proved willing to support this fabulous contemporary architectural development.

Domenig's achievement initially derives from his brilliance and passion as a draftsman. If he had his way, he would build straight from his drawings, in which he believes the finished architecture itself is fully manifested. When you compare his ground plan of the Central Savings Bank office with the built result, you immediately see that a tremendous struggle took place here between organic and engineering thinking, between inner psychological necessity and the dictates of construction. In many respects Domenig is related to Antoni Gaudí, who likewise was an excellent engineer and thought in similarly organic terms. In Domenig's case this tendency had already come to the fore in a number of projects, such as the multipurpose hall in Graz-Eggenberg (1972–77) or the North Restaurant for the Munich Olympic Games (1972).

But in the Central Savings Bank building, terrific shearing forces came into play, solid volumes began to shift and dissolve. Right angles clashed with uterine hollows, rough edges and sharp blades threatened organic shapes resembling aerial roots. Materials and structures lost clear definition. Sculptural qualities were emphasized with liquid, square, and hexagonal structures entering a process of deconstruction on the facade. As Raffaele Raja noted, it was as if the building were protesting against its function, as if form refused to accept content, and the structure no longer wished to conform to generally accepted notions of bank buildings.[53] It was both a technical and an aesthetic experiment, a provocation that not surprisingly drew harsh attacks from numbers of Viennese traditionalists which, despite his success, plunged Domenig into temporary depression. O blissful innocence! For Domenig had done more than merely grate on the aesthetic sensibilities of philistines; he had probed their subconscious, and that is what they could not forgive him, without really knowing why.

The Rikki Reiner Boutique in Klagenfurt (1983–84) employs a deconstructivist idiom similar to that developed by other architects in the 1980s. But again, very original solutions are seen in the dance

Günther Domenig, Rikki Reiner Boutique. Klagenfurt, 1983–84

of elements, materials, and spatial situations Domenig staged — a diagonally laid out, cruciform passageway, illuminated marble columns, a sophisticated and technically elegant basement stairwell with asymmetrical light apertures, a seemingly dysfunctional floating table, and what he calls the "piled up concrete ruins of the dressing-rooms," all of which add up to an architectural cabinet piece. Domenig says his accumulation of materials and structural ramifications were intended to create various, interrelated "drifting bodies" in space, and that he was fascinated by the chance to take optical illusion to the limits of technical feasibility.[84]

Still, Domenig's masterpiece, his life's work, in which the journey becomes the goal, is certainly the Stone House commenced in 1986 on a lot he inherited in Steindorf, on Lake Ossiacher in Carinthia. This is Domenig's Taj Mahal, his Palais Idéal, where he can be his own Faust, Don Quixote, Hamlet, and demiurge rolled into one. The structure is ideal architecture, a place of memory and self-experience, self-determination, and self-representation. Again the temptation arises to apply psychological criteria to a piece of architecture that is as complex and abundant in meanings as a building can be. The Stone House is a sculpture in which rough concrete, glass and steel are in process of being transformed into an homage to the architect's native mountain world, full of reminiscences of Bruno Taut's and Hans Scharoun's crystal and stone structures, a *memento mori* and monument to Domenig's own mental complexity.

But it is also a true, handcrafted masterpiece of highly modern architecture, an experiment to test and explore the limits of the structurally feasible. This becomes obvious in view of the ground plans and cross sections, the sophisticated spatial interlockings, the mutual penetration and superimposition of axes and components. Like every work of art — and here, architecture is the art of building in the original sense of the word — the Stone House takes on a historical significance beyond the individual case, since it embodies a unique aesthetic to which many of the characteristics mentioned at the outset apply.

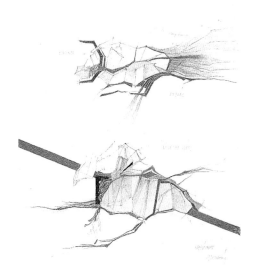

Günther Domenig, preliminary study for Stone House, 1984–85

Günther Domenig, Stone House. Suspended stone, begun 1986

Currently Domenig enjoys considerable success in the field of university, bank, and hospital buildings. It was in the Vienna Central Savings Bank office, however, that his true self shed its chrysalis. In the Stone House in Steinsdorf, which has few windows and only lighting slits in most rooms, it has spun a new cocoon. Whether it will emerge like a butterfly someday from the finished structure, only the future can tell.

DANIEL LIBESKIND

And Daniel Libeskind? If defining architecture in terms of increasing complexity was meaningful, the sequence would read: Zaha Hadid, Günther Domenig, Daniel Libeskind. The impression of complexity may be due partially to the hermetic nature of Libeskind's philosophical and poetic texts on architecture, which despite their claim to absolute validity must be viewed in much the same light as artists' statements. Due to his very personal biographical and cultural background, it is more difficult to enter into Libeskind's individual universe than into the texts and designs of any other architect discussed in this book. In many respects, the cryptical nature and arcane allusions of his writings recall the *Cantos* of Ezra Pound. If anyone ever set out to deconstruct architecture, it was Libeskind

Daniel Libeskind, *Micromegas.* "Leakage," 1979

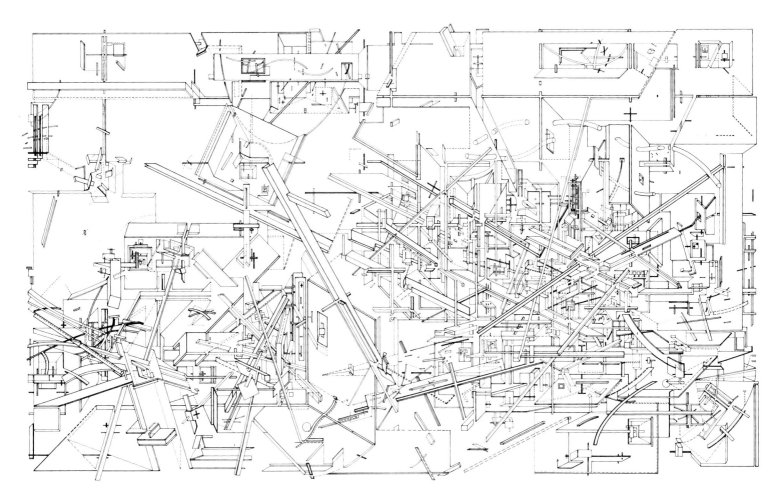

150

in his *Micromegas* (1979). On closer scrutiny these drawings, which initially call to mind city maps, sewing patterns, and puzzles, reveal an abundance of architectural references, from axes, traffic routes, and building fragments to plans and systems of order. As we now know, what goes by the name of chaos is actually merely a higher form of order, whose structure remains inaccessible to immediate sense experience.

Libeskind does little to help the viewer decode his complex structural imagery. Still, his texts and his ingenious reading machine — "Vitruvius and Alberti said, every architect must first make a machine to do architecture"[85] — provide a clue, namely that Libeskind considers everything a text, and that *Micromegas*, too, should be read as a cryptic text. Here is a man in pursuit of the universal mystery, who would deconstruct, unravel the space-time continuum, explode geometries, and proclaim the apocalypse of architecture, which may continue to exist in the form of objects but is devoid of meaning because technology has destroyed its self-identity. And with an eye on catastrophe as only a Jewish eye can be, he plays the endgame, seeking God and transcendence in cosmological contexts. This is a heroic but hazardous undertaking, for the name of the all-consuming Minotaur lurking in this particular labyrinth is Nothingness.

Let us start over again. Here is a man who, out of suffering and pain and anxiety and desire, subjects architecture to vivisection in order to discover its truth, beauty, and meaning. He is a poet and a philosopher. He is familiar with Schopenhauer's likening of architecture to frozen music. He sets out to make architecture ring true again, reverberate. He builds a text-reading and machine architecture. It reverberates, produces text, produces meaning. By so doing it vanquishes Nothingness. Auschwitz.

Let us start over again, again. An architect wins, in the summer of 1989, an international competition for the "Annex to the Berlin Museum, with the Jewish Museum Department," generally known as the Jewish Museum, Berlin, but called by the architect *Between the*

Daniel Libeskind, *Three Lessons in Architecture*, 1985
A. Read Architecture: Reading Machine
B. Remember Architecture: Memory Machine
C. Write Architecture: Writing Machine

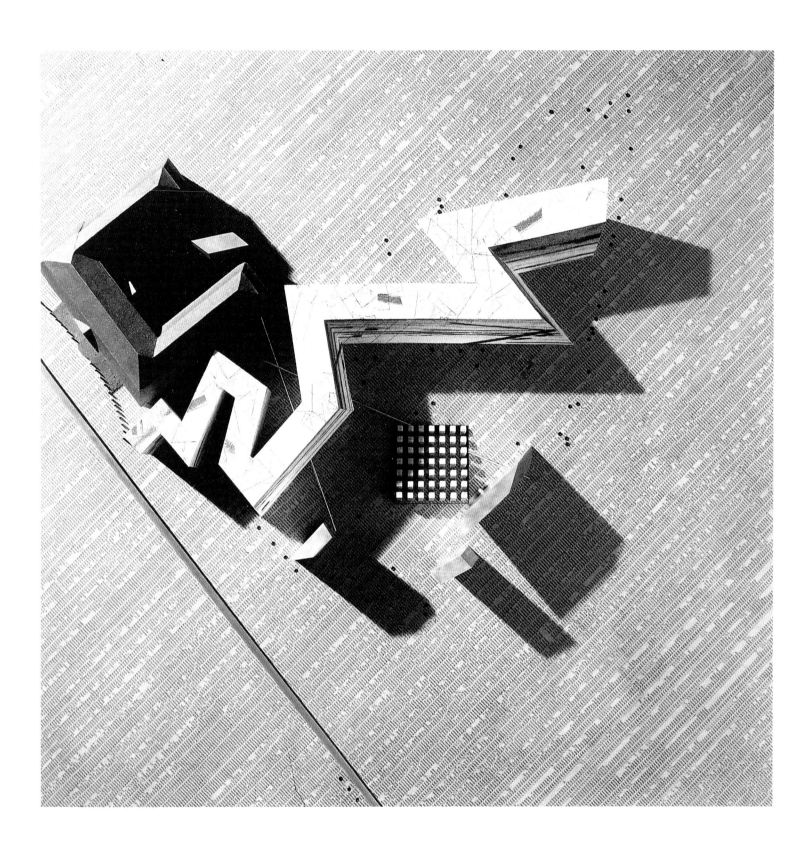

Daniel Libeskind, *Between the Lines*. Expansion
of the Berlin Museum by a Jewish Museum
Department, 1989–96

Lines. He designs a structure of a type that has never before existed.
Next to the original Baroque building of the City Museum, connected with it by an underground passage, a zigzag structure like a frozen lightning bolt, beginning on the street side with a narrow, almost vertical section, becoming wider and more inclined from angle
one to angle ten, is to extend five hundred feet into the cityscape.
The zigzag is traversed on all levels by segments of straight lines.

152

Bizarre geometric fragments are distributed over the building like exploded pavilions in a landscape of ruins. In Libeskind's project description these are called the "discarded void." The zigzag, in Libeskind's eyes the symbol of a broken Star of David, is pervaded by the void. No artifacts; no interpretation of history; only the void, an emptiness intended to evoke a sense of the absence of all of those citizens of Berlin who fell prey to the Holocaust, and who contributed materially to the culture of the city.

This is language and text which arise from the absence of language and text. It is akin to that which arises from Samuel Beckett's texts: Godot, who out of his absence, dialectically becomes flesh and speaks. Libeskind calls it "a conception which is absolutely opposed to reducing the museum or architecture to a detached memorial or to memorable detachment."[86]

What almost no one would have expected comes to pass. The Berlin Senate buries its differences and approves the project, setting 77 million DM aside for it. Then the estimated construction costs increase to over 100 million. In November 1989, the Berlin Wall falls. German reunification becomes the order of the day, funds grow scarce, priorities are redefined. No one wishes to call off the building of the Jewish Museum, which would mean political scandal. So it is merely postponed.

Back to the beginning again. A man deconstructs architecture, inquires into the limits of architecture. Architecture as text. But what he constructs is a text-reading machine which itself is a piece of architecture…

If there is any priority in Germany for a public building, then let it be this one. It is simply more important than any other important building.

In the course of the year 1991, following the Berlin Senate decision to stop the project, this insight began to gain ground. A wave of journalistic and political pressure ensued. Prominent voices like those of Willy Brandt, Simon Wiesenthal, and Jack Lang, as well as that of the Israeli government, made themselves heard in the *New York Times* and the *Herald Tribune*. In Washington, D.C., and several other American cities, Jewish museums were established to prevent

Daniel Libeskind, Jewish Museum, Berlin. Construction site, 1994

Daniel Libeskind, *Cultural Center*, St. Pölten. Northwest elevation, 1992

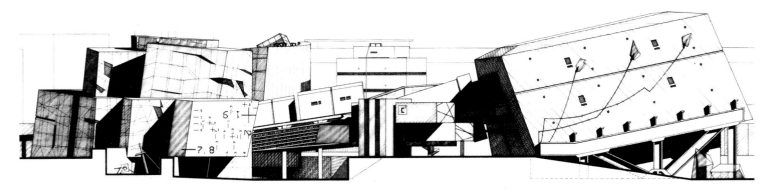

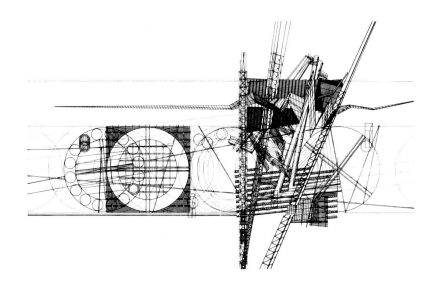

the Holocaust from ever being forgotten. Was Berlin, of all places, not to be among the number?

In September 1991, over the head of the Senate, the Federal German Government decided that the construction of the museum was to begin in 1993. Its cornerstone was laid in November 1992; the basic structure is scheduled for completion by November 1994. The facade, made entirely of zinc, is to be finished by 1995, and after interior work and exhibition installation are done, the Jewish Museum, Berlin, will be inaugurated in 1996 or 1997.

If enough pressure is applied, evidently, architectural visions can indeed be translated into architectural reality.

Endgame, end of time, end of art, end of architecture? Where does the architectural path lead after deconstructivism? Well, the apocalypse has been regularly predicted for millennia now, and history still goes on, including the history of architecture. And both will continue to make some sort of sense, despite Libeskind's objections. In his models for an office building complex in Wiesbaden (1992), and even more clearly in the cultural center envisioned for St. Pölten (1992), he has taken a direction similar to that of Domenig or Behnisch, Gehry, Eisenman, or Coop Himmelblau. Libeskind is apparently growing more and more interested in shaping built architectural history himself. This he does by means of boldly interpenetrating blocks and obliques resembling erratic cliffs, engendering architectural cityscapes of primeval power which continue deconstructivist principles in the direction of greater practicality.

Other potential paths to this end have been suggested by Coop Himmelblau, SITE, the high-tech specialists Rogers and Foster, and by the media architects Nouvel and Ito. First priority in this regard would seem to attach to a synthesis of advanced technology, environmental considerations, and computer-assisted architecture. The result would be yet another utopia, and one worth striving for with the aid of architectural vision.

What form will our lives and work take on tomorrow and the day after tomorrow? What sort of architecture will we live in? Will overpopulation change us into amphibian creatures who build cities half on and half under the water? Or will ozone holes make us cave people who avoid the light of day, build underground dwellings, and are forced to retreat deeper and deeper into the rocky depths? Will we be able to inhabit our planet, robbed of its natural equilibrium and raw materials, shaken by catastrophe after catastrophe, only in specially fortified cities, or will our children and their children, to ensure the survival of the species, be compelled to escape to extraterrestrial settlements equipped with artificial gravity and greenery?

Or will the endless urban sprawls merely continue to grow until cities become festering garbage dumps with no water fit to drink, paralyzed by traffic jams, crime, noise, air pollution, health problems, energy depletion? Will public streets and squares have to be converted into living quarters, or lined with sleeping hole dwellings like those already in existence all over India? Or will birth control, new technologies, electronic traffic guidance systems, recycling processes, and intelligent architecture enable us to cope with our problems to the extent of permitting humanity, if not to live in abundance, at least to continue to totter along the brink of survival?

And how will the high-density cities of the future be designed? Will there be a return to decentralized, smaller units, a continuation of gigantic skyscraper cities, or will the principle of "low rise/high density" come to the fore? What new, energy-saving, recyclable building materials will be discovered, and how will the new and age-old energy sources of sun, wind, and water be employed? What type of structures will be built with the aid of computers and sensor and control systems — intelligent, perhaps even interactive buildings? And how, in terms of architectural aesthetics, can high-tech, environmental considerations and media approaches be best combined?

Many things become evident

Angus McKie, *Hyperspace-Troop Carrier, 5. 16. 2526*

Satirical representation of a utopian airship, end of eighteenth century

from this selection from a much broader range of potential questions. First, the salient issue here is survival. Second, architecture never stands alone, but is embedded in a context of many other and diverse fields of activity. Third, architectural vision is required to find answers to these questions, and futuristic thinking is an absolute necessity. Fourth and finally, while such thinking cannot help but overlap with science fiction, architecture urgently needs an infusion of utopian, visionary spirit to master the enormous tasks which will very soon, as it were, be knocking at its door.

Science fiction is a basically literary genre that grew out of the utopias and projected ideal states of antiquity and the Renaissance. After taking on a scientifically grounded and future-oriented character in the nineteenth century with Jules Verne and other authors, in our own century science fiction has spread to other fields, like film, music, painting, toys, record covers, and computer games. In literature and film, the genre has developed its own unique range of imagery, in which architecture invariably plays a key role, simply because human life runs its course largely in an architectural set-

Lebbeus Woods, *AEON*, 1981–82

Mike Webb, *Wandering Cities on Achamandura*, also known as "Cybertechtonic Animote." Conceived by Pat Hinderis, *Mechanismo*, 1978

ting.[87] This imagery was consequently taken up by the other fields mentioned, generating a very specific iconography of science-fiction architecture, of which almost everybody nowadays carries a picture in his or her mind. I shall illustrate this development by means of a few examples, and then go on to discuss the extent to which science fiction and serious visionary architecture mutually influence, or can be brought into conformance with, one another.

Jonathan Swift's famous novel, *Gulliver's Travels* (1726), is one of those starting points from which an entire train of science-fiction imagery emerged. In his chapter on Gulliver's third journey, Swift describes a country called Laputa, a symbol of England as the oppressor of Ireland. Laputa is a flying ideal city capable of terrorizing entire nations by interposing itself between them and the sun, cutting off the light, and, if they still prove unruly, of crushing them under the weight of its smooth metal floor. In 1838, the caricaturist Grandville envisioned this scene in his woodcut *Gulliver Discovers the Island of Laputa,* and since then it has become the model for countless flying cities in science-fiction illustrations and movies. The notion of a saucer-shaped flying city even entered the planning of NASA and the Russian space program; in the meantime, in order to create artificial gravity, it has metamorphosed into a rotating wheel which can be enlarged by adding modules. If the planners are to be believed, such space stations could provide dwelling and working quarters for tens of thousands of people living in international

Grandville, *Gulliver Discovers the Island of Laputa,* 1838

Robert McCall, *Visitation*, 1986

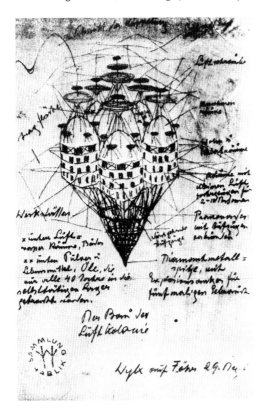

Wenzel August Hablik, *The Building of the Air Colony*, 1908

Opposite page: Frank R. Paul, *City of the Future*, 1942

communities in the not-too-distant future. Further models for space ships and flying cities were offered by Boullée's and Ledoux's ideal architectural configurations. Buckminster Fuller's geodesic domes have involuntarily engendered any number of flying cheese-plate covers whose creators consider them highly progressive images of the mobile space cities of the future.

Science-fiction authors remained largely fixated on space travel and extraterrestrial adventure until the 1960s, when they began to widen their interest to questions of the terrestrial future. Artists and illustrators in the field have since expanded their repertoire, and their depictions of space travel and exploration now include references to military installations, satellites, rockets, and launching ramps, and cities in outer space like monstrous flying battleships.

Unlike the authors, few of the illustrators orient themselves to the scientific realities of incipient space travel and the concomitant research. In their images of cities on strange planets or in extraterrestrial colonies they generally rely on rather simple architectural visions, most of which evoke little more than an overblown New York skyline or Mayan cities in the jungle.

Exceptions prove the rule. In the 1930s and 1940s, Frank R. Paul's illustrations to science-fiction tales in magazines such as *Amazing Stories* and *Wonder Stories* exhibited truly futuristic buildings that were on a level with, and sometimes in advance of, current architectural designs. In recent decades it has been above all Robert McCall who has advanced everything imaginable in the way of high technology and exploited the market of ideas to best effect, combining Wright and Fuller with aircraft supercarriers and exhibition architecture to create his *Floating Cities*. McCall has even been honored by the German Architecture Museum in Frankfurt am Main, which has devoted a postcard series to his work.

The tradition of balloons and early airships, from its fitful beginnings in the eighteenth century to Wenzel Hablik's crystalline *Building of the Air Colony* (1908), leads by way of spherical, balloonish intergalactic warships and space gliders to the bizarre technical-architectural air and space ships of Lebbeus Woods, which in terms of artistic ambitiousness certainly surpass the rest. Woods was also the first architect to try his hand, in visionary drawings like his *Aerial Paris* project, at innovative organic geometries and configura-

tions the likes of which had yet to be seen in architectural history.

As even this brief review shows, however, science-fiction conceptions of architecture generally have very little in common with serious approaches to the architecture of the future.

In film, the situation looks somewhat brighter. Fritz Lang's *Metropolis* (1926) is still unsurpassed as an example of the brilliant employment of futuristic architecture as a protagonist in its own right. It was not until 1982, with Ridley Scott's *Blade Runner*, that another director managed to come close to Lang's achievement.[88] The great science-fiction movies of the 1970s and 1980s — *2001: Space Odyssey, Close Encounters of the Third Kind, Star Wars,* the James Bond film *Moonraker,* or the *Alien* films, to name only a few — had space ships or stations that indeed employed elaborate and effective science-fiction architecture, but it was little more than a translation into three-dimensional terms of the familiar iconology of the magazine and cover illustrators. Truly shockingly new and fantastic architecture has been pursued almost solely by H. R. Giger, in his sets for *Alien I* (1979) and *Dune* (1980), the latter of which unfortunately was never completed. Like the designs of Woods, those of Giger indicate that only an artist of rank can marshal the courage and visionary force to forsake the established conventions. Both men have enriched the architectural canon by new visual metaphors which initially seem so strange that they are capable of changing our visual habits and the way we experience reality.

H. R. Giger, film architecture for *Dune*, 1980 (not realized)

The technology and space-travel euphoria of the late 1950s and early 1960s educed an abundance of megaprojects in the field of futuristic architecture.[89] Understandably, the Japanese were in the forefront of developments, with a group called the *Metabolists.* The country's overpopulation and technological dynamic led to a search for urban planning approaches that would provide living and working opportunities for great numbers of people while conserving land. In keeping with this aim, Arata Isozaki projected both *Space Cities* (1960) and gigantic concrete habitats based on tree houses which would occupy a minimum of ground area, and thus, like Kisho Kurakawa's *Wall Cluster in the City* (1959), would utilize airspace to the utmost. Kenzo Tange in 1960 planned to

build over Tokyo Bay a project of a kind, like Kiyonari Kikutake's *Floating City* of 1958, that has continually cropped up anew at certain intervals. In many respects, such ideas have since begun to take on reality with the huge project for Kansai International Airport, recently opened on an artificial island in Osaka Bay.

A certain aesthetic charm attaches to such projects, as it does to Walter Jonas's *Funnel City for 6,000 Inhabitants,* to Paolo Soleri's *Hexahedron,* to the gigantic pyramid city designs of Buckminster Fuller (1966) and Stanley Tigerman (1968), or to Walter Pichler's, Hans Hollein's, and Raimund Abraham's partially subterranean machine-city designs of the early 1960s. However, the negative consequences of concentrating masses of people in a highly restricted space have yet to be explored on a correspondingly gigantic scale. All the literary analyses in science-fiction novels, with the exception of Stanislav Lem's *Transfer (1970),* have reached extremely pessimistic conclusions. And in Lem's novel, the aggressive genetic potential of man is mitigated by medical means.

Le Corbusier's initially highly praised machine-for-living units (*"unités"*) have since become extremely controversial, not only in Marseille, and those large-scale high-rise prefabricated housing developments since erected in considerable numbers in the East and West have proven such dismal places that the only things they seem to advance are isolation, criminality, alcoholism, and political radi-

Sri Aurobindo, Auroville. Model, 1968

Future Systems, *Green Building with Ecological Temperature and Air Control,* 1990

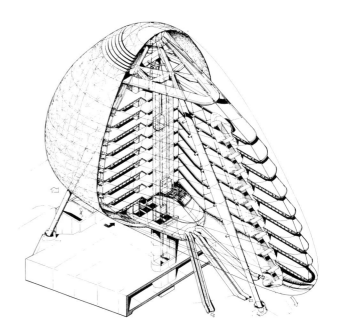

Walter Jonas, *Funnel City*. Various versions since 1960

Arata Isozaki, *Cluster in the Air*, 1962

Kisho Kurakawa, *Wall Cluster in the City*, 1959

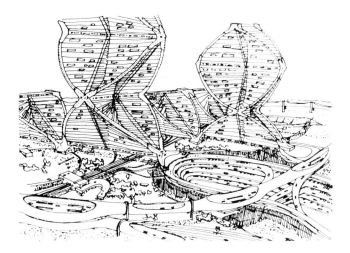

calism. Apparently, however, sheer size alone is not a reliable measure of the success or failure of such projects. Design, quality of furnishing, and general ambience seem to play the key role. Luxurious skyscrapers, estates, and high-rise apartment buildings enjoy the acceptance of their inhabitants, and are treated accordingly. So the subject is still very much up for debate, and in view of population growth and housing shortages, it will be for some time to come.

Space-city projects advanced by Konrad Wachsmann, Yona Friedman, and Eckard Schulze-Fielitz in the late 1950s and early 1960s were included in NASA plans for great space stations, but here, too, initial optimism has since made way for a more sober view of their potentials. On the other hand, grid networks, cantilevered constructions, and module structures of the type envisioned in the 1960s by Archigram have since been employed on a large scale in the armaments industry, for aircraft and rocket production, as well as in university and residential architecture.

Architects around the world experimented in the 1960s with megaprojects involving module construction and frameworks doubling as support and supply systems. In Ontario, for instance, Eberhard Zeidler revolutionized hospital building with his variable prefabricated grid system for McMaster's Health and Science Centre (1967–73), and in Austria, Günther Domenig suggested an *Urban Load-bearing and Utilities Framework* (1965) which was to be divided into public and private zones. In terms of organization, spatial arrangement, and construction the project envisioned horizontal and vertical pedestrian and vehicle traffic by means of ramps, passageways, and vertical nodes, and a support system to which basic elements could be added. This flexibility was intended to ensure a high degree of individuality in terms of furnishing and life-style.

The ostensible inhumanity of such megaprojects was pointed out from the start by young architects and artists, who advanced small-scale, decentralized alternatives. Coop Himmelblau and Haus-Rucker-Co were not immune to the space-travel euphoria of the 1960s, nor, like Archigram, could they ignore the increasing influence on society of telecommunications, television, computers, and increasingly ubiquitous entertainment electronics. Moreover, they experimented with living capsules and pneumatic architectural elements. But they were also sensitive to the dangers associated with increasing air pollution, environmental exploitation, and individual anonymity in the great cities, and held happenings and actions intended to further civil courage and the development of an urban culture. With Haus-Rucker-Co such efforts included space-suits as sources of oxygen in unbreathable city air, and space-colonies in the shape of pulsating yellow hearts, while Coop Himmelblau projected *Feedback Vibration Cities*, Cities *that Beat like Hearts*, or *Cloud Cities*. At the time, the thinking of young Viennese architects was dominated by pneumatic elements, sensors, and television installations that presaged hyper- and multimedia developments to come.

162

They also advanced a number of media-oriented, mobile architectural designs to be worn like a second skin.

Both the technological optimism and the revolutionary spirit of the 1960s were soon dissipated, as over the next decade students and architects turned to small-is-beautiful solutions, which in the 1980s, in turn, gave way to the eclectic narratives of quotation-happy postmodernism. However, the problems remained, or were even exacerbated in the meantime. Rain forests and other long-established forests continued to be cut down, emissions increasingly filled the atmosphere, ozone holes gaped, the world population incessantly rose, the megalopolises grew at breathtaking speed, and the necessity for architectural vision, for the unconventional approaches of cross-current thinkers, became greater than ever before. In all probability, architecture will exhibit, in fact must exhibit, more rapid changes over the next few decades than at any other comparable time period in the past.

Günther Domenig, *Hygrobile Living Capsule*, Ragnitz. Model, 1963

Let us take two remarkable examples to illustrate the role which architectural vision might play in this process. In the future, due to the rapidity of social and economic change, long-term solutions will probably not be as much in demand as short-term, individual, flexible and variable solutions, as these are better adapted to the marginal conditions which are continually growing in importance.

The New York group SITE has been characterized since its inception by an environmental approach applied with humor rather than with sectarian earnestness. As early as 1981, these architects suggested a *Highrise of Homes*, in whose basic structure the individual buyer could integrate his own, personally styled home, thereby turning an entire sprawling suburban housing development into a space-saving vertical estate. Along the same lines, Peter Cook in the 1980s advanced ever-new high-rise variants and eventually developed suggestions on how the old garden-city ideas could be transported in modified form into the twenty-first century. As desirable

James Wines, SITE, *Greened Manhattan*, 1989 (described by Wines as a "humoresque")

side-effects, the urban climate would be improved and nature brought indoors, where it would have better chances of recovery and survival. If politicians still possessed a little visionary spirit instead of merely pragmatically attempting to remedy the worst social omissions, city governments might long ago have been encouraged to redesign their communities along such lines as these. In the early 1990s, SITE transposed similar ideas to megastructures interspersed with vegetation,[90] thus pointing out a way in which life in the cities could indeed be decisively improved.

Tentative endeavors to realize such ideas are found, probably not coincidentally, in the most recent designs of two star British architects: Norman Foster's project for the Commerzbank headquarters in Frankfurt, and Richard Rogers's Brewery and Fountain Building at Zoo Station, Berlin, both of which are atrium constructions with numerous ecological details and lavish greenery. Günther Domenig's 1992–93 design for the Austria Bank headquarters in Vienna included an attractive "green tower," which is sure to find emulators. Yet all of these projects are merely halting starts in the direction pointed out by SITE and Peter Cook. There is still ample room for architectural visionaries and practical thinkers to apply a combined environmental and technological approach to achieve solutions that conserve both energy and resources.

164

Still comparatively unknown on the international scene is Gerald Exline of Los Angeles. Living in Los Angeles, Exline is well acquainted with every aspect of agglomeration, since from traditional downtown to posturban sprawl, every form of urban architectural culture known today occurs within the city limits.

Yet what fascinates Exline to the point of obsession is the design of high-density urban structures, the inevitability of which is suggested by his own, daily experience. With thousands of short, rapid strokes of the pen he records his visions of such evocative structures, in designs that have grown freer and more abstract over the course of the years. A plethora of vertical and horizontal lines tempt the viewer to complete the vision in his own mind, engendering columns and supports, diagonal reinforcements, bridges and window openings, cubic dwelling units, towers and pathways, squares and gardens. The strokes begin to gel, expand, contract and condense, recalling the notations of modern music. They grow darker or lighter, forming gradations and virtual waves that seem to metamorphose into material particles and clusters, condense into architectural vol-

Pyramid City TRY 2004. Designed to provide living and working space for a million inhabitants in the sea off Tokyo

umes that evoke tightly packed computer chips. It is obvious from such drawings that Exline's principal concern lies with the organization of surfaces and open public spaces.

Epistemologically his procedure displays a sophisticated knowledge of the importance of viewer participation. Exline's designs, rather than providing a fixed image, leave various options for interpretation open. No other architect addresses the task of designing future architecture in a visionary mode with a comparable degree of understanding. Exline takes into account the complexities that are certain to occur, and the multilayered analyses that must be performed, if designs of this kind are to be given concrete form. At this point in time, after all, nobody knows how buildings and urban structures will look in the not-too-distant future. Exline leaves room for extrapolation from the familiar, but he also leaves room for completely new approaches and aesthetics. He opens playgrounds for the imagination, and thus fulfils the demands made on the futuristic architect in an ideal way.

In conclusion, a science fiction not exclusively devoted to adventures in outer space has much in common with futuristic architecture, if such architecture does tend to lack the element of adventure as traditionally defined. Good science-fiction authors of the past three decades have proved to be excellent futurologists, as they have not only predicted most of the middle- and long-term trends that have since come to pass but have, as it were, experimentally tested them under laboratory conditions as well. Much the same could be said of futuristic architecture, even if it has not been able to offer global solutions, being satisfied instead with the fragmentary and transitory suggestions of recent years.

For several years now we have been living in an immensely accelerated phase of social and cultural evolution, a widespread reshaping of society into a media, communication, and information culture. An adjunct of the postmodern and post-industrial era, the media are influencing, indeed beginning to dominate, ever broader sectors of our lives. Medialized hybrid cultures and pure media culture will soon prevail, forcing other, more traditional forms to the margins of the cultural system. This development has become dramatically obvious in the visual and performing arts of the 1990s. Accompanying the flood of visual imagery, the buying and selling of data flows, disembodied news, and immaterial commodities have continually increased. The driving force from which these developments have arisen is the computer, the true hypermachine of the waning twentieth and the dawning twenty-first century. Within the decade it will probably lead to the convergence, and eventually to the complete merger, of television systems and other screen media into an interactive, multimedia system.

It would be truly strange if the restructuring process our culture is experiencing thanks to the media should stop at architecture. The computer and its digital networks are already beginning to exhibit previously undreamed-of potentials for mixed text and image processing. Where real photographs and simulations, video and animations, computer graphics and paintings, images and texts of the most diverse provenance, can be combined without transition to create

Brian T. Sullivan, *Spectral 1*. Computer graphic, 1992

image-text surfaces of an entirely new type, this not only expands the range of expression and fields of activity open to media artists but promises to revolutionize design practice in architecture as well. For the architectural imagination, the computer represents an unprecedented challenge.

In the 1970s and 1980s, architectural renderings, previously done largely in black and white, went full color. In addition, architects' offices began to develop increasingly sophisticated methods of presentation aimed at making their work stand out in competitions. The tendency continues, and recently has spread to the field of three-dimensional computer simulation. Some offices have already begun to tempt their clients with cyberspace animations, in which, by donning a data glove or suit, the clients can seemingly

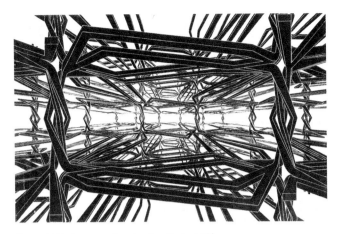

Konrad Wachsmann, *Construction Study*, 1953

Opposite page:
Chicago by night, with Helmut Jahn's Illinois State Center (1979–85)

Doris Vila, *Heaven, home + weightless.* Holographic installation,
PRC, Boston, 1992

walk into a simulacrum of their own, future building. The leap into three-dimensional simulation, the spatial depths of computer-engendered reality, has not only blurred the line between fiction and reality but has lastingly altered the status of the architectural rendering.

Drawings have either become superfluous or they have lost the artistic aura they had only recently attained, with the sophisticated superimpositions, perspectives, and coloring of 1970s and 1980s postmodernist renderings. Marvellous drawings used to convince selection committees and attract clients, as the oeuvre of Helmut Jahn so beautifully illustrates. Now it would appear that the architectural drawing — which, as everyone knows, does not conform to the built result — at best enjoys the status of an artistic visualization of a design idea, if not that of a full-blown work of art. At worst, mediocre architects are in danger of losing their drawing skills altogether, of sacrificing the intuitive, personal touch to the predigested stereotypes of computer software. The challenge at this juncture is to employ the computer creatively, like an extension of the pencil and palette, and, ideally, to tempt new aesthetic and emotional qualities from the electronic maze.

But it is not only the design process that is being radically changed. The screen media are supplemented by holography and the three-dimensional laser. These, with television screens and projected image-walls, with video and audio sculptures, are stretching out ghostly immaterial fingers to get a grasp on architecture. Yet the people who make it, architects, long ignored the media and the media-based arts, and when this became impossible, most tried to repress them. In the meantime, the media had begun to take over architecture from the inside, initially by means of building guidance technology. In the 1980s a redesign of utilities, communications, alarm systems, and internal traffic systems took place, with a rapidity analogous to the increasing acceleration and mobility of social developments. If in the modern age architecture had already learned to walk, ride, and fly, in the postmodern age it became intrinsically dynamic, flexible, mobile, and media-based. In analogy to the human skin and body, architectural bodies learned to see, hear, smell, taste, breathe, speak, sound the alarm — to react with all the sensitivity of a nervous system. In short, we speak

of "intelligent" or "thinking" architectures. These have long surpassed the stage of pure architectural fantasy, though architectural imagination is still capable of opening ever-new fields of activity.

This development has become most obvious in skyscraper construction, where combinations of cameras, terminals, and sensor systems, and computerized control, guidance, and warning systems are employed in ever more complex ways to control access, traffic movements, climate, external and internal illumination, energy flow, and smoke and fire alarms. The potential of these technical media seems virtually unlimited. New subsystems using continually more miniaturized and efficient chips are being devised, and their application is spreading from workplace to residence. In this regard, the *Tron* project in Tokyo, and the Dutch *House of the Future*, both equipped with an abundance of electronic genii, reflect the state of the art in the late 1980s.

The second stage of media influence in building is represented by the effects of communications and entertainment media on the interiors we live in. The examples extend from telephone and fax to television, radio, personal computer, plotter, printer, and paint box, all the way to interactive networks. What is typical of this development is the way in which it increasingly blurs the borderlines among communication, entertainment, work, and artistic production. With the computer at the heart of the system and the screen as integrative element, such equipment proves to be multifunctional. It changes the look of our workplaces and interiors, but it is also highly flexible in application. At present, entirely new generations of office furnishings and media furniture are in the design stage, posing a challenge to the imagination and creativity of architects and interior designers.

The third aspect of the media which has since had a widely visible effect on architecture is that of the aesthetic media mentioned above, each of which has produced an art form specific to it. Common to all of them, again, is the computer, which renders their immaterial products visible and audible on the screen.

Bernard Tschumi, La Villette by night

The crucial role played by this instrument has led many critics, theoreticians, and even practitioners since the late 1980s to believe that the media have caused a crisis in architecture, indeed stricken it to its very roots. This became apparent at the latest, they feel, when the media began to reshape the vocabulary, grammar, and rhetoric of architecture by changing its outward aspect, its face — the facade. For nowhere else does architecture so visibly represent the aesthetics, style, and artistic skill of its creator, or so strongly influence the look of cities. The media, say their critics, have dissolved the hitherto solid ties between form and function, and by means of an endless concatenation of visualizations have caused a crisis of architectural form that has devastated it to the core of its rhetoric.

This is where architectural imagination comes into play. It can advance conservative counterproposals, as in the case of Massimo Scolari and Leon Krier; it can try a progressive strategy and attempt to develop a specific media aesthetic; or, as suitable in a period of transition, it can advance suggestions for an architectural hybrid culture of coexistence, for a dialogue between old and new, which certainly can take place on and within one and the same building.[91]

The media in architecture can look back on a relatively long tradition. At the Bauhaus and in the 1960s, many architects experimented intensively with media applications and means of integration.[92] Every new art, including the media arts and media architecture, must first orientate itself to existing traditions, for or against, and in this case must learn to master the technical difficulties involved in employing the electronic media. No genuine aesthetic ever emerged out of thin air, without relying on some ideal or model from the past. And once a new art or direction in architecture has established itself, it can make a claim to seriousness only if it in fact succeeds in making things and situations, the experience of time and space, the rooms we live in, colors and imagery and sounds and the synaesthetic experience of all of these, visible and tangible in a unique, unprecedented way.

This is a great demand to make, but I think it must be made on the buildings and designs of the new media architecture. At present we are in a hybrid phase, a twilight zone between architecture and architectural fantasy. The term "media architecture" is not even a generally accepted technical term or stylistic category — it is my own neologism. Only a very few actual buildings in this genre exist, and several of them are definitely visionary in character. Many designs have been rejected by selection committees or timid clients who fear the expense, and have thus been relegated to that limbo of "pure" architectural fantasy where unbuilt projects are unjustifiably forgotten. And this despite the fact that the field of media architecture provides an opportunity for wide-ranging innovation.

Those who have tried their hand at media architecture include both newcomers and stars on the international scene, like Jean Nouvel of France, Rem Koolhaas of Holland, the Coop Himmelblau group in Vienna, and Toyo Ito of Japan. For all their individual stylistic differences, they share in common an intellectual approach, a sense of social developments, and a high degree of interest in architectural theory. In the quarter century since the media experiments of Archigram and the young Viennese vanguard, the electronic media have had an increasing influence on the way we experience the urban environment. The media are ever more visibly shaping the public urban space, altering it in terms of their intrinsic aesthetic. In the metropolis above all, this process is continually advanced

Bernard Tschumi, Glass Video Gallery. Groningen, 1990

by neon advertising, electronic image-fields, media facades, holograms, and lasers, new technologies that have made the fantasies of the 1960s real.

Analogously to transformations in philosophy and politics, open, flexible conceptions of space are emerging on all hands. And as in the media arts, the tendency to dematerialization is continually increasing in architecture. This development was postulated as early as 1958, by the painter Yves Klein and the architect Werner Ruhnau, in their joint design for a *Temple of the Elements*, which was to have walls of water and fire, and a roof formed of air. They also published a text called "General Development of the Contemporary Art of Dematerialization" at the time.[93] With reference to Frei Otto's suspended roof and tent constructions, the two authors celebrated walls of fire and water, and roofs of air, as building materials for the "classical city" of tomorrow, which would be correspondingly flexible, spiritual, and immaterial.

While current projects along these lines are informed by a similar philosophy, they are much more practical and less symbolic in nature. Pneumatic architecture, for example, has proven to be anything but a castle in the air. Intrinsically flexible, even partially mobile buildings are now being created in the fields of residential, industrial, and public architecture, buildings as sensitively reacting, sensor- and computer-controlled, dynamic systems with transformable skins and self-regulating walls. Toyo Ito is currently developing complex, flexible space systems in which the rooms, although left indeterminate as regards size and shape, have ceilings, walls, and floors that serve as information transmitters. These generate a unique, media-architectural aesthetic, an art of images and signs. Here, roofs are no longer roofs and walls no longer walls in the traditional sense. As such unprecedented designs show, the meaning of the terms "house" and "building" will have to be redefined. House design appears to be returning to the age-old architectural forms of tent and sail, reflecting a mobile, media-oriented society. Larger buildings, thanks to computerization, are beginning to take the shape of self-regulating, transformable, even learning systems.

In the process, one of the very

Toyo Ito, *The Future of Japan.* Installation, 1991

oldest and imaginatively inspiring media of architecture is again coming in to its own: the medium of light. In the course of changing postmodern living and working habits involving an extension of the day towards a 24-hour day, the illumination required at night is taking on an immense significance. Computer-controlled in modern projectors, refracted by lenses, revelling in color, creating three-dimensional illusions through holograms, light is becoming an immaterial dimension of architecture with a great spectrum of variation and effectiveness. Like hardly any other medium, light is capable of educing emotional, indeed poetic effects. The range of technologies just described, together with huge screens, variable scaffolding structures, and powerful audio equipment, is already being employed in rock and pop music concerts. And comparable effects may even be seen in today's big cities. Viewed by night, especially from the air, cities like Chicago, Los Angeles, and New York are dazzlingly impressive sights. In the 1980s, the art of illumination increasingly came to be recognized as means of lending the urban space a poetic dimension.

When used in conjunction, light and the other electronic media create a new narrative aspect in architecture. What Otto Piene dreamed of as early as the 1960s is gradually coming true, and not only in cinematic computer animations such as those used in *Terminator II*:

> *In the future, interior design and perhaps even exterior architecture will employ light as a building material, to articulate space. It will be used in conjunction with new, electronic noise-proofing. Walking through walls will be completely natural, and doors will become a thing of the past.*[94]

The most experienced architect in this regard is certainly Jean Nouvel. A follower of the post-structuralist philosophers Lyotard, Virilio, and Flusser — but not of Baudrillard — Nouvel's thinking and artistic approach are on the cutting edge of developments. Both sensitive and logical, he has had the impudence to reintroduce into architecture something the critics have unanimously written off for twenty years now: the box. In Nouvel's hands, this minimal configuration becomes a media-controlled, dramatically staged showpiece of high technology. His boxes are multifunctional happening containers that toy with light effects and have facades made of exterior grids and media screens. Their walls are tending to grow ever thinner, becoming membranes equipped with numerous sensors that perform a variety of control functions and are moreover decorated with media images and moving image-text surfaces. The traditional facade is replaced by an interchangeable, sophisticatedly layered and screened image facade. With an ironic and consciously old-fashioned twist, Nouvel in some cases supplements this electronic high tech with painted sailcloth surfaces.[95]

Jean Nouvel, Galeries Lafayette, Berlin. Central media cone, 1994 (under construction)

Jean Nouvel, Galeries Lafayette, Berlin. Model with video facade

The theoretical underpinnings of Nouvel's work certainly correspond to general developments in the application of the media — the trend towards dematerialization to the point of immateriality, to the "disappearance of reality" propagated by Paul Virilio, chief theoretician of speed. In the fields of advertising and design, the corresponding catchwords are "event staging" and "situation design" versus product design. Especially in this area, the use of ever-smaller but ever more efficient chips has brought a tendency to miniaturization and dematerialization in products once considered eminently material in nature.

With Nouvel, the image — or, in the case of his Institut du Monde Arabe, the symbolic, ornamental image-sign — takes the place of traditional architectural canons and symbols as materials of facade design. Nouvel himself speaks of building with the virtual images in the user's mind.[96] "The time that interests me," he says, "is the time of the moment, which I attempt to materialize."[97]

The facade as demarcation between inside and out becomes a skin, a sensitive interface between transmitters and receivers, between sensors and the functional processes they control in the interior of the building. In Nouvel's projects the entrance, traditionally a striking, functional detail, may be marked only by a curtain of light. Or the visitor may be spirited inside the building on escalators and by subterranean access routes. This reduces space, as Nouvel points out, to a secondary parameter. In sum, his approach is experimental, theatrical, highly intelligent, and artistically sensitive. How user-friendly it is will ultimately depend on the ability of the inhabitants of Nouvel's structures to learn to cope with virtuality and media architecture, whether they initially enjoy the sense impressions it conveys or not.

With the Institut du Monde Arabe, despite initial technical difficulties, Nouvel doubtless succeeded in creating a symbiosis of high-tech, electronic media, and ancient ornamental ideas of Islam made fruitful for modern aesthetics. The construction of the Berlin branch of Galeries Lafayette may be expected to set new standards in the field. Other of Nouvel's designs, such as that for the DuMont-Schauberg publishing house in Cologne, or for the Cologne Media Park's central building with media tower, are less certain of being put into practice at this writing. But if media architecture finds the wide acceptance it deserves, Nouvel's aesthetically and philosophically ambitious projects will certainly be in the forefront of architecture as an expression of a media culture and society.

Other paths towards an approach to building based on the media aesthetic, informed by architectural philosophy, and employing the latest technology, have been outlined by Rem Koolhaas. Two of his designs of recent years are among the most progressive examples of the new architectural thinking extant: for the Bibliothèque de France, Paris (1989–90), and for the Center for Art and Media Technology (ZKM), Karlsruhe, from the same period. While the Paris project garnered top honors as an idea, it was not chosen for building. The Karlsruhe design was planned to the point of construction, only to be cancelled in June 1992 by the city fathers, who grew frightened at the expense involved — and at their own initial courage.

Both designs represent enormous, cube-shaped structures. This feature, together with window openings arranged more by aesthetic than by functional criteria, perfectly demonstrates the gap between

Jean Nouvel, Media Park, Cologne.
Central building, model, 1991

Rem Koolhaas, Bibliothèque Nationale, Paris. Model, 1989

Rem Koolhaas, Center for Art and Media Technology (ZKM), Karlsruhe. Interior view, 1989

Rem Koolhaas, Center for Art and Media Technology (ZKM), Karlsruhe. Exterior view and media facade, 1989

form and function characteristic of media architecture. The advantage is that it renders the entire facade transparent, capable of transmitting information about what is happening inside the building.

The Paris design goes even farther than that for Karlsruhe. The solid cube is opened to the outside only by a small number of window apertures, some bizarrely organic in shape. Instead of being divided into floors, the great, empty interior space is conceived as containing special libraries and departments suspended from the ceiling like inner organs and nerve nodes. These are to be connected with each other by a mobile structure of nine large, glazed elevators. Auditoriums and reading rooms represent the sense organs of the cerebral and sensuous structure. The stacks function like arteries and brain convolutions within the body of the libraries. While the public areas form transparent, open spaces, the separate libraries present solid information blocks. A variety of media provide for communication, information, and entertainment, all integrated with one another by the hypermachine — a computer.

The Karlsruhe design, in contrast, still had individual floors connected by means of escalators and ramps, in which museum areas, electronic workshops, and a media theater were to be installed. Otherwise, the design was informed by the same principle of variability that inspired Koolhaas's Paris project, as fitting for a place devoted to the conception and production of immaterial art, as well as to an interchange between traditional and innovative art forms.

To a greater extent than most architects today, Koolhaas realizes that we must accustom ourselves to living without solid ground under our feet, that technological and theoretical innovation alike has become increasingly rapid, and that both individual and collective states, such as the family, working life, and national affairs are growing ever more tenuous, mobile, and open-ended. But he also realizes that these developments contain an opportunity which it would be shortsighted to miss in the face of technology and existential anxiety. What Koolhaas postulates is a media aesthetic for architecture that consciously takes into account the fundamental tension between statics and kinetics, between corporeality and incorporeality. He projects facades as hybrid surfaces, sensitively reacting integuments that at one moment can appear completely neutral and at the next, from the inside out, develop sign character, unfold an electronic narrative. If Koolhaas were at last permitted to realize such a building, it would indeed represent more than an information aesthetic — it would be an architectural translation of a new brand of media-conveyed sense experience. That true media architecture of this type would moreover have the character of a *mise en scène* — theatrical, dramatic, cinematic — really goes without saying.

The radical thinker and designer in the field of media architecture, a well-grounded architect and poetic visionary in one, is Toyo Ito of Japan. In the 1980s his feather-light tent and sail structures for theaters and restaurants, which went back to old nomadic architectural conceptions, caused just as much of a sensation as his statements about the new generation of emancipated, well-salaried, "nomadic" big-city women, for whose sake he felt innovative architecture needed to be developed. For some time now Ito has been advancing media-based projects that have attracted great interest. His *Tower of the Winds* in Yokohama (1986) is an early and superb example of the combination of media and natural environment, and of the aesthetic that can be derived from it. The tower facade reacts like an audiovisual seismograph to every change in wind velocity, light intensity, and ambient street noise, whereby a computer program translates these random impulses into an incessantly scintillating light display. Ito's *Egg of the Winds* (1990) continues such ideas, while at the same time recapitulating venerable notions about the look of unidentified flying objects. An aluminum-clad annex to an

Toyo Ito, *Maison de la Culture du Japon*. Paris, 1991

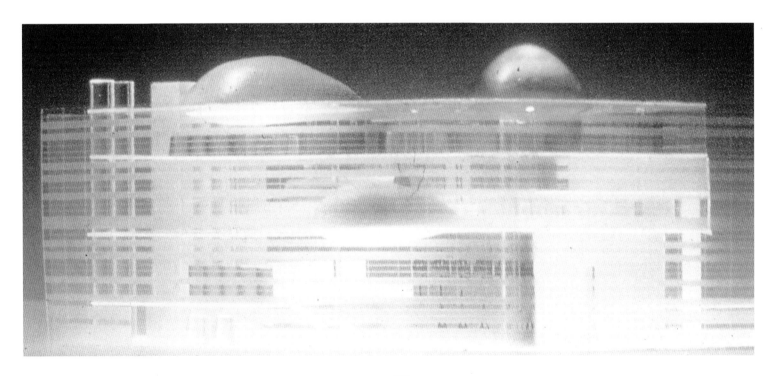

underground garage driveway, the building reflects sunlight by day, but as soon as twilight falls, it begins to exude a magical glow. The interior of the structure contains five liquid crystal projectors that cast images on interior screens and exterior skin, suddenly turning the building into an "outdoor video gallery."

There is probably no other architect who thinks more along the lines of Vilém Flusser's architectural philosophy and considerations on media and communication theory, whether Ito is acquainted with Flusser or not. His most advanced contribution to media architecture has unfortunately remained in the realm of vision — his design for the *Maison de la Culture du Japon* in Paris (1991). Bearing the title "Media Ships Floating on the Seine," the structure possesses an integument facade of electronically controlled glass. Behind it Ito envisions a variety of functional areas that apparently float free in the interior space. Images can be projected on the glazed facade, and even the floors and walls of Ito's house of culture form screens capable of transmitting information. In analogy to Flusser's philosophy, every interior space is created and defined by means of information. This logically renders them temporary in nature. As such, the spaces in Ito's project represent the complex, spatially layered structures and continual flux of global information across existing cultural borders. It is indeed in the nature of the media to contribute to a dissemination of a global aesthetic, including that of architecture. Yet surprisingly, Ito is not entirely in accord with this development, feeling that architecture and life are gradually losing touch with reality, beginning to "float," as he says, under the increasing influence of the media. Ubiquitous imagery and the consumer culture are taking their toll. Yet while this development may be unfortunate for the architect, Ito still believes it must be faced if architecture is to remain at the height of contemporary concerns. And in Japan especially, any other course would mean inevitable bankruptcy.

Media architecture is still at the beginning of its development. But one thing is certain: the cities of the twenty-first century will be increasingly multimedia in character. This will extend from traffic flow control and various administrative functions all the way to shopping, entertainment, and education, not to mention individual building designs and the image of cities as a whole. And if our cities are not to become museums, places devoted solely to historical memory and emotion, we would do well to develop a sense of the aesthetic and poetry potentially contained in the multimedia approach. The media arts are certain to make great strides over the coming decades, either autonomously or in combination with more traditional arts, to produce ever more sophisticated audiovisual worlds. Their integration in architecture can also be expected to increase. In the course of this development, those active in the media would be well advised to look for new alliances both with high-tech approaches and environmental considerations. As things appear now, the environmental discussion is pervading discourses in every other field. In order to achieve a synthesis of the media, high tech, and ecology, it is not enough to develop energy-saving, environmentally compatible technologies; new aesthetics are urgently required as well. This will face planners and architects with extreme challenges. But they must be faced, because the replacement of dino-

Rüdiger Kramm and Axel Strigl, Zeilgalerie les facettes. Frankfurt, 1992

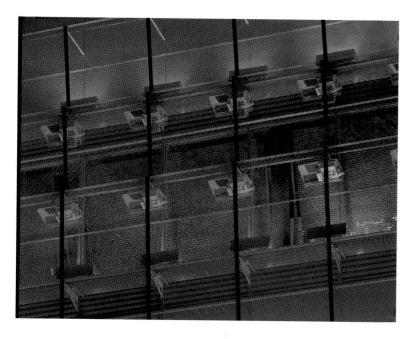

Zeilgalerie les facettes. Detail of media facade

Opposite page:
Toyo Ito, Tower of the Winds. Yokohama, 1986

179

ag4, Office for "Mediatecture," Cologne. Media-Intergrated High-Rise Office Building in Cologne.
Model, 1993. Design by Kronhagel, Lepel, and Singer

saur technologies based on high energy consumption and thoughtless destruction of the natural environment by intelligently combined technologies and control systems will brook no delay.

Hopeful new aesthetic approaches have come from the office of Rüdiger Kramm and Axel Strigl of Darmstadt. In the media facade of their Frankfurt *Zeilgalerie les facettes* (1992), a play of artificial light lends the building an apparent immateriality, divests it of mass. Among others, Frankfurt media architect Christian Möller, who describes himself as an "interactive architect," collaborated on the technical and artistic décor of the kinetic light sculpture. Cologne's ag4, the first "mediatecture" office to term itself a "cooperative for four-dimensional building," develops comprehensive multimedia conceptions for fairground, exhibition, and participatory architecture. Their projects combine audio, visual, and epistemological components with mobile, flexible spaces and environmental friendliness, in the attempt to achieve a new, holistic approach to architecture.

Coop Himmelblau, the Vienna group, were aware of the importance of the media since their inception in the late 1960s, and they

Coop Himmelblau, Model of a Media-Integrated Residential Building.
Exhibition installation, Centre Pompidou, Paris, 1992–93

have repeatedly experimented with media elements. In the 1980s Wolf Prix and Helmut Swiczinsky projected completely configurated media-incorporating large-scale structures, and built architecturally exciting and provocative media follies in Groningen and Osaka. At the great Coop Himmelblau retrospective held in the Centre Pompidou, Paris (December 1992–April 1993), they appeared with a model measuring 49 by 115 feet that once more set new and significant accents. While continuing the group's deconstructive principles, the model revealed an increased dynamic engendered by a series of constructive aspects: winglike elements symbolizing motion; pilasters that penetrated static states and transformed them into dynamic ones; squares and cubes capable of shifting position to redefine spaces; x-shaped, intersecting elements that further contributed to a transformation of static into dynamic aggregate states; and finally, arches as backbone-like links within the construction. The key new aspect of the design, however, was the employment of computer programs which, augmented by searchlights, created on the great expanses of glass flowing, hovering illuminations recalling scudding clouds or rolling waves. These effects produced a compelling contrast between dynamic statics and an incessant flux of movement, which justified Coop Himmelblau in speaking of the principle of "liquid architecture" in connection with the structure.

The implications of such a term, of course, bring Prix and Swiczinsky very close to the hybrid situation of virtual architecture, which now must be briefly addressed. What manner of beast is the virtual reality, the virtual space, about which there has been so much to-do in recent years? It is not a contradiction in terms to speak of immaterial virtuality in connection with something so concrete and static as the architecture in which we live, eat, work, sleep, and make love? Or, if there really is such a thing as virtual architecture, must it not possess entirely unprecedented, media-related poetic and aesthetic qualities? Are three-dimensional computer simulations, animations, and cyberspaces more than a media hoax?

One of the architecturally most interesting artists who passes the international test of mastering the thorny transition and paradigm

Coop Himmelblau, Media Tower. Mariahilfer Platzl, Vienna, begun 1992

Jeffrey Shaw, *The Virtual Museum.* Installation at "Art Frankfurt," 1991, room 3

shift from an analogue to a digital, a material to an immaterial aesthetic — and who can explain this to the layman into the bargain — is the Australian Jeffrey Shaw. After all, it is definitely easier at this point in time to speculate about virtual realities and advance more or less intelligent theories about them than to realize artistically relevant projects. In this field, theory is still far in advance of practice.

Shaw gained a wide reputation in the early 1990s for his projects *Legible City* and *Virtual Museum.* To illustrate his approach, let us describe the latter. In cognizance of the fact that not only historical city areas but large sectors of life and art are increasingly taking on a museum-like character, Shaw set out to counteract this premature conservation by conceiving of a virtual architecture that would be as provisional as the culture around it. He began by outlining modalities of interactive and virtual spaces. Then, localizing these virtual spaces in a close relationship to actual space, Shaw went on to establish — in a manner at once ironical, practical, and immensely theoretical — his discourse on a virtualized, computer-controlled museum as a repository and exhibition venue for immaterial artifacts existing in the twilight zone between apparent and real.

The *Virtual Museum* is a three-dimensional, computerized museum consisting of an immaterial arrangement of rooms and exhibition items. The facility comprises a circular, rotating platform bearing a large video projection monitor, a computer, and an armchair for the viewer. Seated in this chair, the viewer can interactively control his or her movements through the *Virtual Museum.* The architecture consists of five rooms, all of which reproduce the architecture of the real space in which the installation is located (in this case, the Landesmuseum Linz, Austria), which implies a unification of real and virtual spaces.

The combined reality and unreality of these spaces exhibits perceptual and poetic qualities of an intensity previously unknown. The virtual or imaginary spaces that once existed only in our minds, as dreams or edifices of thought, have become virtually real.

The growing incorporation of the media in architecture, and the increasing presence of true media architecture, can be expected to lead to more reflection and experiment in the field of virtual architecture, and inevitably to its acceptance. Virtual architecture will increasingly penetrate into the realm of "real" architecture, partially redefining and replacing it. Habitual ways of thinking, seeing, and experiencing are bound to adapt to this

Jeffrey Shaw, *The Virtual Museum,* 1991, room 5

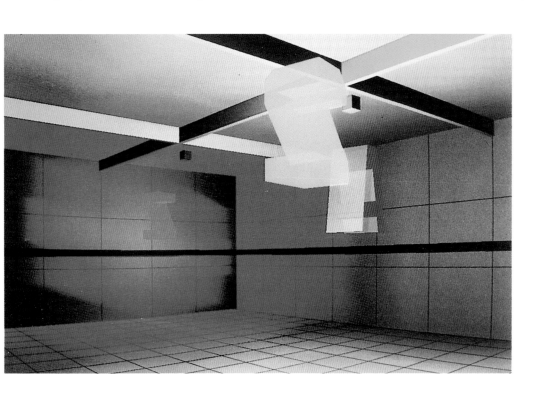

process, which is in fact already very much under way, even though many people, architects and laymen, vehemently deny it or still hope to prevent it.

The situation just described is already real and present in the field of planning and competitions. In addition, models are being used as stand-ins for "real" architecture with ever greater frequency. Computer simulations, transitory, transformable, three-dimensional computer products on hard disk and monitor screen, into which we can physically and mentally enter with the aid of satellites of ourselves, are ultimately bound to supplant "real" architectures to an ever increasing extent.

The recent cyberspace fad has tended to conceal the revolutionary aspects of this and other new technologies, particularly the potentials of networks. Cyberspace has opened out entirely new dimensions of time and space, in which human beings and space not only confront but are capable of mutually influencing one another. Once this circumstance has been accepted and more or less understood, it is capable of altering our perceptual capacity and conception of reality.

Florian Köpp and Michael Willadt, *Imagination Machine IMT2P0*. Third prize at ACS competition, 1992

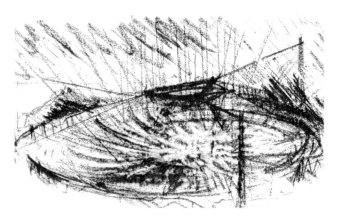

Yann Kersalé, *Arecibo Radio Telescope Project*. Projection variations, 1992

Instead of virtual realities, one can also speak of "artificial environments," meaning that such environments do not occur in nature but must be created by humans aided by the computer. The idea immediately sets off a process in which our apparently solid grasp of reality begins to waver, expand, and take on the form of a continually changing flux. We come to the realization that immaterial, telematic spaces do indeed exist, spaces that interpenetrate with, or are superimposed on, one another to create entire networks which can be rendered graphically visible, audible, tangible as energy fluxes, as media communication spaces, as immaterial art spaces.

The resulting vision is one of an architecture of fluctuating relationships, interdependencies, and interactions, in the context of an expanded conception of architecture. In view of attempts to integrate the variable imagery of the media, their scintillating surfaces, and liquid configurations in the rhetoric of built architecture, there is an apparent need to create new hybrids of pulsating color, pneumatic rooms, and virtual sounds, a new media sensibility implanted with the aid of the computer in actual, material architecture. And logically, architecture will be transformed in the process. Perhaps its most important offshoot at present is the perception of interlayered spaces and realities, the recognition that in future, thinking in terms of process will be all-important. This is a thinking that divorces itself from static notions and realizes what scientists have long known — that mankind can and must be capable of living without solid ground under its feet, and that it is truly possible to settle comfortably into changing, multiplex realities.

By the same token, the computer offers itself perfectly to the associative thinking and shaping processes of artists. Marcos Novak, himself an architect, has found a poetic image that expresses what I mean: "Cyberspace is poetry inhabited, and to navigate through it is to become a leaf on the wind of a dream."[98] People who think such thoughts, and who devote themselves to translating them into reality, are not dreamers at all — they are practical visionaries who conceive of and experiment with new aesthetics, design innovative products that can create new markets and jobs, and open up new dimensions of artistic expression and experience.

The type of experience I refer to is not necessarily predicated on a futuristic environment. A suggestion of it can be had, for instance, by becoming aware of what it means to live in a historically developed city, which implies mentally participating in its various historical strata from the point of view of a modern, contemporary consciousness.

I have no intention of spreading unfounded optimism or uncritical enthusiasm about a brave new media world on the horizon. But I do feel that the new electronic media and virtual realities as applied to architecture and its aesthetic are truly important, because they are capable of suggesting — visually, audibly, and tangibly — altered perceptions of space and time, of our relationship to architecture, and indeed of human relationships in general that conform to the spirit of the contemporary age.

And if the day should come on which we have made architecture too intelligent, as Vilém Flusser once noted, then we will just have to make it more stupid, until we again feel comfortable living and working in it. Even in this hypothetical case, the architectural imagination will still find plenty to occupy it, and all the objections on the part of architectural critics to the contrary, the utopian spirit in architecture will live on.

This will likely be accompanied by a continued dissolution of traditional architectural concepts. Rather than a small number of basic and binding architectural styles, the future will see an increasing pluralism in conformance with the character of society. The field of architecture will probably become more and more of an interface between a great variety of virtual activities. Once again, this tendency can be illustrated by reference to the work of Yann Kersalé, who conceives of himself neither as an architect, light-artist, nor land artist, but as a project artist of the second generation who takes elements from all these fields, combines them, and interlaces them with advanced technology and engineering to create new, hybrid forms. The results reflect some of mankind's age-old dreams with great symbolic concision, and connect the materiality of high-tech architecture with the immateriality of light. By playing on its dual character of particle and wave, Kersalé has managed to instigate a new brand of art, generated from science and technology.

As an example, let us take Kersalé's as yet unrealized project of 1992, which envisioned the temporary transformation of the reflector telescope in Arecibo, Puerto Rico, into an art work in light. This radio telescope with a reflector 984 feet in diameter is one of those listening posts with which we earthlings hope to learn more about the composition, density, and rotation speed of the stars — and also possibly to receive messages from intelligent beings on other planets. The telescope is itself capable of transmitting signals into outer space. Day in and day out, its reflector receives an incessant stream of particles, irradiation, and light waves that issued from distant galaxies thousands of light-years ago.

Fascinated by this apparent galactic chaos, which he knows obeys the laws of probability or some other, as yet undiscovered order, Kersalé set out to render it visible in artistic form. First, 20 to 30 powerful spotlights projecting concentrated or diffuse colored light were to be mounted under the telescope mirror, and the light mixture controlled by a computer and mixing console. The engineering artistry involved in the installation was to link the signals from outer space, the dynamics of their wavelengths, with this computer system to produce a monumental sculpture in light. The variations in light intensity and mixture would depend on laboratory data provided by astronomers and physicists — their analyses of cosmic rays, field strengths, and the frequency and density of the incoming sig-

Yann Kersalé, *Arecibo*, "Lumières d'Ondes," 1992

nals. Kersalé conceived of creating the link by means of the computerized frequency detection used to determine the motion of spiral nebulae. These waves would be transformed into plays of light, whereby operator or observer would be able to influence the computerized process. The time factor would be brought in by means of cameras, and the resulting films and visual records of the cosmic phenomena could be shown at exhibitions and in museums.

Scientists would analyze the impinging data, and the artist Yann Kersalé would transform their measurements into visible, transient sculptures in light whose rhythms would possess their own, intrinsic musicality. They would represent a very personal expression of the aesthetic beauty that resides in science. But instead of dissecting the mysteries of the universe, Kersalé's sculptures would subject its signals to metamorphoses, employ them to create virtual works of art which, in their own way, would pay homage to the beauty of the universal design, raise it to a metaphysical level, and render it an aesthetic experience. Using electronically recorded data from nature, a man and artist could slip into the role of immaterial demiurge. Ultimately, this aim has probably been at the bottom of human strivings from the beginning, whether in philosophy or religion, art or visionary architecture.

FROM THE "WHORE OF BABYLON" TO THE "NEW JERUSALEM" TO THE IDEAL CITIES OF THE RENAISSANCE

1   Preliminary, mainly literary investigations made in preparation for some of the following chapters were published by the author in 1985, under the title "Städtephantasien: Architekturutopien in der Literatur," in the Swiss arts journal *DU* (Zurich), no. 2 (1985), pp. 12–67, 98–99.

2   See also Evelyn Klengel-Brandt, *Der Turm von Babylon* (Leipzig, Vienna, and Munich, 1982), pp. 7–12.

3   John Dos Passos, *Manhattan Transfer* (New York: Bantam Classic, 1959), p. 198.

4   See Barbara Schock-Werner, "Bamberg ist Jerusalem — Architekturporträt im Mittelalter," in *Der Traum vom Raum: Gemalte Architektur aus 7 Jahrhunderten*, exhibition catalogue, Kunsthalle Nürnberg, 13 September–23 November 1986 (Marburg: Hitzeroth, 1986), pp. 45–55.

5   See Leonardo Benevolo, *The History of the City* (Cambridge, Mass.: MIT Press, 1980); especially chap. 6, "European Cities in the Middle Ages," with further reading.

6   James Joyce, *Ulysses* (London: The Bodley Head, 1960), pp. 606–7.

7   See Inken Nowald, "Stadt und Utopie — Beispiele aus der Vergangenheit," in *Stadt und Utopie: Modelle idealer Gemeinschaften* (Berlin: Frölich & Kaufmann, 1982), pp. 21–30.

THE MYTH OF THE TOWER: FROM BABYLON TO THE TOUR DE L'INFINI

8   Stanislaus von Moos, *Turm und Bollwerk: Beiträge zur politischen Ikonographie der italienischen Renaissancearchitektur* (Zurich, 1974), p. 18.

9   Some of the more recent books on skyscrapers and towers to be recommended are: Erwin Heinle and Fritz Leonhardt, *Türme aller Zeiten — aller Kulturen* (Stuttgart: DVA, 1988); Rem Koolhaas, *Delirious New York* (New York: Oxford University Press, 1978); Paul Goldberger, *The Skyscraper* (New York: Alfred Knopf, 1986);

Thomas A. P. van Leeuwen, *The Skyward Trend of Thought* (The Hague: AHA Books, 1986); Ada Louise Huxtable, *The Tall Building Artistically Reconsidered* (New York: Random House, 1984); Johann N. Schmidt, *Wolkenkratzer: Ästhetik und Konstruktion* (Cologne: DuMont, 1991); Heinrich Klotz (ed.), *New York Architecture, 1970–1990* (Munich: Prestel, 1990); Tulvio Irace, *Emerging Skylines: The New American Skyscrapers* (New York: Whitney Library of Design, 1990); John Zukowsky (ed.), *Chicago Architecture, 1872–1922* (Munich: Prestel, 1987); and, by the same author, *Chicago Architecture and Design, 1923–1993* (Munich: Prestel, 1993).

10   One of the most interesting books in this regard is Alison Sky and Michelle Stone, *Unbuilt America: Forgotten Architecture in the United States from Thomas Jefferson to the Space Age* (New York: Abbeville Press, 1983).

CONSCIOUSNESS GOES MODERN: GIOVANNI BATTISTA PIRANESI AND HIS SUCCESSORS

11   Günter Krawinkel, in *Inventionen: Piranesi und Architekturphantasien in der Gegenwart* (Kunstverein Hannover and Werkbund Bremen, 1982), p. 16.

12   Norbert Miller, *Archäologie des Traums: Versuch über Giovanni Battista Piranesi* (Munich: Hanser, 1978).

13   Ibid.; and Martin Christadler, "Giovanni Battista Piranesi und die Architekturmetapher der Romantik," in Armin Paul Frank, Wilhelm Hortmann, and Kurt Schumann (eds.), *Miscellanea Anglo-Americana: Festschrift für Helmut Viebrock* (Munich: Pressler, 1974), pp. 78–108.

14   Quoted in Miller (see n. 12), p. 379.

15   Ibid., p. 380.

16   Thomas De Quincey, "Confessions of an English Opium Eater," in *Complete Writings*, ed. David Masson (Edinburgh, 1890), vol. 3, pp. 438 ff.; quoted in Miller (see n. 12), p. 384.

17   Théophile Gautier, *Contes et Nouvelles* (Paris, n.d.), pp. 494 ff.

18   Peter Greenaway, *Prospero's Books: A Film of Shakespeare's "The

Tempest,"* film script (London: Chatto and Windus, 1991).

REVOLUTIONARY ARCHITECTURE IN FRANCE AND RUSSIA

19   The term "revolutionary architecture" had already been used in passing by François Benoit (1887) and by Siegfried Giedion (1922). For more on the topic, and on the historical debate about this architectural genre, see Klaus Jan Philipp (ed.), *Revolutionsarchitektur: Klassische Beiträge zu einer unklassischen Architektur* (Brunswick and Wiesbaden: Vieweg, 1990).

20   See the extensive monograph by Michel Gallet, *Claude-Nicolas Ledoux* (Paris: Picard, 1980), which includes a comprehensive bibliography.

21   Quoted in Gallet, ibid., p. 27.

22   Archives Nationales, T 163; quoted in Gallet, ibid.

23   *L'Architecture* (1804), p. 21; quoted in Gallet (see n. 20), p. 29.

24   *L'Architecture* (1804), p. 218; quoted in Gallet (see n. 20), p. 29.

25   See Werner Oechslin, "Die Tabuisierung des russischen Beitrags zur modernen Architektur," in *El Lissitzky: Der Traum vom Wolkenbügel*, exhibition catalogue, ETH Zurich, 18 May–24 June 1990 (ETH Zurich, 1991), pp. 9–30.

26   Coop Himmelblau, *Architecture is Now* (New York: Rizzoli, 1983), p. 52.

27   Anatolij Strigalev and Jürgen Harten (eds.), *Vladimir Tatlin: Retrospektive*, exhibition catalogue (Cologne: DuMont, 1993).

28   See Catherine Cook (guest ed.), *Russian Constructivism and Jakov Chernikov*, special issue of *Architectural Design* (London), vol. 59, no. 7/8 (1989). This publication was also the source of the Chernikov quotations given here.

29   Ibid., p. 10.

30   Ibid., pp. 62–63.

31   Ibid.

THE ARCHITECTURE OF DREAMS

32   A review of the many interpretations of this poem is found in Edgar

Mertner, "Samuel Taylor Coleridge: Kubla Khan," in *Die englische Lyrik* (Düsseldorf: Bagel, 1968), vol. 1, pp. 350–61, 430–36.

33 Ibid., p. 356.

34 Peter Weiss, "Der große Traum des Briefträgers Cheval," in *Rapporte I* (Frankfurt am Main: Suhrkamp, 1968), pp. 36–50. All further citations (trans. John William Gabriel) are taken from this source.

35 Italo Calvino, *Invisible Cities*, trans. William Weaver (New York and London: Harcourt Brace Jovanovich, 1972), p. 61.

CRYSTALLINE ARCHITECTURE AND ORGANIC SCULPTURE

36 Iain Boyd Whyte (ed. and trans.), *The Crystal Chain Letters* (Cambridge, Mass.: MIT Press, 1985), p. 19. For the original *Gläserne Kette* correspondence, published nearly entire for the first time, see the German edition, Whyte and Romana Schneider, *Die Briefe der Gläsernen Kette* (Berlin: Ernst und Sohn, 1986). Excerpts from the correspondence were previously translated in Ulrich Conrads and Hans G. Sperlich, *The Architecture of Fantasy* (New York: Praeger, 1962).

37 Dennis Sharp, *Modern Architecture and Expressionism* (London: Longman, 1966), p. 85.

38 Quoted in Dennis Sharp (ed. with intro.), *Glass Architecture by Paul Scheerbart; Alpine Architecture by Bruno Taut* (New York: Praeger, 1972), p. 41.

39 Paul Scheerbart, "Der Architektenkongreß," in *Frühlicht*, no. 1 (autumn 1921); repr. in *Bauwelt Fundamente* (Berlin), vol. 8, 1963, pp. 94–97; here p. 95.

40 Quoted in Wolfgang Reschke, *Wenzel Hablik* (Münsterdorf: Hansen und Hansen, 1981), p. 20. The manifesto was also reprinted in *Wem gehört die Welt? — Kunst und Gesellschaft in der Weimarer Republik*, exhibition catalogue, Berlin (Berlin, 1977), pp. 144 ff.

41 Quoted in Wolfgang Pehnt, "Verstummte Tonkunst: Musik und Architektur in der neueren Architekturgeschichte," in Karin von Maur (ed.), *Vom Klang der Bilder* (Munich: Prestel, 1985), p. 394.

42 Wolfgang Pehnt, *Expressionist Architecture in Drawings*, trans. John William Gabriel (New York: Van Nostrand Reinhold, 1985), p. 7.

43 Quoted in Reinhard Döhl, *Hermann Finsterlin: Eine Annäherung*, exhibition catalogue for "Hermann Finsterlin: Aquarelle und Modelle," Graphische Sammlung der Staatsgalerie Stuttgart, 23 April–31 July 1988 (Stuttgart: Hatje, 1988), pp. 52–53.

44 Finsterlin, "Aphorismen," in Döhl, ibid., p. 375.

45 Finsterlin, "Biographie in großen Zügen," in Döhl (see n. 43), pp. 9–10.

46 See the section "Im Spiegel der Presse," containing articles on Finsterlin's role in Gropius's exhibition "Unbekannte Architektur" (Berlin, April 1919), in Döhl (see n. 43), pp. 143–50; here p. 145.

47 Johannes Langner, "'Seelengletschermühlensystem': Hermann Finsterlin und die Tradition architektonischer Mimesis," in Döhl (see n. 43), pp. 143–50; here p. 145.

48 Moshe Safdie in conversation with the author, Cambridge, Mass., September 1988.

"TO SEEING BORN, TO SCANNING CALLED": WATCHTOWERS, LIGHTHOUSES, IVORY TOWERS

49 Johann Wolfgang von Goethe, *Faust II*, ed. Cyrus Hamlin, trans. Walter Arndt (New York: Norton & Company, 1976).

50 See Heinrich Lichtenberg, *Die Architekturdarstellungen in der mittelhochdeutschen Dichtung* (Göttingen, 1931), pp. 95–114.

51 *The Journal of Christopher Columbus*, trans. with notes and an intro. by Clements R. Markham (reprint, New York: B. Franklin, 1966), p. 36.

52 This and the follwing extract are quoted in Dudley Witney, *The Lighthouse* (Toronto: McClelland and Stewart; Boston: New York Graphic Society, 1975), pp. 28 and 42

53 See Walter Grasskamp, "Elfenbeinsplitter: Zur Baugeschichte des Elfenbeinturms. Ein Glossarium für Einsteiger," in *Der Elfenbeinturm: Ein Reiseführer, Kunstforum*

(Cologne), vol. 51, no. 5 (July 1982), pp. 106–120.

54 Grasskamp, ibid., p. 106.

55 Gérard de Nerval, *Sylvie: Recollections of Valois* (reprint, New York: AMS Press, 1981), pp. 7–8. Quoted in Brigitte Casper, "Rund um den Elfenbeinturm und dann mitten hinein," in *Der Elfenbeinturm* (see n. 53), pp. 15–18; here p. 17.

56 Jacques Lennep, "Eben-Ezer: Ein Turm aus lebenden Steinen," in *Der Elfenbeinturm* (see n. 53), pp. 37–57.

57 Sir Reginald Blomfield, *Modernism* (London, 1934); repr. in H. T. Benton and C. Benton (eds.), *Architecture and Design, 1890–1939* (New York, 1975), p. 175.

58 See also n. 49.

BIZARRE AND GROTESQUE ARCHITECTURE

59 Norbert Miller, "Der verschwundene Garten des Vicino Orsini," in *Daidalos*, no. 3 (15 March 1982), pp. 38–49; here p. 47.

60 Ibid.

61 Jan Pieper, "Gärten der Erinnerung: Im Sacro Bosco von Bomarzo," in *Kunstforum* (Cologne), vol. 69, no. 1 (1984), pp. 91–97; here p. 97.

62 See George R. Collins, "Fantastic Architecture," in Michael Schuyt and Joost Elffers, *Fantastic Architecture: Personal and Eccentric Visions* (London: Thames and Hudson, 1980), pp. 9–29; and Charles Jencks, *Bizarre Architecture* (London: Academy Editions, 1979), pp. 7–15.

63 Jencks, ibid., p. 14.

64 Knowing Cardinal's family, I was struck by the similarity of the mask's features to those of his son, Douglas Jr.

65 Robert Venturi, Denise Scott Brown, and Steven Izenour, *Learning from Las Vegas: The Forgotten Symbolism of Architectural Form* (Cambridge, Mass.: MIT Press, 1977), p. 87.

ADVANCE TO THE PAST — RETURN TO THE FUTURE: CONTEMPORARY VISIONARY ARCHITECTS

66 Krier discusses these notions in *Leon Krier: Drawings, 1967–1980* (Brussels: Aux Archives d'Architec-

ture Moderne, 1980), pp. xxv–xxxi.

67 In this case, too, Krier relies on ancient Roman conceptions, not only of *Roma quadrata, Roma aeterna* but of the urban quarters that developed out of Roman field camps.

68 See Hans-Jürgen and Helga Müller (eds.), *Atlantis Mariposa* (Stuttgart and Vienna: Edition Weitbrecht, K. Thienemanns, 1991).

69 For a more detailed discussion of Hollein, Haus-Rucker-Co, and Raimund Abraham, see the present author's book, *Experimentelle Architekten der Gegenwart* (Cologne: DuMont, 1991).

70 Between 1985 and 1992, Woods had exhibitions in London, Vienna, Berlin, Siegen (Germany), Oslo, and Copenhagen. Among his own publications, the reader is especially referred to *Origins* (London: Architectural Association, 1985); *OneFiveFour* (New York: Princeton Architectural Press, 1989); "Lebbeus Woods: Terra Nova, 1988–1991," *Architecture and Urbanism* (Tokyo), special edition, August 1991; *Anarchitecture* (London: Academy Editions, Architectural Monographs, no. 22, 1992).

71 Exhibited and published in 1993, in connection with the exhibition *Pa kanten af kaos*, Museum Louisiana, Humlebaek, Denmark.

72 "Peter Cook, 1961–1989," *Architecture and Urbanism* (Tokyo), special edition, December 1989. See also Peter Cook (ed.), *Archigram* (London: Studio Vista, 1972; New York: Praeger, 1973; expanded German edition, Basel, Berlin, Boston: Birkhäuser, 1991).

73 See Peter Cook, "Three Effects," in "Peter Cook, 1961–1989" (see n. 72), p. 38.

74 See Arata Isozaki, "First Preface," *Archigram* (see n. 72), p. 4.

75 Heinrich Klotz, *The History of Postmodern Architecture* (Cambridge, Mass.: MIT Press, 1988), pp. 372, 374.

76 Warren Chalk, in *Archigram* (see n. 72), p. 32.

DECONSTRUCTIVE DESIGNS AND BUILT ARCHITECTURAL VISIONS

77 The deconstructivism exhibition held in May 1988 at the Museum of

Modern Art, New York, co-initiated by Philip Johnson, may be said to have jumped on a bandwagon that was long under way. In contrast to the term International Style, coined by Johnson in his famous book and the 1932 exhibition at that museum, the term deconstructivism had become established years before. Still, the exhibition prematurely pigeonholed the movement in architectural history, for it was still in the process of development and needed time to mature.

78   After several discussions and visits to the site in the late 1980s, I was skeptical whether Tschumi's theoretical conception would prove viable in practice. Recent visits to La Villette have shown me wrong, for the buildings are enthusiastically accepted by the public.

79   See the discussion by the present author in *Experimentelle Architekten der Gegenwart* (see n. 69), pp. 121–40; and, on more recent developments, "Bernard Tschumi, 1983–1993," the special Bernard Tschumi edition of *Architecture and Urbanism* (Tokyo), March 1994.

80   See *Terrazzo* (Milan), no. 6, spring/summer 1991. Various authors address the metropolis theme in the form of a visual documentation; pp. 41–204.

81   See Coop Himmelblau, *Architecture is Now* (New York: Rizzoli, 1983), p. 106.

82   *Günther Domenig Werkbuch*, with an essay by Raffaele Raja, ed. Österreichisches Museum für angewandte Kunst (MAK), Vienna (Salzburg: Residenz Verlag, 1991), p. 82.

83   Raja, ibid., p. 29.

84   *Günther Domenig Werkbuch* (see n. 82), p. 108.

85   Daniel Libeskind, in *Daniel Libeskind: Countersign* (London: Academy Editions, Architectural Monographs, no. 16, 1991), p. 39.

86   Ibid., p. 87.

SCIENCE FICTION AND ASPECTS OF FUTURE ARCHITECTURE

87   We cannot go into any further detail here on the literary references to architecture in science-fiction novels. The reader is referred to the relevant chapters in the present author's book, *Literarchitektur: Wechselbeziehungen zwischen Architektur, Literatur und Kunst im 20. Jahrhundert* (Cologne: DuMont, 1989).

88   In the appendix to the exhibition catalogue *Stadt und Utopie: Modelle idealer Gemeinschaften* (Berlin: Frölich & Kaufmann, 1982, pp. 161–75) a number of films relating to the topic of city and utopia are listed, but none of them can match the compellingly evocative *Metropolis* and *Blade Runner*.

89   The first relatively comprehensive presentation of such projects was the exhibition *Stadt und Utopie*, held by the Neuer Berliner Kunstverein at the Staatliche Kunsthalle, Berlin, from 22 October to 28 November 1982 (see n. 88). Another good review, for Vienna, is found in Günther Feuerstein, *Visionäre Architektur Wien, 1958–1988* (Berlin: Ernst und Sohn, 1988). The highly complex subject of science-fiction imagery was treated in a 1984 exhibition at Kassel and the accompanying catalogue: Harald Kimpel and Gerd Hallenberger (eds.), *Zunkunftsräume: Bildwelten und Weltbilder der Science-fiction* (Eberberg: Edition Achteinhalb, 1984).

90   See James Wines, "SITE: Green Architecture," *Terrazzo* (Milan), no. 7, spring 1992, pp. 49–79.

ARCHITECTURE 2000: MEDIA ARCHITECTURE AND VIRTUAL ARCHITECTURES

91   The arguments for and against the media in architecture were reviewed by the present author in a five-part series published in 1993 in the architectural journal *Profil: das architektur magazin*, nos. 3–8 (March–August 1993), and in the annual of the ACS, the Architecture Computer Systems fair, Wiesbaden, under the title "Medienarchitektur und Aspekte der multimedialen Stadt," *CAD im Architektenbüro: ACS-Kompendium* (Wiesbaden, 1993). Since January 1994 I have been outlining the historical background of the topic in what will be a twenty-four part series under the title "Mediarchitecture," in the Tokyo journal *Architecture and Urbanism.*

92   Space prohibits going into the history of the topic at this point. See the articles by the present author, cited above.

93   See Catherine Krahmer, *Der Fall Yves Klein — Zur Krise der Kunst* (Munich: Piper, 1974), pp. 73–74.

94   Otto Piene, quoted in Krahmer, ibid., p. 66.

95   On Nouvel's projects, see Olivier Boissière, *Jean Nouvel* (New York: Rizzoli, 1992), and Gilles de Bure, *Jean Nouvel, Emmanuel Cattani and Associates: Four Projects,* trans. Pamela Johnston (Zurich: Artemis, 1992).

96   See "Ästhetik des Verschwindens: Jean Nouvel im Gespräch mit Patrice Goulet und Paul Virilio," in *ARCH +* (Aachen and Berlin), vol. 108, pp. 32–40; here p. 38.

97   Ibid.

98   Marcos Novak, "Liquid Architectures in Cyberspace," in Michael Benedikt (ed.), *Cyberspace: First Steps* (Cambridge, Mass.: MIT Press, 1991), pp. 225–54; here p. 229.

BIBLIOGRAPHY

"Ästhetik des Verschwindens: Jean Nouvel im Gespräch mit Patrice Goulet und Paul Virilio." In *ARCH* (Aachen and Berlin), vol. 108.

Atlantis: Modell für die Kunst des Lebens. Catalogue of the exhibition at the Deutsches Architektur-Museum, Frankfurt am Main, 12 December 1987–17 January 1988. Frankfurt am Main, 1988.

Benevolo, Leonardo. *The History of the City.* Cambridge, Mass.: MIT Press, 1980.

Benton, H. T., and C. Benton (eds.). *Architecture and Design, 1890–1939.* New York, 1975.

„Bernard Tschumi, 1983–1993." *Architecture and Urbanism* (Tokyo). Special edition, March 1994.

Blomfield, Sir Reginald. *Modernism.* London, 1934.

Boissière, Olivier. *Jean Nouvel.* New York: Rizzoli, 1992.

Bure, Gilles de. *Jean Nouvel, Emmanuel Cattani and Associates: Four Projects.* Translated by Pamela Johnston. Zurich: Artemis, 1992.

Calvino, Italo. *Invisible Cities.* Translated by William Weaver. New York and London: Harcourt Brace Jovanovich, 1972.

Christadler, Martin. "Giovanni Battista Piranesi und die Architekturmetapher der Romantik." In Armin Paul Frank, Wilhelm Hortmann, and Kurt Schumann (eds.), *Miscellanea Anglo-Americana: Festschrift für Helmut Viebrock.* Munich: Pressler, 1974.

Collins, George R. "Fantastic Architecture." In Michael Schuyt and Joost Elffers, *Fantastic Architecture: Personal and Eccentric Visions.* London: Thames and Hudson, 1980.

Columbus, Christopher. *The Journal of Christopher Columbus.* Translated with notes and introduction by Clements R. Markham. Reprint, New York: B. Franklin, 1966.

Conrads, Ulrich, and Hans G. Sperlich. *The Architecture of Fantasy: Utopian Building and Planning in Modern Times.* New York: Praeger, 1962.

Cook, Catherine (guest ed.). *Russian Constructivism and Jakov Chernikov.* Special issue of *Architectural Design* (London), vol. 59, no. 7/8 (1989).

Cook, Peter (ed.). *Archigram.* London: Studio Vista, 1972; New York: Praeger, 1973; expanded German edition,

Basel, Berlin, Boston: Birkhäuser, 1991.

Coop Himmelblau. *Architecture is Now: Projects, (un)buildings, actions, statements, sketches, commentaries, 1968–1983.* New York: Rizzoli, 1983.

De Quincey, Thomas. "Confessions of an English Opium Eater." In *Complete Writings*, edited by David Masson. Vol. 3. Edinburgh, 1890.

Döhl, Reinhard. *Hermann Finsterlin: Eine Annäherung.* Catalogue of the exhibition "Hermann Finsterlin: Aquarelle und Modelle" at the Graphische Sammlung der Staatsgalerie Stuttgart, 23 April–31 July 1988. Stuttgart: Hatje, 1988.

Dos Passos, John. *Manhattan Transfer.* New York: Bantam Classic, 1959.

Feuerstein, Günther. *Visionäre Architektur Wien, 1958–1988.* Berlin: Ernst und Sohn, 1988.

Gallet, Michel. *Claude-Nicolas Ledoux.* Collection "Architectures." Paris: Picard, 1980.

Gautier, Théophile. *Le Pipe d'opium.* In *Contes et Nouvelles.* Paris, n.d.

Goldberger, Paul. *The Skyscraper.* New York: Alfred Knopf, 1986.

Grasskamp, Walter. "Elfenbeinsplitter: Zur Baugeschichte des Elfenbeinturms. Ein Glossarium für Einsteiger." In *Der Elfenbeinturm: Ein Reiseführer. Kunstforum* (Cologne), vol. 51, no. 5 (July 1982).

Greenaway, Peter. *Prospero's Books: A Film of Shakespeare's "The Tempest."* London: Chatto and Windus, 1991.

Günther Domenig Werkbuch, with an essay by Raffaele Raja. Edited by Österreichisches Museum für angewandte Kunst (MAK), Vienna. Salzburg: Residenz Verlag, 1991.

H. R. Giger Retrospektive, 1964–1984. Zurich: ABC, 1984.

Heinle, Erwin, and Fritz Leonhardt. *Türme aller Zeiten – aller Kulturen.* Stuttgart: DVA, 1988.

Huxtable, Ada Louise. *The Tall Building Artistically Reconsidered.* New York: Random House, 1984.

Irace, Tulvio. *Emerging Skylines: The New American Skyscrapers.* New York: Whitney Library of Design, 1990.

Jencks, Charles. *Bizzare Architecture.* London: Academy Editions, 1979.

Joyce, James. *Ulysses.* London: The Bodley Head, 1960.

Kimpel, Harald, and Gerd Hallenberger (eds.). *Zukunfträume: Bildwelten und Weltbilder der Science-fiction.* Eberberg: Edition Achteinhalb, 1984.

Klengel-Brandt, Evelyn. *Der Turm von Babylon: Legende und Geschichte eines Bauwerkes.* Leipzig, Vienna, and Munich, 1982.

Klotz, Heinrich. *The History of Postmodern Architecture.* Cambridge, Mass.: MIT Press, 1988.

——— (ed.). *New York Architecture, 1970–1990.* Munich: Prestel, 1990.

Koolhaas, Rem. *Delirious New York: a Retroactive Manifesto for Manhattan.* New York: Oxford University Press, 1978.

Krahmer, Catherine. *Der Fall Yves Klein – Zur Krise der Kunst.* Munich: Piper, 1974.

Krawinkel, Günter et al. (eds.). *Inventionen: Piranesi und Architekturphantasien in der Gegenwart.* Catalogue of the exhibition at the Kunstverein Hannover and the Werkbund Bremen, 13 December 1981–10 February 1982. Bremen, 1982.

Krier, Leon. *Leon Krier: Drawings, 1967–1980.* Brussels: Aux Archives d'Architecture Moderne, 1980.

"Lebbeus Woods: Terra Nova, 1988–1991." *Architecture and Urbanism* (Tokyo). Special edition, August 1991.

Leeuwen, Thomas A. P. van. *The Skyward Trend of Thought.* The Hague: AHA Books, 1986.

„Leon Krier: Houses, Palaces, Cities." AD profile, 54. London: Architectural Design, 1984.

Libeskind, Daniel. *Daniel Libeskind: Countersign.* Architectural Monographs, no. 16. London: Academy Editions, 1991.

Lichtenberg, Heinrich. *Die Architekturdarstellungen in der mittelhochdeutschen Dichtung.* Göttingen, 1931.

Mertner, Edgar. "Samuel Taylor Coleridge: Kubla Khan." In *Die englische Lyrik.* Vol. 1. Düsseldorf: Bagel, 1968.

Miller, Norbert. *Archäologie des Traums: Versuch über Giovanni Battista Piranesi.* Munich: Hanser, 1978.

———. "Der verschwundene Garten des Vicino Orsini." In *Daidalos*, no. 3 (15 March 1982).

Moos, Stanislaus von. *Turm und Boll-werk: Beiträge zur politischen Ikono-graphie der italienischen Renais-sancearchitektur.* Zurich, 1974.

Müller, Hans-Jürgen, and Helga Mül-ler (eds.). *Atlantis Mariposa: Eine Zwischenbilanz.* Stuttgart and Vienna: Edition Weitbrecht, K. Thienemanns, 1991.

Nerval, Gérard de. *Sylvie: Recollec-tions of Valois.* Reprint, New York: AMS Press, 1981.

Novak, Marcus. "Liquid Architectures in Cyberspace." In Michael Benedikt (ed.), *Cyberspace: First Steps.* Cam-bridge, Mass.: MIT Press, 1991.

Nowald, Inken. "Stadt und Utopie – Beispiele aus der Vergangenheit." In *Stadt und Utopie: Modelle idealer Ge-meinschaften.* Catalogue of the exhibition held by the Neuer Berliner Kunstverein at the Staatliche Kunst-halle, Berlin, 22 October–28 Novem-ber 1982. Berlin: Frölich & Kaufmann, 1982.

Oechslin, Werner. "Die Tabuisierung des russischen Beitrags zur modernen Architektur." In *El Lissitsky: Der Traum vom Wolkenbügel.* Catalogue of the exhibition held at the ETH Zurich, 18 May–24 June 1990. Zurich: ETH Zurich, 1991.

Pehnt, Wolfgang. "Verstummte Ton-kunst: Musik und Architektur in der neueren Architekturgeschichte." In Karin von Maur (ed.), *Vom Klang der Bilder: Die Musik in der Kunst des 20. Jahrhunderts.* Munich: Prestel, 1985.

———. *Expressionist Architecture in Drawings.* Translated by John

William Gabriel. New York: Van Nostrand Reinhold, 1985.

"Peter Cook, 1961–1989." *Architec-ture and Urbanism* (Tokyo). Special edition, December 1989.

Philipp, Klaus Jan (ed.). *Revolutions-architektur: Klassische Beiträge zu ei-ner unklassischen Architektur.* Bruns-wick and Wiesbaden: Vieweg, 1990.

Pieper, Jan. "Gärten der Erinnerung: Im Sacro Bosco von Bomarzo." *Kunstforum* (Cologne), vol.69, no. 1 (1984).

Reschke, Wolfgang. *Wenzel Hablik.* Münsterdorf: Hansen und Hansen, 1981.

Scheerbart, Paul. "Der Architekten-kongreß." In *Frühlicht,* 1921, no. 1, repr. in *Bauwelt Fundamente* (Berlin), vol. 8 (1963).

Schmidt, Johann N. *Wolkenkratzer: Ästhetik und Konstruktion.* DuMont paperback 256. Cologne: DuMont, 1991.

Schock-Werner, Barbara. "Bamberg ist Jerusalem – Architekturporträt im Mittelalter." In *Der Traum vom Raum: Gemalte Architektur aus 7 Jahrhunderten.* Catalogue of the exhi-bition conceived by Kurt Löchner and organized by the Albrecht Dürer So-ciety in cooperation with Kunsthalle Nürnberg, 13 September–23 Novem-ber 1986. Marburg: Hitzeroth, 1986.

Sharp, Dennis. *Modern Architecture and Expressionism.* London: Longman, 1966.

———. (ed. with intro.). *Glass Archi-tecture by Paul Scheerbart; Alpine Architecture by Bruno Taut.* New York: Praeger, 1972.

Sky, Alison, and Michelle Stone. *Un-built America: Forgotten Architecture in the United States from Thomas Jefferson to the Space Age.* New York: Abbeville Press, 1983.

Stadt und Utopie: Modelle idealer Ge-meinschaften. Catalogue of the exhi-bition held by the Neuer Berliner Kunstverein at the Staatliche Kunst-halle, Berlin, 22 October–28 Novem-ber 1982. Berlin: Frölich & Kaufmann, 1982.

Strigalev, Anatoliy, and Jürgen Har-ten (eds.). *Vladimir Tatlin: Retrospek-tive.* With essays by Dmitrij Dimakov and Anatoliy Strigalev. Cologne: DuMont, 1993.

Terrazzo (Milan), no. 6 (spring/sum-mer 1991).

Thomsen, Christian W. "Städtephan-tasien: Architekturutopien in der Lite-ratur." *DU* (Zurich), no. 2 (1985).

———. *Literarchitektur: Wechselbe-ziehungen zwischen Architektur, Literatur und Kunst im 20. Jahr-hundert.* Cologne: DuMont, 1989.

———. *Experimentelle Architekten der Gegenwart.* Cologne: DuMont, 1991.

———. Five-part series of articles on media architecture in *Profil: das ar-chitektur magazin,* nos. 3–8 (March–August 1993), and, from January 1994, a 24-part series under the title "Mediarchitecture" in *Archi-tecture and Urbanism* (Tokyo).

Venturi, Robert, Denise Scott Brown, and Steven Izenour. *Learning from Las Vegas: The Forgotten Symbolism of Architectural Form.* Cambridge, Mass.: MIT Press, 1977.

Weiss, Peter. "Der große Traum des Briefträgers Cheval." In *Peter Weiss, Rapporte I.* Edition Suhrkamp 276. Frankfurt am Main: Suhrkamp, 1968.

Wem gehört die Welt? Kunst und Gesellschaft in der Weimarer Repu-blik. Catalogue of the exhibition at Berlin. Berlin, 1977.

Whyte, Iain Boyd (ed. and trans.). *The Crystal Chain Letters: Architectural Fantasies by Bruno Taut and His Circle.* Cambrige, Mass.: MIT Press, 1985.

Whyte, Iain Boyd, and Romana Schneider. *Die Briefe der Gläsernen Kette.* Berlin: Ernst und Sohn, 1986.

Wines, James. "SITE: Green Architec-ture." *Terrazzo* (Milan), no. 7 (spring 1992).

Witney, Dudley. *The Lighthouse.* With a foreword by Thomas H. Raddall. Toronto: McClelland and Stewart; Boston: New York Graphic Society, 1975.

Woods, Lebbeus. *Origins.* London: Architectural Association, 1985.

———. *OneFiveFour.* New York: Princeton Architectural Press, 1989.

———. *Anarchitecture: Architecture is a Political Act.* Architectural Mono-graphs, no. 22. London: Academy Edi-tions; New York: St. Martin's Press, 1992.

———. *The New City.* New York: Simon & Schuster, 1992.

Zukowsky, John (ed.). *Chicago Archi-tecture, 1872–1922.* Munich: Prestel, 1987.

———. *Chicago Architecture and Design, 1923–1993.* Munich: Prestel, 1993.

PHOTOGRAPH CREDITS

The author and publishers wish to thank those ar-chitects and artists who provided photographs of their works. All other photographs were taken from the author's archives, except in the following cases:

Akademie der Künste, Berlin: pp. 81 (bottom), 82, 86 (top)
Architektenkammer Hessen: p. 183
Archives d'Architecture Moderne, Brussels: p. 120 (top)
Lala Aufsberg, Sonthofen: p. 93 (bottom)
Bayerische Verwaltung der Staatlichen Schlösser, Gärten und Seen, Munich: pp. 70 (top), 74
Bildarchiv Preussischer Kulturbesitz, Berlin: pp. 17, 50, 69
Blasdel, Burlington: p. 110
Tom Bonner, Venice, CA: pp. 144 (bottom), 145, 146 (top, bottom)
A. Buonomo: p. 43 (bottom)

Kenneth Champlin: p. 38 (bottom)
concoup: p. 174
Ulrich Conrads and Hans G. Sperlich, *Phan-tastische Architektur* (Stuttgart, 1960): p. 58 (center left)
DAM Deutsches Architektur-Museum, Frankfurt am Main: p. 158 (top)
Derbi: pp. 173, 174
Erco: pp. 88 (bottom), 89
Harry Foster: p. 91 (top, bottom)
Georges Fessy: p. 44
Mark Gabor: p. 109 (bottom)
Michel Gallet, *Claude-Nicolas Ledoux* (Paris, 1980): p. 58 (bottom), 59 (top right, center left), 60 (top)
Gaston: p. 175 (top)
Thomas Heinle: p. 37 (bottom)
Herzog August Bibliothek, Wolfenbüttel: p. 28 (top)
Udo Hesse: p. 154 (bottom)
Indra, Grenoble: pp. 75–77
Christian Kandzia: p. 135

Klenberger, Lechbruck: p. 73 (top)
Kunsthistorisches Museum, Vienna (Artothek): pp. 11, 12 (bottom)
Dieter Leistner, Mainz: p. 179 (top, bottom)
Massimo Listri: p. 70
J.M. Monthiers: p. 170
George Mott: p. 94
Museum of Fine Arts, Boston: p. 53
Petra Nettelbeck: p. 108 (top, bottom)
Werner Neumeister: p. 72 (bottom)
Newspeed: cover, p. 165
Ostdeutsche Galerie, Regensburg: p. 80
A. and J. Picard Collection: p. 60 (bottom)
Pinacoteca Comunale, San Gimignano (SCALA): p. 15
Pinkster + Thal: p. 171
Revolutionsarchitektur, ed Winfried Nerdinger et al. (Munich, 1990): pp. 56, 57 (bottom), 58 (top)
Rheinisches Bildarchiv, Cologne: p. 19
Christian Richters: p. 142
H. Roger-Viollet, Paris: p. 115
Michael Schuyt: pp. 102 (bottom), 111

Staatliche Kunstsammlungen, Gemäldegalerie, Kassel: p. 54
Staatsgalerie, Stuttgart: p. 55
Wim Swan: pp. 92, 93 (top)
Terrazzo, Milan: p. 159
Frank Thiel: p. 96 (top)
Der Traum vom Raum: Gemalte Architektur aus sieben Jahrhunderten (Marburg, 1986): pp. 59 (bottom), 72 (top)
Antonio Trimarco: p. 134
Tim Trimbur: p. 35
Elfi Tripamer, Vienna: p. 149 (bottom)
Uffizi, Gabinetto dei Disegni e Stampe, Florence: p. 57 (top)
J. Uhl: p. 37 (top)
United States Coast Guard Photo: p. 97
D. Vila: p. 168 (top)
Van der Vlugt & Claus, Amsterdam: pp. 113, 143
Paul Warchol: p. 141
Dudley Witney: pp. 98 (top), 99 (top left, bottom left, right)
Gerald Zugmann, Wien: p. 144 (top)

INDEX OF NAMES